HENRY T. BLACKABY
CLAUDE V. KING

FRESH ENCOUNTER

EXPERIENCING GOD
IN REVIVAL AND
SPIRITUAL AWAKENING

BROADMAN
& HOLMAN
PUBLISHERS

Nashville, Tennessee

Printed in the United States of America

4262-54
0-8054-6254-6

Published by
Broadman & Holman Publishers
Nashville, Tennessee

Dewey Decimal Classification: 269.24
Subject Heading: REVIVALS
Library of Congress Card Catalog Number: 95-53177

Unless noted otherwise, Scripture passages are from the New King James Version, copyright © 1979, 1980, 1982, Thomas Nelson, Inc., Publishers. Other Bibles used are the Holy Bible, New International Version (NIV), copyright © 1973, 1978, 1984 by International Bible Society; and the King James Version KJV).

Fresh Encounter: Experiencing God in Revival and Spiritual Awakening is a compilation, reorganization, and expansion of messages by Henry Blackaby and Claude King in the following resources published in 1993 by LifeWay Press (127 9th Ave., N., Nashville, TN 37234)—*Fresh Encounter: God's Pattern for Revival and Spiritual Awakening, Fresh Encounter Leader's Manual,* and *Fresh Encounter: A Plumb Line for God's People.*

Library of Congress Cataloging-in-Publication Data
Blackaby, Henry T.
      Fresh encounter : experiencing God in revival and spiritual awakening /
  Henry T. Blackaby and Claude V. King
        p. cm.
     ISBN 0-8054-6254-6
      1. Revivals. I. King, Claude V., 1954– . II. Title.
  BV3790.B53   1996
  269—dc20   95–53177
                                             CIP

00 99 98 97 96 5 4 3 2 1

CONTENTS

PREFACE

From across America and around the world, an intensifying cry is being raised to God for a fresh encounter with Him in revival. Almost everywhere we go we hear churches cry out for revival. They are saying that what they are experiencing is so bad, so dry, and so empty, they want a fresh touch from God. They want to experience God in the ways God's people experienced His mighty power and presence in the Scriptures and in history. Some are experiencing a fresh wind of God's Spirit blow in revival. But, many are saying, "We don't know what to do." Their heart cry is, "Is there a word from the Lord? What does God say we need to do?" We sense that God is hearing and responding to that cry.

Just as it was in Bible times, standing in the presence of Holy God is an awesome experience. To stand before Him is to stand before the One who created the entire universe. He is the One who worked out eternal salvation for all humankind when His Son died on a very cruel cross, bearing the sin of a whole world in Himself. Therefore, any encounter with God carries with it a serious accountability. No one can be in God's presence without a serious response. The response required is not a response to a concept, a law, or a principle. It is a response to a Person. This is always very serious.

This book will bring you face to face with Scripture—key Scripture. We have included the text along with the references so you can read what God Himself has said. As you read God's Word, the Spirit of God is present to assist you. He not only will bring you understanding, but He also will bring you face to face with God, who is revealing Himself to us through the Scriptures. Every encounter with God's Word by God's people is an encounter with God. Our response to what He reveals to us always requires a serious and personal response to Him. He takes our response to Him very seriously. So must we.

As you study this book, we encourage you to do the following:

- Take your time with God in His Word very seriously.
- Expect to encounter God as you study.
- Spend personal time encountering God in prayer after each chapter.
- Meet together with one or more other believers to discuss and share what God is revealing to you.
- Agree to respond to Him with immediate and thorough obedience to everything He calls you to do or to be.

♦ Agree to help each other work out into your lives all that God has said to you, adjusting, repenting, and obeying Him.

♦ Share with each other regularly, even daily (they did in the early church in the Book of Acts) what God is doing in your lives.

♦ Continue praying, studying together, and responding to Him until revival is a very real part of your lives and your church.

This book is a resource to encounter God through His Word in such a way that God's people may experience true, deep, and lasting revival in their lives. Then they will see God work through their changed lives to touch the rest of their world with His salvation.

WARNING!

Whenever God speaks, it is never for observation or discussion; it is for obedience. Do you want God to speak to you, your family, and your church? Then you, your family, and your church need to be prepared to obey Him when He does speak. To hear the Creator of the Universe speak to you and then refuse to obey is a terrible offense to God. He is your Creator. Christ is Head of His church. He is the Sovereign Ruler of the Universe. He has every right to be Lord of your life. He has a right to expect obedience, and He does.

We want to issue a clear warning to you. *Do not* start this study unless you mean business with God. If the Holy Spirit takes the Word of God and brings you face to face with God, you are accountable for responding to the relationship. At that point you either have to reject Him or obey Him. To sin in ignorance is one thing, but God judges much more severely those who sin with knowledge of the Truth (2 Pet. 2:20–21). Jesus asked His followers this penetrating question: "Why do you call me, 'Lord, Lord,' and do not do what I say?" (Luke 6:46, NIV).

You will not be able to go through this material without gaining a clear knowledge of what God requires for His people to return to Him and become His instrument to reach a lost world. If you complete this study and then decide not to obey God, you will be far worse off afterward than before. In one respect you will be better off not reading this book than reading it and saying no to God's will. If you encounter God and say no, you will be deeply hardened in heart.

Count both costs, however. Do not count only the cost if you do study the materials and refuse to obey. Ask God to help you grasp the cost of not returning to Him. What will it cost your family or your church if you refuse to even seek God's directions? What will happen if you fail to experience revival? Moses warned God's people that the words of God "are not just idle words for you—they are your life" (Deut. 32:47, NIV).

JEREMIAH AND ISRAEL

Jeremiah 41–42 recounts a tragic story from Israel's history. Jerusalem had just fallen to the Babylonians. The leaders gathered a remnant of the people and began a journey to Egypt to escape the Babylonians. On the way they decided to seek God's counsel.

> Now all the captains of the forces . . . and all the people, from the least to the greatest, came near and said to Jeremiah the prophet, "Please, let our petition be acceptable to you, and pray for us to the LORD your God, for all this remnant (since we are left but a few of many, as you can see), that the LORD your God may show us the way in which we should walk and the thing we should do."
>
> Then Jeremiah the prophet said to them, "I have heard. Indeed, I will pray to the LORD your God according to your words, and it shall be, that whatever the LORD answers you, I will declare it to you. I will keep nothing back from you."
>
> So they said to Jeremiah, "Let the LORD be a true and faithful witness between us, if we do not do according to everything which the LORD your God sends us by you. Whether it is pleasing or displeasing, we will obey the voice of the LORD our God to whom we send you, that it may be well with us when we obey the voice of the LORD our God." (Jer. 42:1–6)

The people took an oath to obey whatever God directed. After ten days the Lord sent word that the people were to stay in the land He had given them. God also sent this warning:

> "Then hear now the word of the LORD, O remnant of Judah! Thus says the LORD of hosts, the God of Israel: 'If you wholly set your faces to enter Egypt, and go to dwell there, then it shall be that the sword which you feared shall overtake you there in the land of Egypt; the famine of which you were afraid shall follow close after you there in Egypt; and there you shall die.'" (Jer. 42:15–16)

God knew that the hearts of the people were bent on going their own way. They went through the motions of seeking God's directions, but they had already made up their minds to go to Egypt. Jeremiah gave this warning to the people:

> "The LORD has said concerning you, O remnant of Judah, 'Do not go to Egypt!' Know certainly that I have admonished you this day. For you were hypocrites in your hearts when you sent me to the LORD your God, saying, 'Pray for us to the LORD our God, and according to all that the LORD your God says, so declare to us and we will do it.' And I have this day declared it

to you, but you have not obeyed the voice of the LORD your God, or anything which He has sent you by me. Now therefore, know certainly that you shall die by the sword, by famine, and by pestilence in the place where you desire to go to dwell." (Jer. 42:19-22)

The people sought God's directions, but they had no intention of changing their own plans. According to Jeremiah, that was a fatal mistake that would cost them their lives in Egypt.

Studying *Fresh Encounter* will bring you face to face with God's requirements for revival. Make sure that you, your family, and your church are prepared to do whatever God requires of you. Remember that God will judge you based on your actions and not on your words alone.

GOD IS UP TO SOMETHING BIG

Many conditions around us seem so bad. In reality, however, we are living in a most exciting time to be alive. God is moving mightily worldwide to break down long-standing barriers to the gospel. Modern technology is making possible the preaching of the gospel to the nations of the world. People worldwide seem to have a greater spiritual hunger today than at any time in history, and they are responding to the gospel message in numbers hard to believe. Nations once closed to Christian witness are now begging for Bibles and people to teach them about Jesus. From this perspective, we live in a world filled with opportunity and responsiveness to the gospel. The great question we face is this: Will we submit to God's refining fire so He can make us clean vessels through which He can work to redeem a lost world? We pray that your answer will be yes!

May we continue to "tremble" with holy fear when God speaks (Isa. 66:2), and may we continue to quicken with hope and anticipation for what God is going to do among His people for His glory alone.

Henry T. Blackaby and Claude V. King
November 1995

PART I

REVIVAL AND
SPIRITUAL AWAKENING

CHAPTER 1

An Invitation to a
Fresh Encounter

Uzziah was a popular and powerful king who ruled Judah for fifty-two years (792–740 B.C.). During his early years, Uzziah "did what was right in the sight of the LORD" (2 Chron. 26:4). "As long as he sought the LORD, God made him prosper" (2 Chron. 26:5). These were years of relative peace and prosperity for Judah. "But after Uzziah became powerful, his pride led to his downfall" (2 Chron. 26:16, NIV). In his pride Uzziah decided he could enter the temple and offer incense to God just like the priests. God struck Uzziah with leprosy in the middle of this rebellion. The final days of his life were spent in a separate house. He was excluded from the temple, and his son had to govern the people in Uzziah's place.

Isaiah was a prophet of God living in Jerusalem at the time of King Uzziah's death. God had already begun to reveal to the prophet how wicked and rebellious the people of God had become. Isaiah realized that his nation was in a severe spiritual crisis. Isaiah thought about Uzziah's recent death from leprosy. Troubled with the sins of his nation, Isaiah went to the temple to worship.

In the year that King Uzziah died, I saw the Lord sitting on a throne, high and lifted up, and the train of His robe filled the temple. Above it stood seraphim; each one had six wings: with two he covered his face, with two he covered his feet, and with two he flew. And one cried to another and said:

> "Holy, holy, holy is the LORD of hosts;
> The whole earth is full of His glory!"

And the posts of the door were shaken by the voice of him who cried out, and the house was filled with smoke.

So I said:

> "Woe is me, for I am undone!
> Because I am a man of unclean lips,
> And I dwell in the midst of a people of unclean lips;
> For my eyes have seen the King,
> The LORD of hosts."

Then one of the seraphim flew to me, having in his hand a live coal which he had taken with the tongs from the altar. And he touched my mouth with it, and said:

> "Behold, this has touched your lips;
> Your iniquity is taken away,
> And your sin purged."

Also I heard the voice of the Lord, saying:

> "Whom shall I send,
> And who will go for Us?"

Then I said, "Here am I! Send me."
And He said, "Go, and tell this people." (Isa. 6:1–9)

In the temple, Isaiah experienced a fresh encounter with God. It actually began as a terrifying experience. When Isaiah became aware of God's holiness, his mind must have immediately turned to remember that God struck Uzziah down with leprosy in this very place. Isaiah was so terrified he trembled in God's presence. In Isaiah's fresh encounter with God:

- ♦ God revealed His holiness.
- ♦ Isaiah became dreadfully aware of his sinfulness.
- ♦ Isaiah confessed his sin in deep repentance.
- ♦ God forgave Isaiah, removed his guilt, and cleansed him.

♦ God announced that He had a mission for which He needed a messenger.
♦ Isaiah, in his renewed state, quickly volunteered, "Here am I! Send me."
♦ God commissioned Isaiah to "Go, and tell this people . . ."

Though Isaiah lived over twenty-seven hundred years ago, his fresh encounter with God reveals a pattern that can instruct us and give us great hope. Even though you live in a sinful nation, you can have a fresh encounter with God. A fresh encounter with God will reveal His holiness and your sinfulness. God will call you to return to Him in purity and holiness that only He can grant you. In His way and in His timing, God will guide you to join Him in His redemptive mission to reconcile a lost world to Himself.

EXPERIENCING DARK AND DESPERATE TIMES

Many Christians and churches are in despair over the spiritual and moral condition of our nation and our churches. In many places the world seems to be growing darker and darker. Wickedness is increasing rapidly. Perversions are multiplying. Actions that once were criminal are becoming fashionable. Moral values seem to have disappeared as people do what is right in their own eyes. People, organizations, and even governments actively are opposing Christians, and few seem to fear God any more. Our nation is at a point of moral and spiritual crisis much like Isaiah's. We may be surprisingly close to God's judgment on our nation.

Christians should not be surprised by the spiritual darkness around us. That is all it can be. Darkness is dark. The greater problem is not with the darkness. The problem is with the light. When light shines, it dispels darkness. We face a growing spiritual darkness in our land because the light is not shining brightly.

Jesus said that His disciples are the light of the world (Matt. 5:14–16). When the light of Christ in us is dimmed by the sins and cares of the world, darkness increases. When God's people are clean vessels, the light displayed causes darkness to flee. Darkness itself cannot overcome light. Light overcomes darkness!

Conditions in our nation, our cities, and even in many of our churches are desperate, but don't be discouraged. You may be like Jerusalem: you think God has forgotten you but God does not forget His people. Read what God said to Zion:

> But Zion said, "The LORD has forsaken me,
> And my Lord has forgotten me."
> "Can a woman forget her nursing child,

And not have compassion on the son of her womb?
Surely they may forget,
Yet I will not forget you.
See, I have inscribed you on the palms of My hands;
Your walls are continually before Me." (Isa. 49:14–16)

Can you see the picture God describes? A mother cannot forget her new-born at her breast, and He cannot forget His people——He has engraved us on the palms of His hands. Can you see Jesus with the nail prints from the cross standing with open arms? He is saying, "I will never forget you. Look at my hands." Through Isaiah, this is what God said:

"In an acceptable time I have heard You,
And in the day of salvation I have helped You;
I will preserve You and give You
As a covenant to the people,
To restore the earth,
To cause them to inherit the desolate heritages;
That You may say to the prisoners, 'Go forth,'
To those who are in darkness, 'Show yourselves.'" (Isa. 49:8–9)

Though times seem dark and desperate, God still reigns on the throne of the universe! Never have we seen a deeper, more profound hunger among the people of God for a spiritual revival than we see right now. God is at work stirring the hearts of His people to pray and seek His face. We are getting closer and closer to the turning point. Perhaps you are reading this book because you, too, have such a burden for revival. May God grant you eyes to see the coming of genuine, heaven-sent revival in our land.

GOD'S INVITATION

Is your church thirsty for more of God than you are experiencing? Are you like a desert because of a period of spiritual dryness? Do you sense a desperate need for revival in your church? Do you feel a sense of urgency about the moral decay of the world around you? Has this touched the lives and homes of close family and friends? Many believe that revival is our only hope. God has given us the requirements for revival: "'When I shut up heaven and there is no rain, or command the locusts to devour the land, or send pestilence among My people, if My people who are called by My name will humble themselves, and pray and seek My face, and turn from their wicked ways, then I will hear from heaven, and will forgive their sin and heal their land'" (2 Chron. 7:13–14).

The healing of our nation is waiting on the repentance and revival of God's people. God is looking for a holy people through whom He can work to reveal Himself to a watching world. He needs clean vessels—people and churches. "What manner of persons ought you to be in holy conduct and godliness, looking for and hastening the coming of the day of God . . .? be diligent to be found by Him in peace, without spot and blameless" (2 Pet. 3:11–12,14).

We believe God is now in the process of calling His people to return to Him. He is saying, "'If anyone thirsts, let him come to Me and drink. He who believes in Me, as the Scripture has said, out of his heart will flow rivers of living water'" (John 7:37–38).

"Everyone who thirsts, Come to the waters; And you who have no money, Come, buy and eat. . . .

"Seek the LORD while He may be found, Call upon Him while He is near. Let the wicked forsake his way, And the unrighteous man his thoughts; Let him return to the LORD, And He will have mercy on him; And to our God, For He will abundantly pardon. . . .

"So shall My word be that goes forth from My mouth; It shall not return to Me void, But it shall accomplish what I please, And it shall prosper [in the thing] for which I sent it. For you shall go out with joy, And be led out with peace; The mountains and the hills Shall break forth into singing before you, And all the trees of the field shall clap their hands." (Isa. 55:1,6-7,11-12)

The Spirit and the bride say, "Come!" And let him who hears say, "Come!" And let him who thirsts come. Whoever desires, let him take the water of life freely. (Rev. 22:17)

"Come to Me, all you who labor and are heavy laden, and I will give you rest." (Matt. 11:28)

"Return to me, and I will return to you," says the LORD of hosts. (Mal. 3:7)

"Repent therefore and be converted, that your sins may be blotted out, so that times of refreshing may come from the presence of the Lord." (Acts 3:19)

When God's people come before Him with an open Bible, in the presence of His Spirit, with a willingness to repent of sins as individuals and as a group, God stands ready to send genuine revival to His people. He is calling us to return to Him. Then He will return with His mighty power and presence to forgive, to cleanse, to heal, and to restore His people to a right relationship with Him and begin the healing of multitudes.

Dear brothers and sisters in Christ, the healing of our nation is waiting on the repentance of God's people. We are seeing some significant moves of God in communities, churches, colleges, and universities. Now seems to be a time of God's favor. For the sake of God's glory, because of His Love, to honor His Son Jesus in His body, for the sake of our children and relatives, for the sake of our neighbors and friends, for the healing of our nation—for all these things—let us, as God's chosen people, humble ourselves, pray, cry out to Him and seek His face, turn from our wicked ways, and return to our love relationship with Jesus.

For your own encouragement, read the following testimony of what God did in the first great revival in the American colonies.

A TESTIMONY OF GOD'S GRACE: THE FIRST GREAT AWAKENING

The First Great Awakening in the American colonies is often dated 1740–43. Like other great revivals, the spiritual climate of the churches had reached a low point. Practices like the Half-Way Covenant brought many into church membership without requiring any indication of saving faith. Consequently, churches were a mixture of believers and unbelievers. The Christian testimony had been watered down, and the church was mixed with the world.

Traveling evangelists like George Whitefield and Gilbert Tennent were used of God to quicken the spirits of His people. Under their preaching, many church members and even preachers came under the conviction of the Holy Spirit that they had never been converted. They were greatly distressed until they had made their salvation sure. Historians estimate that 25,000 to 50,000 persons were added to the churches in New England alone, amounting to 7 to 14 percent of the population. New churches were started in record numbers, and colleges like Dartmouth and Princeton were started to train missionaries and ministers to carry the gospel to the lost world. This revival also laid the foundation of cooperative relationships between denominations. The religious liberties guaranteed in the new republic had their birth in this revival.

Sometime around 1734 revival began to occur in several locations in New England. God used these early revivals and awakenings to prepare the soil for the sowing of the gospel that would follow.

Northampton, Massachusetts, was the site of a citywide awakening in 1734–35. Jonathan Edwards was pastor of the Congregational church. Prior to the revival the town experienced a "degenerate time" with a "dullness of religion." According to Edwards, the young people were addicted to night walking, tavern drinking, lewd practices, and frolics among the sexes the greater part of the night. "Family government did too much fail in the town." And for a long period the town was sharply divided between two parties who jealously opposed one another in all public affairs.

In a nearby village two young people died in the spring of 1734. People began to think soberly about spiritual and eternal matters. In answer to the prayers of His people, God began to move. In the fall Edwards preached on justification by faith alone. In December 1734, five or six persons were converted. One of them was a young woman who was "one of the greatest company keepers in the whole town." Her life was so radically changed that everyone could tell it was a work of God's grace. During the following six months, three hundred persons were "hopefully converted" in this town of eleven hundred. Edwards said:

> God has also seemed to have gone out of his usual way in the quickness of his work, and the swift progress his Spirit has made in his operation, on the hearts of many. . . . There was scarcely a single person in the town, either old or young, that was left unconcerned about the great things of the eternal world. . . . The town seemed to be full of the presence of God: it never was so full of love, nor so full of joy. . . . It was a time of joy in families on the account of salvation's being brought unto them. . . . Our public assemblies were then beautiful; the congregation was alive in God's service, every one earnestly intent on the public worship. . . . Our public praises were then greatly enlivened; God was then served . . . in the beauty of holiness.[1]

SUMMARY

- Even though you live a sinful nation, you can have a fresh encounter with God.
- Our nation is at a point of moral and spiritual crisis much like Isaiah's. We may be surprisingly close to God's judgment on our nation.
- The fact that we face a growing spiritual darkness in our land indicates that the light is not shining brightly.
- When God's people are clean vessels, the light displayed causes darkness to flee.
- God still reigns on the throne of the universe.
- Revival is our only hope.
- "'Return to me, and I will return to you,' says the LORD of hosts" (Mal. 3:7).
- The healing of our nation is waiting on the repentance of God's people.

ENCOUNTERING GOD IN PRAYER

Take some time to move carefully into God's presence in prayer.

- Ask the Holy Spirit to reveal any sin, pride, or impurity in your life and seek forgiveness and cleansing for all He reveals.

♦ Ask the Lord to help you see the condition of our nation, cities, and churches from His perspective. Ask Him to help you feel the grief that He feels.

♦ Focus your attention on Jesus with outstretched hands, and thank Him for not forgetting you. Thank Him for saving you.

♦ Tell the Lord about your burden for personal and corporate (church) revival. Ask Him to give you understanding as you read this book. Ask Him to bring you to a personal fresh encounter with Him.

ENCOUNTERING GOD WITH OTHERS

As you have opportunity in a small group, consider these discussion questions for chapter 1:

1. In your opinion, how significant was Isaiah's fresh encounter with God at the temple? Why?

2. What are some examples of the evidence you see that our nation is in a moral and spiritual crisis?

3. How close do you sense our nation is to experiencing greater judgment from God for our wickedness?

4. Why is the healing of our nation waiting on the repentance of God's people?

5. What are some of the similarities of sin and wickedness in our day as compared to Northampton, Massachusetts, in the 1730s?

CHAPTER 2

God Sets His Plumb Line

God created His people for an intimate and personal love relationship with Him. Jesus said the most important commandment of God is this: ""You shall love the LORD your God with all your heart, with all your soul, with all your mind, and with all your strength." This is the first commandment'" (Mark 12:30).

More than anything, God wants you to love Him. This is God's desire for your life—a love relationship with Him. Those who have placed their faith in Jesus Christ's saving grace and have surrendered their lives fully to Him as Lord have new life in Him. Jesus said, "'This is eternal life, that they may know You, the only true God, and Jesus Christ whom You have sent'" (John 17:3). You come to know God when you experience the love relationship with Him for which you were created.

Also notice that Mark 12:30, which Jesus called the greatest commandment, is addressed to God's people, not to individuals. The full dimensions of God's love are experienced only within the context of God's people. God has fashioned His people into a living body of Christ—the church. His ideal is for His people to love Him with their total being. In that love relationship, God will reveal Himself and His mighty power. In a love relationship with God, God's people will have a similar quality of love for one another, revealing to the world that they are Jesus' disciples. That is what Jesus prayed:

> "I do not pray for these alone, but also for those who will believe in Me through their word; that they all may be one, as You, Father, are in Me, and I in You; that they also may be one in Us, that the world may believe that You sent Me. And the glory which You gave Me I have given them, that they may be one just as We are one: I in them, and You in Me; that they may be made perfect in one, and that the world may know that You have sent Me, and have loved them as You have loved Me." (John 17:20–23)

SIN BRINGS DISCIPLINE

Even if you have a love relationship with God, you and your church will tend to depart from that relationship because of sin. You break the intimate fellowship with God. Churches also can sin, breaking fellowship with God. But God is love (1 John 4:16). He continues to love His people even when they rebel against His lordship—His rule over them.

When you move out of fellowship and away from the love relationship with God, He disciplines you. "'For whom the LORD loves He chastens, And scourges every son whom He receives'" (Heb. 12:6). Because of His holiness and His justice, God must punish sin and rebellion. God disciplines individuals, families, and churches so that they will come back to the love relationship that brings abundant life and makes them a "highway" over which God's salvation can go to the rest of the world (Isa. 35:8).

God disciplines His children because of His love. God knows that the best life possible for you is found only in an intimate love relationship with Him. God's rebuke or discipline is His invitation for you to return to Him. The salvation of a world is at stake. Are you experiencing the discipline of the Lord? Is your church experiencing the rebuke or punishment of God? God disciplines those He loves. The discipline is God's invitation for you to return to Him so a world can be brought to reconciliation with God through you.

Many Christians and churches have grown so familiar with sin and with living apart from intimacy with God that they do not realize how far away from Him they are living. Because they do not know the Scriptures, they don't see how their lives and actions fail to measure up to God's standards. They may even be experiencing God's discipline and shrug it off as "spiritual warfare." How does God get the attention of people who are so disoriented to Him?

GOD'S PLUMB LINE

In Scripture God uses the idea of a plumb line to describe what He does with His rebellious people:

> Behold, the Lord stood on a wall made with a plumb line, with a plumb line in His hand. And the LORD said to me, "Amos, what do you see?" And I said, "A plumb line." Then the Lord said: "Behold, I am setting a plumb line In the midst of My people Israel; I will not pass by them anymore." (Amos 7:7–8)

God built His people like a straight wall—true to plumb. When we depart from Him, we often do not realize how far we have departed. We may not realize how close we are to complete collapse or destruction. In order to help His people, God holds a plumb line beside them so they can see how far they have departed.

The Leaning Tower of Pisa is a physical example of our problem. A bell tower was built in Pisa, Italy. The tower is 179 feet tall and made from solid

marble. The ground beneath the tower was not solid enough to support the weight of the tower, and it began to sink on one side. Now the tower leans more than seventeen feet off center. The walls are straight, but the whole building leans. The problem is with the foundation. If the foundation were firm and in line, the walls would be in line as well. If we had a huge crane that could pull the walls to plumb again, the problem would return just as soon as we let the tower loose. Without a solid foundation, the tower will sink and be crooked again.

In a similar way, your spiritual life has its foundation in a love relationship with God. The way you live your life, your practice of your faith, and your obedience to God's commands can be represented by the tower. If your life (or your church) is out of line with God's plan, that is merely a visible symptom of a root problem. The problem is in your love relationship. Jesus said, "'If anyone loves Me, he will keep My word'" (John 14:23).

God's Word reveals God Himself, His purposes, and His ways. The Scriptures serve as God's plumb line for us. When we can see that we have departed from His Word to us, His purposes, His ways, and His commands, we can know clearly that we have a problem. The problem is that we have left our love relationship with Him. You cannot love God correctly and not obey Him fully. It is spiritually impossible. If you are disobeying God, it is because you do not love Him. "'He who does not love Me does not keep My words'" (John 14:24).

GOD'S PLUMB LINE FOR EPHESUS

In His first letter to the churches in Revelation, the risen Christ invited the church in Ephesus to hear and respond to him. Jesus commended their hard work, perseverance, and intolerance of evil. Yet they had a fatal flaw. Jesus set a "plumb line" alongside their church so they would clearly know what was wrong.

> "I have this against you, that you have left your first love. Remember therefore from where you have fallen; repent and do the first works, or else I will come to you quickly and remove your lampstand from its place—unless you repent. . . . He who has an ear, let him hear what the Spirit says to the churches. To him who overcomes I will give to eat from the tree of life, which is in the midst of the Paradise of God." (Rev. 2:4–7)

The primary reason we need revival is that we have forsaken our love relationship with God—our first love. God invites us to repent and return to our first love. His word to the church at Ephesus indicates that failure to repent is fatal. He said he would remove their lampstand (representing the church: Rev. 1:20) if they refused to return to their first love for Him. To the extent that we fail to return to our first love, we will miss out on the abundant life He intends for His people, and a lost world will continue its march into a lost eternity.

As you continue to read, let the Lord begin to set the plumb line of Scriptures alongside your life, your family, your church, your denomination, and even your nation. Let Him show you any place you have departed. When you see the signs of departure, remember that restoration must begin in the heart. You need to let God bring you to a place of experiencing a broken heart over your broken relationship. "For godly sorrow produces repentance leading to salvation, not to be regretted" (2 Cor. 7:10).

Read the following testimony about a time when God set a plumb line among some missionaries and other leaders.

A TESTIMONY OF GOD'S GRACE:
THE SHANTUNG REVIVAL

In the 1920s Christian missionaries in North China were grieved over the spiritual condition of the churches. Members showed little or no spiritual sensitivity or concern. The missionaries began to wonder if many people had accepted Christianity mentally but had never been born again.

In 1920 missionaries began to devote one day a month to prayer for revival. In March 1927, the southern revolutionary army burned Nanking, and all missionaries were ordered to Chefoo for possible evacuation. They began to study the Scriptures and ask the Lord why they had been removed from their work. God began to speak through His Word.

A group of Baptist missionaries asked Marie Monsen, an Evangelical Lutheran missionary from Norway, to join their prayer meetings. God began to use her to challenge missionaries and others to get right with Him. The missionaries spent days before the Lord. They confessed every known sin. They sought to be reconciled with one another. God was getting a people right with Himself. Marie was used of the Lord as she asked the missionaries and others three penetrating questions:

1. Have you been born of the Spirit?

2. What evidence do you have of the new birth?

3. Have you been filled with the Holy Spirit?

The hunger for spiritual vitality caused people to do much soul-searching. Christians, especially the leaders, were revived and filled with the Holy Spirit and power. Once Christians were revived, God had clean vessels through which to work. By 1932, revival was spreading.

Many came to realize they were only "head" Christians, but they had never placed their trust in Christ. An evangelist for twenty-five years, Mr. Chow realized he was trusting in his good works for salvation but not in Christ. After he was saved, he refused to be paid for his preaching. Lucy Wright, a missionary nurse for nine years, realized she had only joined the church. She trusted Christ for the first time. In 1932, masses of people were coming to Christ. In one school all six hundred girls and nine hundred out of one thousand boys trusted Christ during ten days of meetings.

The revival produced many results. Saved people went everywhere telling everyone what Jesus had done for them. Those who turned to Christ took down their "house gods" and burned them. The hearts of God's people were full of praise and thanksgiving. Joyful singing filled the services. New songs were written and the Scripture was put to music. All believers had a great hunger for God's Word. Bible classes met nightly. Enrollments in the Bible schools and seminaries increased significantly. Spiritually dead churches were revived. Church attendance multiplied, and the members paid close attention to worship, prayer, and discipleship. Prayer meetings lasted two or three hours as people got right with God and prayed for the lost. Broken families and relationships were healed.[1]

HAVE YOU BEEN BORN AGAIN?

Marie Monsen's questions caused many to carefully examine their spiritual lives. This would be a good time for you to do the same.

As you read the stories of revival and spiritual awakening, you may realize that you have never had that kind of experience. Perhaps at some time you answered an invitation to respond to Christ but feel you don't seem to have a real and personal relationship to Him. Maybe you "grew up" in the church and have become a church member but you realize something is missing. You need an answer to the question: *Have I been born again by God's Spirit?*

If you have not been born again, that is the beginning place for your repentance. You can turn to Christ and experience a new life in Him. His Kingdom is right next to you, waiting on your repentance. If you have been born again and things don't seem quite right, you may stand in need of personal revival.

Ask God to help you understand your true condition before Him. According to Romans 8:16, "The Spirit Himself bears witness with our spirit that we are children of God." Under God's guidance, ask yourself two questions: (1) Have I been born again by the Spirit of God? (2) What is the evidence that I experienced the new birth?

Question #1: Have I been born again by the Spirit of God? To help you probe deeper, ask yourself:

♦ Have I been born again by the Spirit of God?

♦ Have I confessed that I am a sinner?

♦ Have I agreed with God that Jesus' death on the cross and His resurrection from the dead is my only hope for salvation?

♦ Have I asked God to forgive me of my sin and to cleanse me by Jesus' shed blood?

♦ Have I surrendered my will and life to the lordship of Jesus Christ?

♦ Have I received God's free gift of eternal life?

According to 2 Corinthians 5:17, "If anyone is in Christ, he is a new creation; old things have passed away; behold, all things have become new." If you have been born again, you will see the evidence in your life.

Question #2: What is the evidence that I have experiencedthe new birth? To help you probe deeper, ask yourself:

♦ Has Christ taken up residence in my life?

♦ Is the Holy Spirit affirming to me that I am God's child?

- Do I hear God's voice (spiritually) and follow Him?

- Do I love my brothers and sisters in Christ?

- Does the Holy Spirit reveal spiritual truths to me?

- Is God's power and presence evident in my life?

- Is God bearing spiritual fruit through my life?

Read the contrasts between the old nature and the new. Which one best describes you?

OLD LIFE

The works of the flesh are evident, which are: adultery, fornication, uncleanness, lewdness, idolatry, sorcery, hatred, contentions, jealousies, outbursts of wrath, selfish ambitions, dissensions, heresies, envy, murders, drunkenness, revelries, and the like; of which I tell you beforehand, just as I also told you in time past, that those who practice such things will not inherit the kingdom of God. (Gal. 5:19–21)

Those who live according to the flesh set their minds on the things of the flesh, but those who live according to the Spirit, the things of the Spirit. . . . Because the carnal mind is enmity against God; for it is not subject to the law of God, nor indeed can be. So then, those who are in the flesh cannot please God. (Rom. 8:5, 7–8)

NEW LIFE

The fruit of the Spirit is love, joy, peace, longsuffering, kindness, goodness, faithfulness, gentleness, self-control. Against such there is no law. And those who are Christ's have crucified the flesh with its passions and desires. (Gal. 5:22–24)

You are not in the flesh but in the Spirit, if indeed the Spirit of God dwells in you. Now if anyone does not have the Spirit of Christ, he is not His. And if Christ is in you, the body is dead because of sin, but the Spirit is life because of righteousness. (Rom. 8:9–10)

God created you for a love relationship with Him. You will never know true peace and joy apart from that intimate love relationship. It is a real and personal relationship with the God of the universe. It also is an eternal relationship, everlasting. It can begin here and now, and it will continue in heaven for all eternity.

If God is drawing you to Himself, would you respond to Him? Because of sin, all humanity is separated from God and spiritually dead. God, however, has paid the penalty for your sin through the death of Christ on the cross. Yes, He loved you that much! He wants your love and devotion in return.

God says, "If you confess with your mouth the Lord Jesus and believe in your heart that God has raised Him from the dead, you will be saved" (Rom. 10:9). When Jesus began His earthly ministry, His message was: "'Repent, for the kingdom of heaven is at hand'" (Matt. 4:17). To repent, you turn from your self-centered life to a Christ-centered life where Jesus rules in your mind, heart, and life. Jesus said, "'If anyone desires to come after Me, let him deny himself, and take up his cross daily, and follow Me'" (Luke 9:23).

You can turn to a love relationship with God right now. He is listening. Just talk to Him.

♦ Tell God of your desire to know and experience Him.
♦ Agree with Him about your sin and your need for His forgiveness.
♦ Ask Him to forgive you.
♦ Surrender your will to Him, and make Him Lord of your life.

When you do, God will place His Spirit in you. You will be a new creation. Your old life will be put away and a newness of life will take its place (2 Cor. 5:17).

SUMMARY

♦ God created His people for an intimate and personal love relationship with Him.

♦ The full dimensions of God's love are experienced only within the context of God's people.

♦ Because of His holiness and His justice, God must punish sin and rebellion.

♦ God disciplines His children because of His love.

♦ The Scriptures serve as God's plumb line for us. When we can see that we have departed from His Word to us, His purposes, His ways, and His commands, we can know clearly that we have a problem.

♦ You cannot love God correctly and not obey Him fully.

♦ The primary reason we need revival is that we have forsaken our love relationship with God—our first love.

ENCOUNTERING GOD IN PRAYER

Take some time in prayer to focus you heart on your love relationship with God.

♦ Thank God for inviting you to a love relationship through His Son, Jesus.

♦ Tell God how much you love Him.

♦ Ask the Lord to reveal anything in your life, family, or church that may be evidence of God's discipline. Respond to anything He reveals.

♦ Following the example in the Shantung Revival, ask the Lord to help you examine your own relationship with Him. Use the three questions as you examine your relationship with God.

ENCOUNTERING GOD WITH OTHERS

As you have opportunity in a small group, consider these discussion questions for chapter 2:

1. How important is an intimate and personal love relationship with God to a Christian? To a church? Why?

2. How can obedience be an indicator of the quality of the love relationship with God?

3. In your opinion, what are some examples of evidence that God may be disciplining our nation? Your church?

4. How serious would the problem be if God tried to discipline a church but the church members called it "spiritual warfare"?

5. Why do you think failure for a church to return to its first love can be fatal?

CHAPTER 3

Experiencing God in Revival

The word *revival* has a variety of meanings for Christians. For some it means a series of meetings in the spring or fall. Some think of revival as a time when people place their faith in Christ and receive Him as Savior and Lord. Other people have used the term *revival* to describe a spiritual awakening where large numbers of people are converted.

In recent history we have tended to use the term *revival* to describe a time of evangelistic services. That has not always been the case. In fact, not many decades ago, churches usually held two-week revival meetings. The first week focused on God's people getting right with Him; that was the revival if they really returned to a right relationship with the Lord. The second week focused on evangelistic preaching to the lost. As churches have accommodated their plans to the pressures on family schedules, revival services have been reduced to three of four days. With the limited time, churches have chosen to emphasize evangelism rather than focusing on getting God's people right with the Lord. Consequently, we have lost our understanding of what revival really is.

REVIVAL FOR GOD'S PEOPLE

What is genuine revival? The word *revive* is made up of two parts: *re* meaning "again" and *vive* meaning "to live." Thus, *revive* means "to live again, to come or be brought back to life, health, or vitality." Revival is a time when spiritual life and vitality is restored. Someone quoted an old country preacher as saying, "You can't be *re*vived unless you have first been vived!" Those who are dead in trespasses and sins don't need revival; they need life that comes by being born again. Revival is a return to spiritual health after a period of spiritual decline into sin and broken fellowship with God. We will use the word *revival* to describe what God does to restore His people to a right relationship with Him. Revival is for God's people when they need to be forgiven and restored to life, spiritual health, and vitality. Thus, *revival occurs when God restores spiritual health and vitality to His people.*

Revival is for God's people who need a fresh encounter, a fresh love relationship with Him. Genuine revival does not come simply by reforming or changing behavior. Just changing your ways is not enough. Unless your love relationship with God is repaired, you will eventually go back to your old ways of living. The only lasting motivation for obedience to God is a sound love relationship with Him. If your love relationship with God is right, your life will line up with His standards. Jesus said, "'If anyone loves Me, he will keep My word'" (John 14:23).

Do you see the connection? A right love relationship with God is the prerequisite for obedience. Correct behavior comes because of the love relationship. To reform behavior without a change in the relationship with God is only temporary and superficial. Revival requires a change of heart as well as a change in actions in such a way that God's fullness returns to His people.

Revival is God putting the plumb line of His Word right down the middle of His people. He calls us to repent of our wicked ways and return to holiness and a love relationship with Him. When we repent and return to Him, He turns our hearts back to Him. He forgives. He cleanses. He restores His fullness of life. He gives renewed life. In fact, He *is* our life. This is revival.

Revival has not taken place unless a change of character has occurred, not unless a change of heart has taken place. When your love for the Lord compels you to obey Him, then revival has occurred. When God returns to His people in power, His presence will be known and felt. Let's take a look at an example of revival from the Bible.

REVIVAL UNDER KING ASA

Asa, King of Judah, had a heritage of faith. He was the great-great-grandson of King David. Asa's father, King Abijah, trusted in the Lord and guided the people to follow the requirements of the Lord. Asa was brought up to trust the Lord and faithfully serve Him. When Asa became king, he "did what was good and right in the eyes of the LORD his God, for he removed the altars of the foreign gods and the high places, and broke down the sacred pillars and cut down the wooden images. He commanded Judah to seek the LORD God of their fathers, and to observe the law and the commandment" (2 Chron. 14:2–4).

God gave them victory over their enemies. God prospered them. Then, evidently, their hearts departed from the Lord, for the Bible tells us that they had been "without the true God" (2 Chron. 15:3). Then, God sent a word to Asa through the prophet Azariah.

> Now the Spirit of God came upon Azariah the son of Oded. And he went out to meet Asa, and said to him: "Hear me, Asa, and all Judah and Benjamin. The LORD is with you while you are with Him. If you seek Him, He will be found by you; but if you forsake Him, He will forsake you. For a long time Israel has been without the true God, without a teaching priest, and without law; but when in their trouble they turned to the LORD God of Israel, and sought Him, He was found by them. And in those times there was no peace to the one who went out, nor to the one who came in, but great turmoil was on all the inhabitants of the lands. So nation was destroyed by nation, and city by city, for God troubled them with every adversity. But you, be strong and do not let your hands be weak, for your work shall be rewarded!" (2 Chron. 15:1–7)

God did not overrule the people's choice to forsake Him. He did, however, allow them to suffer the consequences of their sin. They were without the true God. The priests were not teaching the law, so the people got farther and farther from God. Crime increased so much it was unsafe to travel. Nations and cities were at war with each other, and God was troubling the people to get their attention. (Does any of this sound familiar?)

King Asa needed this reminder from the Lord. God did not leave Israel; they left Him. God would be with His people when they returned to Him. God was calling them back into a right relationship with Him. If they would seek the Lord, He would be found. But, if they forsook the Lord, He would forsake them. Asa heard the words from the Lord and responded.

> And when Asa heard these words and the prophecy of Oded the prophet, he took courage, and removed the abominable idols from all the land . . . and he restored the altar of the LORD that was before the vestibule of the LORD. Then he gathered all Judah and Benjamin, and those who dwelt with them from Ephraim, Manasseh, and Simeon, for they came over to him in great numbers from Israel when they saw that the LORD his God was with him.

So they gathered together at Jerusalem in the third month, in the fifteenth year of the reign of Asa. And they offered to the LORD at that time seven hundred bulls and seven thousand sheep from the spoil they had brought. Then they entered into a covenant to seek the LORD God of their fathers with all their heart and with all their soul; and whoever would not seek the LORD God of Israel was to be put to death, whether small or great, whether man or woman. Then they took an oath before the LORD with a loud voice, with shouting and trumpets and rams' horns. And all Judah rejoiced at the oath, for they had sworn with all their heart and sought Him with all their soul; and He was found by them, and the LORD gave them rest all around. (2 Chron. 15:8–15)

Asa prepared for the return to the Lord by removing the detestable idols and repairing the altar of the Lord. He then called all the people together. This was serious business, and the future of the nation depended on the wholehearted response of the people. According to this passage, the people did not come as a result of pressure from the King. They were not reluctant or sad. They sought the Lord with all their heart and soul, eagerly, with shouting and trumpets and horns, and with rejoicing. God met His people and restored peace on every side.

Do you see a pattern for revival? God's people forsook Him. He disciplined them. Then he called them to return to Him. All the people sought God with all their hearts, and He was found. The great joy of revival came after the repentance.

QUICK OR PROGRESSIVE

Revival is a sovereign act of God. We cannot force Him to do anything. Yet, in His sovereignty God has set forth the requirements for revival. He has said, "'Return to me, and I will return to you'" (Mal. 3:7). The essence of revival is returning to the Lord. This can happen quickly or it can take place over a period of time.

For instance, Church A needs revival. Sin and compromise have become common, even among the members. Even though the church hears preaching and studies the Bible Sunday after Sunday, people are not repenting and returning to the Lord. They may even resist the whole idea of repenting of sin. But then God gets the attention of His people. They recognize how displeasing they are to the Lord. In deep brokenness and shame they come before the Lord confessing sin and seeking forgiveness, cleansing, and restoration. When God sees that they are returning with their hearts, He sends genuine revival.

Church B has similar spiritual needs, but God begins to convict the people of Church B of sin through preaching and Bible study. When God surfaces sin, the people respond to the Lord with repentant hearts. God peels off a layer of sin, like a layer of skin of an onion. Then, He begins peeling away another layer. With each step along the way, the people of Church B respond to the Lord by repenting of their sin and returning to God and His ways. With no special event and with no ability to pinpoint a day or time that revival came, this church eventually comes to understand that things are different. They say, "We are not the people we used to be. God's presence and power have returned. We love each other and are experiencing unity again!"

God sent revival to Church A and to Church B. Revival came quickly to Church A, but it came to Church B in a slow process over a period of time. Either way, when God's people return to Him and God returns to His people, revival has come. A time of gradual building to revival began in the 1790s and led to the Second Great Awakening. Read the following testimony of God's grace.

A TESTIMONY OF GOD'S GRACE: THE SECOND GREAT AWAKENING

The Second Great Awakening began in England around 1792, but its roots went back earlier. In 1784 the pastors of the Northhampton Association issued a Call to Prayer for the first Monday of each month. Prayer meetings began to spread to other areas and across denominational lines. They explained the objective for the prayer concerts in these words: "That the Holy Spirit may be poured down on our ministers and churches, that sinners may be converted, the saints edified, the interest of religion revived, and the name of God glorified. At the same time . . . let the whole interest of the Redeemer be affectionately remembered, and the spread of the Gospel to the most distant parts of the habitable globe."

Revival did come to ministers and churches. Word of the revival spread across the Atlantic, and by 1797 the revival fires began to break out in the United States. This awakening was different than the first. In the First Great Awakening, God worked through outside evangelists. In the Second Great Awakening, he worked through pastors in their own congregations.

Pastors preached great doctrines from God's Word with a focus on God's sovereignty and the necessity of redemption. The Holy Spirit brought deep conviction of sin, and people surrendered to Christ and were converted. These revivals were long-lasting, covering two to three decades. Revival and spiritual awakening swept many college campuses. At Yale, 75 out of 230 students were converted. Half of those surrendered to the gospel ministry.

By 1800 the movement crossed the mountains to Kentucky and Tennessee. James McGready preached in open-air meetings (later known as camp meetings). The presence of a holy God so gripped people that they experienced physical anguish often resulting in collapse, groans, and piercing shrieks. Individuals confessed their sins and prayed fervently for forgiveness and salvation. Many were joyously converted.

This period of spiritual quickening lasted for decades. It covered Britain and the United States and spread to other countries around the globe. Lives and communities were so transformed in morals and spirit that outside observers were struck by the radical differences they saw. College campuses were reclaimed from unbelief to once again prepare missionaries and ministers of the gospel. Churches were revived in spirit and flooded with new converts. No one has been able to estimate the total results of the Second Great Awakening. Kentucky Baptists saw an increase of ten thousand (one of every twenty in the state). The Methodist Episcopal church saw a national increase of forty thousand between 1800 and 1803. Many other denominations experienced similar growth.

Perhaps the greatest impact of God's sovereign work was the launching of the modern missions movement. William Carey began his preaching ministry in the Northhampton Association during the days of the Call to Prayer. In 1792 he led the organization of the Baptist Missionary Society and went to India as its first missionary. Other organizations coming to life during this time included the London Missionary Society; Congregational, Baptist, and Methodist foreign missions societies; home missions societies of several denominations; national and international Bible and tract societies; many Christian colleges; seventeen theological seminaries; and many other Christian organizations. When God's people are revived, He gives them a new heart with His compassion for a lost world.[1]

SUMMARY

+ We have lost our understanding of what revival really is.
+ Revival is a return to spiritual health after a period of spiritual decline into sin and broken fellowship with God.
+ Revival occurs when God restores spiritual health and vitality to His people.
+ The only lasting motivation for obedience to God is a sound love relationship with Him.
+ God calls us to repent of our wicked ways and return to holiness and a love relationship with Him.
+ "'The LORD is with you while you are with Him. If you seek Him, He

will be found by you; but if you forsake Him, He will forsake you'"
(2 Chron. 15:2).

♦ Revival is a sovereign act of God. We cannot force Him to do anything.
♦ Revival can happen quickly, or it can take place over a period of time.
♦ When God's people are revived, He gives them a new heart with His
   compassion for a lost world.

ENCOUNTERING GOD IN PRAYER

♦ Thank God that He is merciful, patient, loving, and long-suffering.
♦ Ask the Lord to show you the true spiritual condition of your own life,
   your family, and your church.
♦ Ask the Lord to begin the process of calling you back to Him in every
   way you need to return.
♦ Pray that your pastor and other leaders would respond to a word from
   the Lord the way Asa did.

ENCOUNTERING GOD WITH OTHERS

As you have opportunity in a small group, consider these discussion questions
for chapter 3:

1. Prior to studying this lesson, how would you have defined *revival?* Has
   your definition changed? If so, in what way?

2. Can you remember a time when your church experienced a genuine
   revival among God's people that left its mark on the lives touched? If
   so, share a testimony of what God did.

3. How is love for the Lord related to obedience?

4. What similarities do you see between the need for revival in Asa's day
   and the need for revival today?

5. What was the most meaningful insight you gained about revival from
   the story of the revival under Asa?

6. What are two ways God might bring revival in a church? How are they
   different? How are they similar?

CHAPTER 4

EXPERIENCING GOD IN SPIRITUAL AWAKENING

In John 3, Jesus discussed with Nicodemus a spiritual truth. "'Unless one is born again, he cannot see the kingdom of God'" (John 3:3). He went on to explain two births—one physical birth and one spiritual.

> "That which is born of the flesh is flesh, and that which is born of the Spirit is spirit. . . .
>
> "For God so loved the world that He gave His only begotten Son, that whoever believes in Him should not perish but have everlasting life. For God did not send His Son into the world to condemn the world, but that the world through Him might be saved. 'He who believes in Him is not condemned; but he who does not believe is condemned already, because he has not believed in the name of the only begotten Son of God. . . .'
>
> "He who believes in the Son has everlasting life; and he who does not believe the Son shall not see life, but the wrath of God abides on him." (John 3:6, 16–18, 36)

Through this new birth a person comes to experience spiritual life. Without it a person "shall not see life." This birth comes through the Holy Spirit. God's desire is that all people experience this new birth. Because of His love, God sent Jesus as a sacrifice for our sin so that, through Him, we might be saved instead of condemned. People who have not been born again don't need revival. They need life.

WHAT IS SPIRITUAL AWAKENING?

Spiritual awakening occurs when large numbers of people (or a high percentage of people in an area) experience this new birth to spiritual life in a short period of time. Spiritual awakenings are not just times of mass decisions for Christ. Decisions may or may not reflect a new birth. In a spiritual awakening people's lives are changed radically. Often a spiritual awakening results in a changed society in a city or a nation. Major social reforms often have accompanied spiritual awakening. When people put off the old life of sin and put on the new life in Christ things are different. "If anyone is in Christ, he is a new creation; old things have passed away; behold, all things have become new" (2 Cor. 5:17).

Here are some examples of things that take place during a spiritual awakening:

♦ Bars and taverns close for lack of business.
♦ Police and law enforcement personnel face a drop in work due to decreases in crime.
♦ Businesses receive money and merchandise from thieves, employees, and shoplifters who are seeking to return stolen goods.
♦ Christians and churches begin serious efforts at helping the poor and needy in the community through orphanages, rescue missions, and other needs-based ministries.
♦ Laws change or are enacted to protect the oppressed and to uphold justice.
♦ Reconciliation takes place between races and ethnic groups.
♦ Foul language is replaced by civil and wholesome talk.
♦ Evil practices cease and often are outlawed.
♦ Private and public acts of immorality decrease dramatically.
♦ Marriages are restored and family life is strengthened.

SPIRITUAL AWAKENING AT PENTECOST

Prior to Jesus' coming, Israel had declined to a low point in her history. For over four hundred years, God's people had not heard a word from the Lord through His prophets. The Pharisees had developed a legalistic spirit based on keeping the letter of the law without considering the spirit of the law or a personal and real relationship with the Lord. Temple worship had become an action of the head rather than a response of the heart. God's people desperately needed revival. "But when the fullness of the time had come, God sent forth His Son" (Gal. 4:4). God was preparing to call His people to repentance and revival. When Jesus first began to preach, His message was: "'Repent, for the kingdom of heaven is at hand'" (Matt. 4:17). Many did begin repenting and returning to the Lord. Revival was beginning among those who were God's people.

When Jesus was arrested, tried, and crucified, the disciples deserted Him. Peter, with curses, even denied knowing Jesus. In a sense, the days between Jesus' resurrection and return to heaven provided time for renewal or revival of the disciples' relationships with Him. These days also provided time for Jesus to further prepare the disciples. "He also presented Himself alive after His suffering by many infallible proofs, being seen by them during forty days and speaking of the things pertaining to the kingdom of God" (Acts 1:3). Jesus returned them to the Scriptures and explained everything the Scriptures had to say about Him. "Beginning at Moses and all the Prophets, He expounded to them in all the Scriptures the things concerning Himself" (Luke 24:27).

When the Holy Spirit came on the Day of Pentecost, He empowered the early church for the first time. At this point the church did not need revival (renewal of life). They had been revived. As a newly empowered church, they were just beginning to experience the fullness of life God intended for His people.

> When the Day of Pentecost had fully come, they were all with one accord in one place. And suddenly there came a sound from heaven, as of a rushing mighty wind, and it filled the whole house where they were sitting. . . . And they were all filled with the Holy Spirit and began to speak with other tongues, as the Spirit gave them utterance. And there were dwelling in Jerusalem Jews, devout men, from every nation under heaven. And when this sound occurred, the multitude came together, and were confused, because everyone heard them speak in his own language. Then they were all amazed and marveled, saying to one another, "Look, are not all these who speak Galileans? And how is it that we hear, each in our own language in which we were born? . . . We hear them speaking in our own tongues the wonderful works of God." So they were all amazed and perplexed, saying to one another, "Whatever could this mean?" (Acts 2:1–12)

When God's people surrender themselves fully to the work of the Holy Spirit, God will draw a watching world to Himself. Peter answered the questions of the crowd by preaching from the Old Testament Scriptures about the coming of the Holy Spirit. He then proclaimed Jesus as the Christ. The message was brief; but, since God was working through him, the results had God-sized dimensions.

"Therefore let all Israel be assured of this: God has made this Jesus, whom you crucified, both Lord and Christ." When the people heard this, they were cut to the heart and said to Peter and the other apostles, "Brothers, what shall we do?" Peter replied, "Repent and be baptized, every one of you, in the name of Jesus Christ for the forgiveness of your sins. And you will receive the gift of the Holy Spirit." . . . Those who accepted his message were baptized, and about three thousand were added to their number that day. (Acts 2:36–38, 41, NIV)

This is the purest example we have in Scripture of what God will do in spiritual awakening when He has a people rightly related and fully surrendered to Him. God displayed His power through the believers as they spoke foreign languages they had not learned. After only a brief message, people "were cut to the heart" by the convicting work of the Holy Spirit. Three thousand accepted the message, repented, were baptized, and received the gift of the Holy Spirit. The church began with 120 believers, and God added 3,000 in a single day. That is spiritual awakening!

This is God's pattern—revival among God's people and then spiritual awakening among the lost. This "first" spiritual awakening continued in the first century:

> They continued steadfastly in the apostles' doctrine and fellowship, in the breaking of bread, and in prayers. Then fear came upon every soul, and many wonders and signs were done through the apostles. Now all who believed were together, and had all things in common, and sold their possessions and goods, and divided them among all, as anyone had need. So continuing daily with one accord in the temple, and breaking bread from house to house, they ate their food with gladness and simplicity of heart, praising God and having favor with all the people. And the Lord added to the church daily those who were being saved. (Acts 2:42–47)

The people in the early church were filled with awe as they observed the miraculous way God was working. Their lives were changed. They lived unselfishly with glad and sincere hearts. They praised God and enjoyed the favor of all the people. Wouldn't you like to be part of a church like that? As the people of God maintained a right relationship with Him, it was reflected in their love for one another. Their God-like love for one another attracted the lost people of Jerusalem, and the spiritual awakening continued! Here are some of the summary statements of what God was doing through His people:

♦ "Many of those who heard the word believed; and the number of the men came to be about five thousand" (Acts 4:4).

- ◆ "Believers were increasingly added to the Lord, multitudes of both men and women" (Acts 5:14).
- ◆ "The word of God spread, and the number of the disciples multiplied greatly in Jerusalem, and a great many of the priests were obedient to the faith" (Acts 6:7).
- ◆ "Then the churches throughout all Judea, Galilee, and Samaria had peace and were edified. And walking in the fear of the Lord and in the comfort of the Holy Spirit, they were multiplied" (Acts 9:31).
- ◆ "It became known throughout all Joppa, and many believed on the Lord" (Acts 9:42).
- ◆ "When the Gentiles heard this, they were glad and glorified the word of the Lord. And as many as had been appointed to eternal life believed. . . . And the disciples were filled with joy and with the Holy Spirit" (Acts 13:48, 52).
- ◆ "So the churches were strengthened in the faith, and increased in number daily" (Acts 16:5).
- ◆ "This became known both to all Jews and Greeks dwelling in Ephesus; and fear fell on them all, and the name of the Lord Jesus was magnified. And many who had believed came confessing and telling their deeds. Also, many of those who had practiced magic brought their books together and burned them in the sight of all. And they counted up the value of them, and it totaled fifty thousand pieces of silver. So the word of the Lord grew mightily and prevailed" (Acts 19:17–20).

A TESTIMONY OF GOD'S GRACE: SPIRITUAL AWAKENING IN WALES

In the fall of 1904, a revival broke out in Wales. During the next six months, one hundred thousand people were saved in a great spiritual awakening. No one organized the campaign. They did not use advertising, public relations, radio broadcast, or great soul-winning and witnessing campaigns. God did a sovereign work that captured the attention of the world. When the Spirit of God fell on a people who were right with Him, the lights came on all over the place. Without anybody witnessing to them, people cried out: "What must I do to be saved?"

Wales is a principality of Great Britain west of London. The area has a wonderful history of revivals among God's people. By the beginning of this century, the Welsh people had a longing for a fresh wind of God's Spirit. The last great revival had taken place in 1859 and 1860. Church membership was declining. People were indifferent to religious matters. The churches were formal. God's people needed revival.

By 1904 God was at work in many places and in many people throughout Wales leading up to the revival. The nation was like a tinderbox God had prepared for the quick spread of revival fires. God chose to use a young man named Evan Roberts in a special way. Evan worked in the coal mines of Wales, but he had a great burden for revival. For thirteen years he prayed for an outpouring of God's Spirit. Prayer meetings with different groups of God's people became a major emphasis in his life. Early in 1904 Evan accepted God's call on his life to preach, and he went to school to prepare.

Following a Sunday School service, Seth Joshua led in prayer. One of his requests was, "Lord, bend us." The Spirit of God used that simple statement to touch Evan's heart. On his way out the door he kept praying, "O Lord, bend me!"

God gave Evan a burden to go to his home church in Loughor for a week of services with the young people. Following a Monday night prayer meeting on October 31, 1904, seventeen young people stayed to hear Evan's message. His message had four points:

1. You must put away any unconfessed sin.
2. You must put away any doubtful habit.
3. You must obey the Spirit promptly.
4. You must confess Christ publicly.

That night all seventeen responded to his appeal. They decided to continue meeting. Crowds increased nightly. The Spirit was poured out on the whole area as God's people returned to Him. Lost people were dramatically converted—seventy thousand in two months, eighty-five thousand in five months, and over one hundred thousand in the six months following that October meeting.

These were life-changing commitments. Taverns closed for lack of business. Crime dropped drastically, leaving the police with little to do. People paid old debts and made restitution for thefts and other wrongs. There was even a work slowdown in the coal mines as the mules had to learn a new language of the converted miners. (They quit cursing!) News of the revival spread to other countries, and Christians were stirred to prayer. Soon God was at work in nations around the world bringing people to Him.[1]

SUMMARY

♦ People who have not been born again don't need revival. They need life.
♦ Spiritual awakening occurs when large numbers of people (or a high percentage of people in an area) experience this new birth to spiritual life in a short period of time.

+ When Jesus first began to preach, His message was: "'Repent, for the kingdom of heaven is at hand'" (Matt. 4:17).
+ As a newly empowered church, they were just beginning to experience the fullness of life God intended for His people.
+ When God's people surrender themselves fully to the work of the Holy Spirit, God will draw a watching world to Himself.
+ The church began with 120 believers, and God added 3,000 in a single day. That is spiritual awakening!
+ God used that demonstration of God-like love among human beings as a real attraction to the lost people of Jerusalem and the spiritual awakening continued!
+ "Lord, bend us." "Lord, bend me."

ENCOUNTERING GOD IN PRAYER

+ Pray about your own church. Ask God what changes He would want from your church in order for it to be used in the spiritual awakening of your community. As God reveals insights, write them in the margins of this book.
+ Ask the Lord to allow you to feel His burden for the lost people in your community and world.
+ Read through the four questions of Evan Roberts and ask the Lord to reveal anything you need to do in response to Him.
+ Pray: "Lord, bend me."

ENCOUNTERING GOD WITH OTHERS

As you have opportunity in a small group, consider these discussion questions for chapter 4:

1. What does it mean to be born again?

2. What is the difference between revival and spiritual awakening?

3. How can the events of the Gospels and Acts be seen as a revival and spiritual awakening?

4. What kinds of changes might God make in our community if we were to experience revival and spiritual awakening?

CHAPTER 5

BIBLICAL FOUNDATIONS FOR REVIVAL SERVICES

In Old Testament times, God knew that His people would depart from their fellowship with Him. Their hearts would lose their whole-hearted love for the Lord. Consequently, God made provision for regular times to be set aside for corporate renewal of fellowship. These times of renewal were called holy convocations or sacred assemblies (solemn assemblies in KJV).

Sacred assemblies were days for God's people to come together for a sacred task. They were prescribed as times to:

♦ demonstrate obedience to God and His commands and decrees
♦ remember God's provisions for His people
♦ acknowledge God's ownership of all one's resources (time and material)
♦ offer sacrifice
♦ recognize God in His holiness
♦ confess and repent of personal and corporate sin
♦ renew fellowship and the covenant with God

SCHEDULED TIMES FOR REVIVAL

Leviticus 23 and Numbers 28–29 identify seven prescribed days each year that were to be celebrated as sacred assemblies. These days were:

1. First day of the Feast of the Passover (15th day of the first month)

2. Seventh day of the Feast of the Passover (2lst day of the first month)

3. Feast of Firstfruits (Pentecost—50 days after Passover)

4. Feast of Trumpets (First day of the seventh month)

5. Day of Atonement (Tenth day of the seventh month)

6. First day of the Feast of Tabernacles (15th day of the seventh month)

7. Eighth day of the Feast of Tabernacles (22nd day of the seventh month)

Several of the Old Testament revivals took place on these scheduled days. In addition to these seven annual events designed to maintain close fellowship with God, the Sabbath Day also was to function as a sacred assembly. When these prescribed days accomplished their intended purpose, God's people stayed in right relationship to Him. When they became mere ritual or religious tradition, they did not do the intended work of bringing the people back into fellowship with God. God condemned these evil assemblies (Isa. 1:13, NIV). Consequently, God often had to bring judgment on His people as a loving discipline in order to call them back to Him.

In the face of God's remedial judgments, the prophet Joel knew the people needed to return to the Lord quickly. He issued a call to an emergency assembly for the people to hurry back to the Lord. God answered by forgiving and restoring His people; and He said, "'I will restore to you the years that the swarming locust has eaten'" (Joel 2:25). God revives His people when they repent. God's desire, however, is that His people would renew their fellowship with Him on a regular, continuing basis so He would not have to discipline them.

NEW TESTAMENT ASSEMBLIES

The term "sacred assembly" does not appear in the New Testament. Because the Jerusalem Christians were primarily of Jewish ancestry, they continued to practice the Jewish customs and laws. Up until the time of Constantine, Jewish Christians continued to celebrate the times of the Jewish feasts, but with a focus on the fulfillments brought through Christ. Two New Testament events occurred in connection with prescribed Jewish sacred assemblies. Both were occasions of great importance to the early church.

PENTECOST

After Jesus ascended to heaven, the Jerusalem Christians spent ten days praying and waiting on the coming of the Holy Spirit. On the Day of Pentecost, these Jewish Christians would have been observing a prescribed sacred assembly. During this assembly in the upper room, the Holy Spirit came and the church was empowered. Three thousand converts came to Christ that first day (see Acts 2).

PETER'S DELIVERANCE

When King Herod began to persecute the church and executed James, it so pleased the Jews that he arrested Peter with the intention of executing him, also. Because it was the Feast of Unleavened Bread (Passover week), Herod put Peter in prison to try him the day after the Passover celebrations ended. The last day of Passover (the seventh day) was a scheduled day of sacred assembly. Again, the Jerusalem Christians would have been observing the prescribed sacred assembly, especially in light of this sense of persecution they were facing. That evening, following the day of sacred assembly, the Christians stayed together to pray for Peter. God dramatically intervened and delivered Peter from prison. Shortly thereafter, the Lord struck King Herod down and he died; but Peter lived to provide strong leadership for the early church (see Acts 12).

SOME APPLICATIONS IN OUR DAY

These biblical foundations for scheduled times for revival point us to several issues today's churches need to address.

REGULAR TIMES FOR RENEWAL

Christians need to look at the calendar and find days and times to dedicate as regular days for returning to fellowship with the Lord. Christian holidays, scheduled "revival" services, and observance of baptism and the Lord's supper are examples of times that can help members remember and respond to the Lord. (For more suggestions for Continuing Renewal, see chapter 19.)

THE LORD'S DAY

The Christian observance of the Lord's Day needs to be a regular time to return to fellowship. The Lord's Day ought to be kept holy to the Lord and used as a day to do good (Matt. 12:12). We do not need the legalism of the

Pharisees, but we do need a fresh call to dedicate and consecrate the day to the Lord. We need to focus special attention on the Father, His Word, and fellowship with His people. We need to avoid self-indulgent pleasure seeking and, when possible, regular work on the Lord's Day. God knows that we need times to rest from our work, just as He rested in creation (Gen. 2:1–3). The Lord's Day provides a time to examine the past week, confess any unconfessed sin, and return to seek God's forgiveness and cleansing. This also should be a positive day of celebration and festival. It should be a day for ministry to the needy in Christ's name. It should be a day dedicated wholly to the Lord.

Sacrifice and Offering

Because of prosperity, we have forgotten the Lord (see warning in Deut. 6:10–12). The tithe and proportional giving of sacrifices and offerings were instituted by God to call His people to remember God's ownership and our stewardship of all. Because of greed and in disobedience, many Christians are robbing God. For this reason, many Christians and churches are unknowingly living under the curse and wrath of God as idolaters (Mal. 3:6–12; Eph. 5:5–6).

Gathering the People

In sacred assemblies all the people were gathered. Churches may be satisfied to hold "sacred assemblies" with a whosoever-will-may-come attitude. God is looking for corporate repentance. Churches need to ask the Lord to show them ways to summon the people to come together and return to the Lord.

God's Judgment

Leaders need to be able to identify expressions of God's discipline and judgments. When judgment comes on God's people, they need to know they are being judged so that they will respond immediately. A common error is to call everything bad that happens to a church "spiritual warfare." Spiritual warfare does occur, but so does God's discipline. If we mistake discipline for Satan's attack, God will not be able to get our attention and call us to repent. Developing this spirit of discernment requires dependence on the Lord and a close personal walk with Him in prayer and a thorough study of God's Word.

Sacred assemblies (like the one called in Joel 1–2 in response to judgment) ought to be the exceptions. If regular times of renewal were faithfully observed, fellowship with God would be maintained. Today, we immediately need to respond to God's present judgments on His people and our nation by calling God's people to gather corporately before the Lord and return to Him. In the long term, we need to find regular times to renew fellowship with God.

LESSONS FROM BIBLICAL REVIVALS

Because the church was still young when the New Testament was written, we do not have many details about corporate repentance. We see the call for repentance in the New Testament. The Old Testament, however, is the foundation of our understanding about how God relates to His people. We can see several factors that seem to be common to these corporate revival experiences in the Old Testament. In the next chapter, we will examine several of these revival experiences in the Old Testament. Let us look at some common elements of these experiences so we can be watching for them in the various revival experiences.

1. *Revivals began with leaders.* They began at the top. Other leaders were drawn in as the revival spread. There was no pride about knowing what to do. Leaders depended on others to help them. The king would call on the help of the prophet. Nehemiah, the governor, called leaders of all the families together to seek their counsel. One person might miss a needed cue. With several leaders working together, they gained the benefit of the wisdom and counsel of the others and their sensitivity to the Lord.

2. *Revival often came after God's people had experienced severe discipline and judgment or after they were warned of coming judgment.* In most cases the discipline had already come. The people were crying out to God for help in the middle of their difficulty. Sometimes recognition of serious sin caused the people to fear God's judgment and they responded to the Lord. For Nineveh, Jonah preached a one-sentence message announcing God's coming judgment, and the king, all the people, and even the animals were compelled to repent in sackcloth and ashes!

3. *Many revivals occurred at times scheduled for revival or for covenant renewal.* These included the Feasts of Trumpets, Tabernacles, and Passover. God can honor a scheduled time for returning to Him. Revival does not have to be spontaneous only. But the scheduled time must be a time of sincerely seeking the Lord, not just tradition or ritual.

4. *All God's people were expected to attend these scheduled meetings.* This was serious business; no excuses were acceptable. The life of the nation depended on their response. The leaders knew that the sin of one person could bring God's judgment on the nation (Achan, for example, in Joshua 7). Leaders called all the people to return to the Lord. On one occasion they threatened to remove a

person from the genealogies of Israel if they did not report at the appointed time. On another occasion, God's coming judgment was so close that the leaders threatened to kill anyone who did not join in returning to the Lord. We, of course, would not recommend that approach! But it does point out that the leaders of Israel knew well that God dealt with them corporately as well as individually, and it was very serious with God.

5. *Leaders gave clear guidance to the people about revival.* As part of these worship experiences, the leaders helped the people

♦ remember what God had done for them in the past;
♦ express worship and praise with rejoicing;
♦ offer offerings and sacrifices; and
♦ renewing and affirming their covenant with God as His holy people.

6. *Revivals began with worship.* After the repentance, the joy of worship and praise was great. These are the fruits of revival. This is the experience of "revival" for which we often pray. However, the difficulty of repentance and a refining process must come first. Then the joy comes.

7. *The Scriptures were a vital part of the revival experience.* Through God's Word the people came to know God's requirements. They also understood the consequences if they did not return to the Lord. The Scriptures were not the end. They pointed the people to the Lord. He was the One to whom they were to return. The Scriptures must have a central place, but whom we seek in revival is the Lord Himself.

8. *The leaders and the people confessed and repented of their sins and the sins of their fathers before them.* Confessing the sins of their fathers was an important step in the process, because God was dealing with the nation corporately. When a people or nation sins, that sin must be dealt with in this generation or the next. However, the most important factor was to confess (agree with God about) the seriousness of the sin. After confession the people determined not to walk in the ways of their father's sin. Confession is a beginning place, but that alone is not enough. The people followed through by repenting.

9. *The people demonstrated their repentance by removing idols, cleansing places of worship, and changing their ways.* They took action to bear the fruits of repentance.

10. *The people did all these things wholeheartedly with joy.* They did not have to be forced into response. Somehow, God communicated to the people the seriousness of their condition. Once they recognized the situation, the people joined the process of returning to the Lord. This is humanly impossible, but with God all things are possible. God granted them repentance.

11. *God responded by cleansing, forgiving, restoring, and blessing His repentant people.* This is where God does the sovereign work of revival that no human can do. Only God can forgive, cleanse, purify, and restore. When He does this, revival has occurred!

T. W. Hunt, prayer leader and author of *The Mind of Christ*, has made these related observations about the biblical revivals:

♦ Most were preceded by high wickedness.
♦ Most were attended by multiple leadership.
♦ They spread from the high officials downward.
♦ Previously established divine criteria were restored.
♦ They were attended by great love of the written Word of God.
♦ Worship, especially as expressed in the great Jewish festivals, had a primary place. It was worship from the heart.
♦ The temple and the people were purified.

Hunt adds, "The scriptural evidence indicates that if established leaders will not assume their God-given responsibility in revival, then God will produce new leaders in a major social upheaval."[1]

SUMMARY

♦ God made provision for regular times to be set aside for corporate renewal of fellowship.
♦ When these prescribed days accomplished their intended purpose, God's people stayed in right relationship to Him.
♦ When they became mere ritual or religious tradition, they did not do the intended work of bringing the people back into fellowship with God.
♦ Christians need to look at the calendar and find days and times to dedicate as regular days for returning to fellowship with the Lord.
♦ The Lord's Day ought to be kept holy to the Lord and used as a day to do good, not evil.
♦ Because of prosperity, we have forgotten the Lord.
♦ Leaders need to be able to identify expressions of God's discipline and judgments.
♦ They began at the top with the leadership. Other leaders were drawn in as the revival spread.
♦ The leaders knew that the sin of one person could bring God's judgment on the nation.
♦ Through God's Word the people came to know God's requirements. They also understood the consequences if they did not return to the Lord.

- They demonstrated their repentance by removing idols, cleansing places of worship, and changing their ways.
- They did all these things wholeheartedly with joy.
- "If established leaders will not assume their God-given responsibility in revival, then God will produce new leaders in a major social upheaval."

ENCOUNTERING GOD IN PRAYER

- Spend some time remembering the times and ways God has blessed you in the past. Think about the high points of your Christian experience. Are you as close to the Lord now as you were at those points?
- If so, tell the Lord how much you love Him. Thank Him for the love and mercy He has shown.
- If you are not at such a high point, ask the Lord to show you where you have departed. Confess any unconfessed sin. Pray and seek the Lord's face.
- If you are a spiritual leader, ask the Lord to teach you His ways. Ask Him to guide you to know when and how to lead His people to renew their fellowship with Him regularly.

ENCOUNTERING GOD WITH OTHERS

As you have opportunity in a small group, consider these discussion questions for chapter 5:

1. Why would God plan for regular times for His people to return to Him?

2. What are some appropriate times in the Christian calendar for renewing fellowship with God?

3. What are some ways the Lord's day is no longer honored and kept holy? What are some ways that we can set the Lord's Day apart as a holy day and make its observance meaningful?

4. Why would multiple leadership of times of revival be valuable?

5. Why is it important that churches try to gather all God's people for times of revival?

CHAPTER 6

Revivals in Scripture

We already have looked at the revival under King Asa (pp. 21–23). In this chapter, we want to examine some of the other revivals in Scripture. We will look at several that are very instructive about how God's people return to Him as a corporate group. Then you will be given references for other revivals that you may want to study on your own.

A REVIVAL UNDER SAMUEL

During the days of Eli the Priest, the Israelites had departed from the Lord. They went to battle against the Philistines and lost four thousand men. The leaders returned to camp and asked, "'Why has the LORD defeated us today before the Philistines? Let us bring the ark of the covenant of the LORD from Shiloh to us, that when it comes among us it may save us from the hand of our enemies'" (1 Sam. 4:3).

The Israelites made a serious mistake. They thought they could take the initiative and control God's actions in their behalf. They did not seek their directions from the Lord. They used their own human reasoning.

Then they turned to a substitute for God. They substituted the ark of the covenant for God Himself. The ark was to represent God's presence among His people. However, they made a subtle but significant shift in their thinking. They shifted their trust from God Almighty to the ark itself. They took "it" with them so "it" would save them.

It did not save them, and they lost thirty thousand soldiers in the next battle. The ark was captured and Eli's two sons were killed. Upon hearing the news, Eli himself fell over, broke his neck, and died.

Seven months later, the Philistines returned the ark to Israel, and it was taken to Kiriath Jearim for safe keeping. During the time that followed, Israel was without the manifest presence of God. Twenty years later the people finally cried out to God. They "lamented after the Lord." Samuel led them to repent by getting rid of their foreign gods and returning to the Lord.

> Samuel spoke to all the house of Israel, saying, "If you return to the LORD with all your hearts, then put away the foreign gods and the Ashtoreths from among you, and prepare your hearts for the LORD, and serve Him only; and He will deliver you from the hand of the Philistines." So the children of Israel put away the Baals and the Ashtoreths, and served the LORD only.
>
> And Samuel said, "Gather all Israel to Mizpah, and I will pray to the LORD for you." So they gathered together at Mizpah, drew water, and poured it out before the LORD. And they fasted that day, and said there, "We have sinned against the LORD." And Samuel judged the children of Israel at Mizpah. Now when the Philistines heard that the children of Israel had gathered together at Mizpah, the lords of the Philistines went up against Israel. And when the children of Israel heard of it, they were afraid of the Philistines. So the children of Israel said to Samuel, "Do not cease to cry out to the LORD our God for us, that He may save us from the hand of the Philistines."
>
> And Samuel took a suckling lamb and offered it as a whole burnt offering to the LORD. Then Samuel cried out to the LORD for Israel, and the LORD answered him. (1 Sam. 7:3–9)

Israel met together as a group to fast, confess their sin, and offer sacrifices of water and a lamb. Samuel, as a spiritual leader, prayed for the people and God answered him.

> Now as Samuel was offering up the burnt offering, the Philistines drew near to battle against Israel. But the LORD thundered with a loud thunder upon the Philistines that day, and so confused them that they were overcome before Israel. And the men of Israel went out of Mizpah

and pursued the Philistines, and drove them back as far as below Beth Car. Then Samuel took a stone and set it up between Mizpah and Shen, and called its name Ebenezer, saying, "Thus far the LORD has helped us."

So the Philistines were subdued, and they did not come anymore into the territory of Israel. And the hand of the LORD was against the Philistines all the days of Samuel. (1 Sam. 7:10–13)

Do you see how God related to His people? When they departed from Him, He disciplined them. When they cried out to Him and repented of their wickedness, God heard their cry, delivered them from their enemy, and restored them to a right relationship with Himself.

REPENTANCE IN NINEVEH

Because of God's great love and mercy, He does not delight in the death of the wicked. We see a clear picture of God's mercy in the story of Jonah and a significant repentance at Nineveh. "Now the word of the LORD came to Jonah the son of Amittai, saying, 'Arise, go to Nineveh, that great city, and cry out against it; for their wickedness has come up before Me'" (Jon. 1:1–2).

God called Jonah to be a prophet and carry a message to a wicked city that was on the verge of destruction. The people of Israel would have hated this capitol city of their enemies, the Assyrians. Jonah did. He did not want to see this city repent and be spared from destruction, so he tried to run from God's call. God pursued Jonah and finally got his attention in the belly of a great fish.

Now the word of the LORD came to Jonah the second time, saying, "Arise, go to Nineveh, that great city, and preach to it the message that I tell you." So Jonah arose and went to Nineveh, according to the word of the LORD. Now Nineveh was an exceedingly great city, a three-day journey in extent. And Jonah began to enter the city on the first day's walk. Then he cried out and said, "Yet forty days, and Nineveh shall be overthrown!" (Jon. 3:1–4)

Can you imagine how Jonah must have felt preaching a message of judgment in the city of Israel's enemy? His message was one sentence long. He preached it walking one-third of the way into the city, and the people immediately began to respond.

So the people of Nineveh believed God, proclaimed a fast, and put on sackcloth, from the greatest to the least of them. Then word came to the king of Nineveh; and he arose from his throne and laid aside his robe, covered himself with sackcloth and sat in ashes. And he caused it to be proclaimed and published throughout Nineveh by the decree of the king and his nobles, saying, Let neither man nor beast, herd nor flock, taste anything; do not let them eat, or drink water. But let man and beast be covered with sackcloth, and cry mightily to God; yes, let every one turn from his evil way and from the violence that is in his hands. Who can tell if God will turn and relent, and turn away from His fierce anger, so that we may not perish? (Jon. 3:5–9)

Do you see the major role of this leader? As king, he called the entire city to fast, humble themselves in sackcloth and ashes, cry out to God (pray), and repent. When they did respond to God, He relented. "God saw their works, that they turned from their evil way; and God relented from the disaster that He had said He would bring upon them, and He did not do it" (Jon. 3:10).

Jonah had the privilege of seeing a city of 120,000 people repent. This salvation of a pagan city should give us hope and cause us to cry out all the more for God to spare us because of His mercy. We can pray that God will get the attention of our nation and our leaders so that we, too, might repent and return to the Lord.

REVIVAL UNDER HEZEKIAH

Ahaz was a very wicked king who shut up the temple of the Lord and worshiped other gods openly. He even sacrificed some of his own sons by fire. Because of his wickedness, "The LORD his God delivered him into the hand of the king of Syria. They defeated him, and carried away a great multitude of them as captives, and brought them to Damascus. Then he was also delivered into the hand of the king of Israel, who defeated him with a great slaughter" (2 Chron. 28:5).

The nation reached a low point spiritually under Ahaz's leadership. Hezekiah, his son, became king of Judah following the sixteen-year reign of Ahaz. He did not follow the pattern of his father Ahaz.

> Hezekiah became king when he was twenty-five years old, and he reigned twenty-nine years in Jerusalem. . . . And he did what was right in the sight of the LORD, according to all that his father David had done.
>
> In the first year of his reign, in the first month, he opened the doors of the house of the LORD and repaired them. Then he brought in the priests and the Levites, and gathered them in the East Square, and said to them: "Hear me, Levites! Now sanctify yourselves, sanctify the house of the LORD God of your fathers, and carry out the rubbish from the holy place. For our fathers have trespassed and done evil in the eyes of the LORD our God; they have forsaken Him, have turned their faces away from the dwelling place of the LORD, and turned their backs on Him. . . .

"Therefore the wrath of the LORD fell upon Judah and Jerusalem, and He has given them up to trouble, to desolation, and to jeering, as you see with your eyes. For indeed, because of this our fathers have fallen by the sword; and our sons, our daughters, and our wives are in captivity. Now it is in my heart to make a covenant with the LORD God of Israel, that His fierce wrath may turn away from us." (2 Chron. 29:1–6, 8–10)

A wise spiritual leader will recognize the symptoms of spiritual sickness in the people of God. Hezekiah knew that their fathers had forsaken the Lord. He saw the destruction, death, and captivity of Judah and Jerusalem as God's judgments on His people for their sin. Hezekiah knew that it was time to cry out to the Lord. To prepare for revival, Hezekiah had the place of worship repaired, cleansed, and dedicated to the Lord once again.

The Levites spent sixteen days consecrating the temple and removing all the unclean things. Hezekiah then gathered all the city officials, and they went to the temple to offer sacrifices to the Lord. The temple musicians were called into service to assist with the worship. "The service of the house of the LORD was set in order. Then Hezekiah and all the people rejoiced that God had prepared the people, since the events took place so suddenly" (2 Chron. 29:35–36).

Hezekiah sent word to all Israel and Judah calling them to assemble for the Passover celebration. The time had already passed for the celebration, but the leaders sensed that they could not wait another year.

Then the runners went throughout all Israel and Judah with the letters from the king and his leaders, and spoke according to the command of the king: "Children of Israel, return to the LORD God of Abraham, Isaac, and Israel; then He will return to the remnant of you who have escaped from the hand of the kings of Assyria. And do not be like your fathers and your brethren, who trespassed against the LORD God of their fathers, so that He gave them up to desolation, as you see. Now do not be stiff-necked, as your fathers were, but yield yourselves to the LORD; and enter His sanctuary, which He has sanctified forever, and serve the LORD your God, that the fierceness of His wrath may turn away from you. For if you return to the LORD, your brethren and your children will be treated with compassion by those who lead them captive, so that they may come back to this land; for the LORD your God is gracious and merciful, and will not turn His face from you if you return to Him.'" (2 Chron. 30:6–9)

Hezekiah called the people to return to the Lord. This was a call to worship. Not everyone wanted to return to the Lord. Those who did not scorned and ridiculed the messengers. Others, however, humbled themselves and gathered to worship. And "the hand of God was on Judah to give them singleness of heart to obey the command of the king and the leaders, at the word of the LORD" (2 Chron. 30:12). The people gathered to return to the Lord. Hezekiah prayed for the people.

"And the LORD listened to Hezekiah and healed the people" (2 Chron. 30:20). When the people had returned to the Lord and worshiped Him, the covenant relationship of love had been reestablished. The people experienced great joy in their worship. In fact, they decided to celebrate the feast seven more days because of their great joy. Their "practice" and "obedience" changed once the relationship with God was restored. "Then the whole assembly agreed to keep the feast another seven days, and they kept it another seven days with gladness. . . . a great number of priests sanctified themselves. The whole assembly of Judah rejoiced . . . So there was great joy in Jerusalem, for since the time of Solomon the son of David, king of Israel, there had been nothing like this in Jerusalem. Then the priests, the Levites, arose and blessed the people, and their voice was heard; and their prayer came up to His holy dwelling place, to heaven" (2 Chron. 30:23–27).

As a demonstration that they had repented, the people went forth from the assembly to cleanse the land: "Now when all this was finished, all Israel who were present went out to the cities of Judah and broke the sacred pillars in pieces, cut down the wooden images, and threw down the high places and the altars—from all Judah, Benjamin, Ephraim, and Manasseh—until they had utterly destroyed them all" (2 Chron. 31:1).

During the next five months, the people generously brought tithes "of everything" to the Lord. "And when Hezekiah and the leaders came and saw the heaps, they blessed the LORD and His people Israel" (2 Chron. 31:8). When a people have returned to their love for the Lord, their giving reflects that love. Often a giving problem is just one clear symptom of a broken relationship with God. To solve the giving problem, lead the people to return to the Lord. Here is a summary of Hezekiah's work: "He did what was good and right and true before the LORD his God. And in every work that he began in the service of the house of God, in the law and in the commandment, to seek his God, he did it with all his heart. So he prospered" (2 Chron. 31:20–21).

Think about the joy in worship and the signs of revival that took place under Hezekiah's leadership. Does your church obey this way? Does your church experience this kind of joy with the Lord in worship? If not, pray for your spiritual leaders as they guide your church to return to the Lord.

REVIVAL UNDER JOSIAH AND HILKIAH

Because of the sins of his fathers, Josiah came to the throne of Judah while the temple was in shambles. The Book of the Law had been lost. King Josiah did not even know the requirements of the Lord. In the eighteenth year of Josiah's reign, he began to repair the temple of the Lord. While cleaning the temple Hilkiah, the priest found the Book of the Law. When Josiah heard the Law read, he looked at all they were doing as a nation in light of God's Law—God's plumb line. Josiah cried out to God. He tore his robes in brokenness before God.

He was fearful because He now knew that God had promised to punish His people if they did not keep His covenant and His Law. Josiah must have felt betrayed by his fathers who were kings before him. "How could they have been so irresponsible?" he must have asked. Josiah now saw clearly the symptoms of a people who had departed from the Lord. As leader, he immediately went to the Lord for directions. Josiah sought a word from the Lord through the prophetess Huldah. "'Go, inquire of the LORD for me, and for those who are left in Israel and Judah, concerning the words of the book that is found; for great is the wrath of the LORD that is poured out on us, because our fathers have not kept the word of the LORD, to do according to all that is written in this book'" (2 Chron. 34:21).

She sought the Lord and brought back a word from Him.

> "Thus says the LORD: 'Behold, I will bring calamity on this place and on its inhabitants, all the curses that are written in the book which they have read before the king of Judah, because they have forsaken Me and burned incense to other gods, that they might provoke Me to anger with all the works of their hands. Therefore My wrath will be poured out on this place, and not be quenched.'" (2 Chron. 34:24–25)

First God told Josiah it was too late for the nation. His final judgment was going to come on the nation. God is very patient, but He does not withhold His anger forever. About forty years later, God told Jeremiah: "'Do not pray for this people, for their good. When they fast, I will not hear their cry; and when they offer burnt offering and grain offering, I will not accept them. But I will consume them by the sword, by the famine, and by the pestilence'" (Jer. 14:11–12).

By the days of Jeremiah, God told Jeremiah it was too late to even pray about the matter any longer. God's call to His people is: "repent or perish." When we hear that call, we had better respond. The time will come when repentance is no longer an option. At that point our only expectation is judgment. Fortunately for Josiah, God saw His brokenness and delayed sending the judgment.

"Because your heart was tender, and you humbled yourself before God when you heard His words against this place and against its inhabitants, and you humbled yourself before Me, and you tore your clothes and wept before Me, I also have heard you," says the LORD. "Surely I will gather you to your fathers, and you shall be gathered to your grave in peace; and your eyes shall not see all the calamity which I will bring on this place and its inhabitants." (2 Chron. 34:27–28)

God doesn't just look on our outward actions. He looks on our heart. He saw that Josiah truly was brokenhearted because of the sins of the people. His response saved a whole generation from God's final judgment. One very significant fact in this revival account is that God decided to spare that generation from His judgment after Josiah responded but *before* the people repented. When the leader repented, God heard and responded. Josiah then guided the people as they all returned to the Lord.

Then the king sent and gathered all the elders of Judah and Jerusalem. The king went up to the house of the LORD, with all the men of Judah and the inhabitants of Jerusalem—the priests and the Levites, and all the people, great and small. And he read in their hearing all the words of the Book of the Covenant which had been found in the house of the LORD. Then the king stood in his place and made a covenant before the LORD, to follow the LORD, and to keep His commandments and His testimonies and His statutes with all his heart and all his soul, to perform the words of the covenant that were written in this book. And he made all who were present in Jerusalem and Benjamin take a stand. So the inhabitants of Jerusalem did according to the covenant of God, the God of their fathers. Thus Josiah removed all the abominations from all the country that belonged to the children of Israel, and made all who were present in Israel diligently serve the LORD their God. All his days they did not depart from following the LORD God of their fathers. (2 Chron. 34:29–33)

Josiah guided the people to repent. They gave evidence of their return to the Lord by removing all the false gods. They followed the Lord with their whole heart. Once the people had repented, Josiah guided the people in the celebration of the Passover and the Feast of Unleaven Bread. This was a time of celebration and praise for all the things God had done for Israel in delivering the people from Egyptian bondage. After repentance, joy returns to worship. "There had been no Passover kept in Israel like that since the days of Samuel the prophet" (2 Chron. 35:18).

REVIVAL UNDER EZRA AND NEHEMIAH

During one of the cycles of sin in the Old Testament, God judged Judah by sending them into exile in Babylon. After seventy years, God began to bring the people back to Jerusalem. A significant revival took place under the leadership of Ezra the priest/scribe and Nehemiah the governor. This revival began on the day for the Feast of Trumpets.

> Now all the people gathered together as one man in the open square that was in front of the Water Gate; and they told Ezra the scribe to bring the Book of the Law of Moses, which the LORD had commanded Israel. So Ezra the priest brought the Law before the assembly of men and women and all who could hear with understanding on the first day of the seventh month. Then he read from it in the open square that was in front of the Water Gate from morning until midday, before the men and women and those who could understand; and the ears of all the people were attentive to the Book of the Law. So Ezra the scribe stood on a platform of wood which they had made for the purpose . . . And Ezra opened the book in the sight of all the people, for he was standing above all the people; and when he opened it, all the people stood up. And Ezra blessed the LORD, the great God. Then all the people answered, "Amen, Amen!" while lifting up their hands. And they bowed their heads and worshiped the LORD with their faces to the ground. (Neh. 8:1–6)

Can you imagine being part of a crowd that stood for six hours (daybreak to noon) listening attentively to God's Word being read? Amazing! Another amazing fact from our modern perspective is that *all* the people assembled, all that could understand. This was not an optional event. The people heard how God had called them out as a nation. They heard about all the miracles and mighty acts God had performed for them. They couldn't help but worship Him. This revival experience began with a reading of God's Word and a meaningful time of worship. "The Levites, helped the people to understand the Law; and the people stood in their place. So they read distinctly from the book, in the Law of God; and they gave the sense, and helped them to understand the reading" (Neh. 8:7–8).

When the people understood the words of the Law, however, they realized how miserably they and their fathers had failed the Lord. They began to weep and mourn. Notice the unusual response of the spiritual leaders:

> Nehemiah, who was the governor, Ezra the priest and scribe, and the Levites who taught the people said to all the people, "This day is holy to the LORD your God; do not mourn nor weep." For all the people wept, when

they heard the words of the Law. Then he said to them, "Go your way, eat the fat, drink the sweet, and send portions to those for whom nothing is prepared; for this day is holy to our LORD. Do not sorrow, for the joy of the LORD is your strength." (Neh. 8:9–10)

The leaders did not want to cut short the worship and praise that was ascending to the Lord. They knew the people needed to experience the joy of His presence. Genuine worship would strengthen them for the work of repentance to follow. The Israelites experienced great joy. Worship alone, however, could not bring about revival. No amount of prayer, feasting, fasting, or Scripture study could. God required repentance—a turning away from wrong and returning to Him.

On the day following the Feast of Trumpets, multiple leaders gathered together to see how to continue in their return to the Lord:

> Now on the second day the heads of the fathers' houses of all the people, with the priests and Levites, were gathered to Ezra the scribe, in order to understand the words of the Law. And they found written in the Law, which the LORD had commanded by Moses, that the children of Israel should dwell in booths during the feast of the seventh month. (Neh. 8:13–14)

Knowing the Jewish calendar is important here. The next event for the Jews to observe was the Day of Atonement on the tenth day of the seventh month (Lev. 23:27). Then the Feast of Tabernacles was to be celebrated the fifteenth day of the seventh month through the twenty-second day (Lev. 23:34–43). The leaders must have realized that the people were so discouraged and weak that they were not ready to deal thoroughly with their sin the way the Day of Atonement required. So they decided to skip the Day of Atonement and celebrate the Feast of Tabernacles.

For eight days they celebrated all the mighty deeds of God's provision for the people during their wandering in the wilderness. "And their joy was very great" (Neh. 8:17, NIV). Do you remember what the leaders said earlier about joy? They said, "the joy of the Lord is your strength" (Neh. 8:10). Now (and not until now) the people were strong and ready to deal with their sin through repentance. Two days later, the people assembled for a special time of repentance.

> Now on the twenty-fourth day of this month the children of Israel were assembled with fasting, in sackcloth, and with dust on their heads. Then those of Israelite lineage separated themselves from all foreigners; and they stood and confessed their sins and the iniquities of their fathers. And they stood up in their place and read from the Book of the Law of the

LORD their God for one-fourth of the day; and for another fourth they confessed and worshiped the LORD their God. (Neh. 9:1–3)

The people fasted, wore sackcloth, confessed and turned from their sins, and worshiped the Lord. Following the time of confession, Nehemiah rehearsed all the mighty acts God had performed for His people; he recounted the spiritual markers for the nation. He detailed God's judgment on the land because of the sins of the nation. He agreed that God was justified in all the ways He had acted in judgment. Then Nehemiah guided the people in reaffirming their covenant relationship with God. Revival began with genuine worship and ended with worship.

This revival experience is very instructive for us in seeing how spiritual leaders guided the people to return to the Lord. It also raises a caution for us. Because the people wanted to help each other keep the covenant in the future, they signed a binding agreement that stated how they would keep the commands of the Lord (Neh. 9:38–10:39). As far as we know, God had no problem with this agreement.

But the next generation that came along did not have the personal experience with God that this generation had experienced. That new generation began to keep the written laws and develop other written laws to help them keep the commands faithfully. By the time Jesus came to the Jews, the sect of the Pharisees had become a strong influence in the religious life of the people. They emphasized keeping the letter of the law but missed the spirit of it. They studied the Scriptures diligently but refused to come to a personal relationship with the Christ of the Scriptures. Revival is fragile, and it cannot be passed on from one generation to the next. The next generation must be led to experience God in a personal way themselves.

FOR FURTHER STUDY

The list below includes some of the other times in Scripture where God's people returned to Him or renewed their relationship with Him. You may want to read these also:

❑ Jacob leads his family to repent: Genesis 34–35
❑ Elijah on Mount Carmel: 1 Kings 18:16–46
❑ Jehoshaphat points the people to the Lord in time of crisis: 2 Chronicles 20
❑ Reforms of Jehoiada and Joash: 2 Chronicles 23–24
❑ Joel calls a sacred assembly: Joel 1–2
❑ Ezra dealt with the sin of intermarriage: Ezra 9–10
❑ Nehemiah's reforms: Nehemiah 13

SUMMARY

♦ "'If you return to the LORD with all your hearts, then put away the foreign gods . . . and prepare your hearts for the LORD, and serve Him only; and He will deliver you'" (1 Sam. 7:3).

♦ This salvation of a pagan city should give us hope and cause us to cry out all the more for God to spare us because of His mercy.

♦ A wise spiritual leader will recognize the symptoms of spiritual sickness in the people of God.

♦ "'The LORD your God is gracious and merciful, and will not turn His face from you if you return to Him'" (2 Chron. 30:9).

♦ When a people have returned to their love for the Lord, their giving reflects that love. Often a giving problem is just one clear symptom of a broken relationship with God.

♦ The time will come when repentance is no longer an option.

♦ God decided to spare that generation from His judgment after Josiah responded but *before* the people repented.

♦ Genuine worship would strengthen them for the work of repentance.

♦ They said, "'the joy of the Lord is your strength'" (Neh. 8:10). Now (and not until now) the people were strong and ready to deal with their sin through repentance.

♦ Revival is fragile, and it cannot be passed on from one generation to the next. The next generation must be led to experience God in a personal way themselves.

ENCOUNTERING GOD IN PRAYER

♦ Through the Scriptures the Lord may surface specific requirements for you to experience genuine revival in your life, family, or church. Are you willing to obey whatever God may require? (Consider very carefully.) If you are, tell God. If you are not yet willing to make such a serious commitment, would you consider asking God to help you become willing? If so, ask Him. Search the Scriptures and listen to the Spirit of God.

♦ Begin to pray to the Lord for your church. Pray that they will do all that God requires to experience revival. Pray especially for your pastor as he leads God's people. Pray that the Scriptures will lead to God's plumb line in your life and your church.

♦ Ask God to give your church a unity of mind to return to Him with all their heart. Humble yourself before God in prayer. Ask Him what you need to do to get ready for revival. Let "the washing of water by the word" (Eph. 5:26) cleanse you.

ENCOUNTERING GOD WITH OTHERS

As you have opportunity in a small group, consider these discussion questions for chapter 6:

1. What is the most unusual fact you read in one of the revivals in Scripture?

2. What was the role of spiritual leaders in these revivals?

3. What are some of the common elements you see in these revivals?

4. Why is worship an important element in revival?

5. Why was the reading of the Law (Scripture) so important?

6. Why do you think it was important for Nehemiah to rehearse the mighty acts of God during this "revival meeting"? How meaningful would it be for your church to remember all the ways God has worked in your church in years past?

7. What were some examples of the evidence that people genuinely had repented?

8. What were some of the fruits of revival?

PART II

GOD'S PATTERN FOR REVIVAL AND SPIRITUAL AWAKENING

CHAPTER 7

SEVEN PHASES IN GOD'S PATTERN

Spiritual awakening took place on the Day of Pentecost. God had a people rightly related to Himself, so He was able to display His glory to a watching world. He exalted His Son Jesus through His people and drew the lost to saving faith in Christ. The early church at Pentecost is the example of what God intends for the church to be. Churches, however, don't always stay in right relationship with God. They tend to depart from Him. When God's people have departed from a right relationship with Him, they need revival.

A CYCLE OF SIN AND REVIVAL

A church departs from God and eventually returns to Him seeking revival. God's people have often gone around this circle. The Book of Judges chronicles this cycle of departure and return, describing the first cycle in Judges 2:

1. *The People Served the Lord:* "The people served the LORD all the days of Joshua, and all the days of the elders who outlived Joshua, who had

seen all the great works of the LORD which He had done for Israel" (Judg. 2:7).

2. *The People Forsook the Lord:* "Then the children of Israel did evil in the sight of the LORD, and served the Baals" (Judg. 2:11).

3. *God Defeated Them Through Enemies:* "The anger of the LORD was hot against Israel. So He delivered them into the hands of plunderers who despoiled them; and He sold them into the hands of their enemies all around, so that they could no longer stand before their enemies" (Judg. 2:14).

4. *The People Cried Out for Help:* "They were greatly distressed. . . . [and] the LORD was moved to pity by their groaning" (Judg. 2:15, 18).

5. *God Had Compassion and Delivered:* "The LORD raised up judges who delivered them out of the hand of those who plundered them. . . . for the LORD was moved to pity" (Judg. 2:16,18).

The second cycle is seen in Judges 3:

So the children of Israel did evil in the sight of the LORD. They forgot the LORD their God . . . Therefore the anger of the LORD was hot against Israel, and He sold them into the hand of Cushan-Rishathaim king of Mesopotamia; and the children of Israel served Cushan-Rishathaim eight years. When the children of Israel cried out to the LORD, the LORD raised up a deliverer for the children of Israel, who delivered them: Othniel . . . The Spirit of the LORD came upon him, and he judged Israel. He went out to war, and the LORD delivered Cushan-Rishathaim king of Mesopotamia into his hand; and his hand prevailed over Cushan-Rishathaim. So the land had rest for forty years (Judg. 3:7–11).

NEW TESTAMENT CHURCHES THAT DEPARTED

This problem, however, is not just an Old Testament problem for Israel. New Testament churches also departed from a right relationship with God. In Revelation 2–3 we read the words of the resurrected Christ as he calls different churches to repent and return to Him.

♦ *To the Church at Ephesus:* "'I have this against you, that you have left your first love. . . . repent and do the first works, or else I will come to you quickly and remove your lampstand from its place—unless you repent'" (Rev. 2:4–5).

♦ *To the Church at Pergamos:* "'I have a few things against you, because you have there those who hold the doctrine of Balaam, who taught Balak to put a stumbling block before the children of Israel, to eat things sacrificed to idols, and to commit sexual immorality. Thus you also have those who hold the doctrine of the Nicolaitans, which thing I hate. Repent, or else I will come to you quickly and will fight against them with the sword of My mouth'" (Rev. 2:14–16).

♦ *To the Church at Sardis:* "'I know your works, that you have a name that you are alive, but you are dead. . . . Remember therefore how you have received and heard; hold fast and repent. Therefore if you will not watch, I will come upon you as a thief, and you will not know what hour I will come upon you'" (Rev. 3:1–3).

♦ *To the Church at Laodicea:* "'I know your works, that you are neither cold nor hot. I could wish you were cold or hot. So then, because you are luke-warm, and neither cold nor hot, I will vomit you out of My mouth. . . . As many as I love, I rebuke and chasten. Therefore be zealous and repent'" (Rev. 3:15–19).

This cycle of departure and return to the Lord is a sad characteristic of God's people throughout the ages. The way God deals with His people in this cycle forms a pattern. In the following chapters we will examine the seven phases in this pattern as seen in the Scriptures. This is not just a study of the history of Israel or a history of the church. It is a study of God and how He works with His people to accomplish His mission to bring a world to Him. The following diagram illustrates the pattern we see in Scripture:

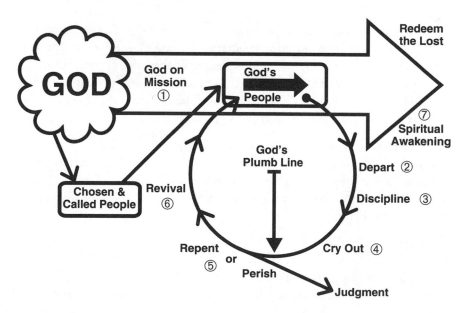

Let's take a quick look at the seven phases in God's pattern for revival and spiritual awakening. Then we will look at each phase in more detail in the chapters that follow.

♦ PHASE 1: *God is on mission to redeem a lost world. He calls a people into a relationship with Him, and He accomplishes His work through them.* God has called the churches to be His people. He wants to work through them to proclaim Christ and bring lost men, women, and children to faith in Him.

♦ PHASE 2: *God's people tend to depart from Him, turning to substitutes for His presence, His purposes, and His ways.* Churches tend to depart from the Lord and begin to accept substitutes for God, His purposes, and His ways. For instance, some churches made a subtle shift from depending on God to depending on an important leader or a program for "successful church growth." That shift can be fatal.

♦ PHASE 3: *God disciplines His people because of His love.* God knows that churches can only experience fullness of life in a right relationship with Him. Because of His love, He disciplines wayward Christians and churches to bring them back to Him. He also disciplines because His plan for world redemption slows down when His people have departed.

♦ PHASE 4: *God's people cry out to Him for help.* God's discipline becomes more and more intense until His people cry out to Him. He is patient and long-suffering. Like the Father of the Prodigal Son, God waits eagerly for His children to return to Him.

♦ PHASE 5: *God calls His people to repent and return to Him or perish.* God clearly defines the requirements for repentance. He doesn't give options. Churches can return to Him or suffer the consequences of their sin. He sets before His people a choice of life and death. When a church continues to refuse to repent, it is no longer of any use for the Kingdom. Like the church at Ephesus, God may remove the church from usefulness or existence.

♦ PHASE 6: *God revives His repentant people by restoring them to a right relationship with Him.* God stands ready to receive His people when they return. He cleanses and forgives. He gives them a new heart to serve Him and fullness of the Holy Spirit to empower them for His work. He restores the joy of being in the family of God.

♦ PHASE 7. *God exalts His Son Jesus among His people and draws the lost to saving faith in Him.* When God has a people rightly related to Himself, He is able to display His glory to a watching world. When a people experience the mighty power of God bringing wholeness to their lives, others will notice and want a similar experience of life. Spiritual awakening becomes a natural by-product of a revived people.

A TESTIMONY OF GOD'S GRACE: THE PRAYER REVIVAL OF 1857–58

With little in the way of human planning, a nationwide revival broke out among God's people in "union prayer meetings" beginning in 1857. In the awakening that followed, nearly a million people accepted Christ and became involved in churches in a single year. Someone has estimated that a similar move of God in our day would result in thirty million people turning to Christ.

The years leading up to 1857 were years of tremendous growth and prosperity for America. The population was booming. People and businesses were becoming wealthy. The "cares of the world" captured the minds and hearts of Americans, choking out their interest in God and His kingdom. Churches were declining in numbers, strength, and influence.

The growth of New York City began to force the wealthy residents out of the downtown area. They were replaced by unchurched masses of common laborers. Many churches decided to move to "more fruitful" locations. In a state of decline, the North Dutch Church decided to stay and reach the lost masses around them. They employed a businessman, Jeremiah Lanphier, as a lay missionary. He began to visit homes, distribute Bibles and tracts, and advertise church services. Facing a discouraging response, he found comfort in prayer.

One day Lanphier prayed, "Lord, what wilt thou have me to do?" He sensed God's leadership to begin a weekly prayer service for workers and business people to retire from their work at the noon hour for communion with God. He began on Wednesday, September 23, 1857, with six people attending. The second week, twenty attended, and forty came the third week. The hunger and thirst after God was evident, and they began daily "union prayer meetings" the fourth week. People of all classes of society and from every denomination attended.

God had a praying people in place when the financial crash of 1857 hit, just weeks after the prayer meetings began. "Merchants by the thousands all over the country were forced to the wall, banks failed, and railroads went into bankruptcy."[1] In New York City alone, thirty thousand lost their jobs. Added to the financial crisis, the nation was gripped by tensions over slavery. The future of the nation was bleak indeed.

In the midst of disaster and with a great hunger for God, people flooded the prayer meetings by the thousands. The meetings spread across New York City and then across the nation. Businesses even closed to allow their employees time for prayer. The newspapers gave front-page coverage of "Revival News," and revival spread like wildfire across the country. Religion became the common topic of conversation.

When the revival/awakening was at its peak, fifty thousand people were converted every week. Within a year nearly one million people were converted. "Bishop McIlvaine, in his annual address before the Diocesan Convention of Ohio, said . . . 'I rejoice in the decided conviction that it [the revival/awakening] is "the Lord's doing;" unaccountable by any natural causes, entirely above and beyond what any human device or power could produce; an outpouring of the Spirit of God upon God's people, quickening them to greater earnestness in his service; and upon the unconverted, to make them new creatures in Christ Jesus.'"[2]

SUMMARY

+ The early church at Pentecost is the example of what God intends for the church to be.
+ When God's people have departed from a right relationship with Him, they need revival.
+ The problem of departing from a right relationship with God is a problem for New Testament churches as well.
+ God is on mission to redeem a lost world. God calls His people into a relationship with Him, and He accomplishes His work through them.
+ God's people tend to depart from Him, turning to substitutes for His presence, purposes, and ways.
+ God disciplines His people out of His love for them.
+ God's people cry out to Him for help.
+ God calls His people to repent and return to Him or perish.
+ God revives His repentant people by restoring them to a right relationship with Him.
+ God exalts His Son Jesus in His people and draws the lost to saving faith in Him.

ENCOUNTERING GOD IN PRAYER

Take some time to pray about the phases in God's pattern to seek where you, your family, and your church may be in that cycle.

+ Ask the Lord to reveal your personal condition related to Him and His redemptive work in the world. Then ask Him about your family and your church. Ask the Lord which phase you are in.

- Ask the Lord to begin preparing your heart to cry out in behalf of your family, church, or nation.
- Would you be willing to pray like Jeremiah Lanphier, "Lord, what wilt thou have me to do?" Would you be willing to wait on the Lord until He tells you what He wants to do through you for revival in our day? If so, pray that now.

ENCOUNTERING GOD WITH OTHERS

As you have opportunity in a small group, consider these discussion questions for chapter 7:

1. Where do you sense our nation is in this cycle of sin and revival? Why?

2. Judges 2:14 says, "The anger of the LORD was hot against Israel. So He delivered them into the hands of plunderers who despoiled them; and He sold them into the hands of their enemies all around, so that they could no longer stand before their enemies." Who are some of the "plunderers" or raiders God may use in our day to discipline His people?

3. In which of the seven phases in God's pattern for revival and spiritual awakening do you sense your church is? Why?

4. When have you been part of a time of repentance in your church? What was it like?

5. What affect did financial disaster have on the beginning of revival in 1857? How would people respond today with a similar disaster?

6. What was the relationship of prayer and the beginning of revival in 1857?

CHAPTER 8

GOD IS ON MISSION TO REDEEM A LOST WORLD

Let's begin to look in detail at the seven phases in God's pattern for revival and spiritual awakening. The first and seventh phases describe God's ideal plan to

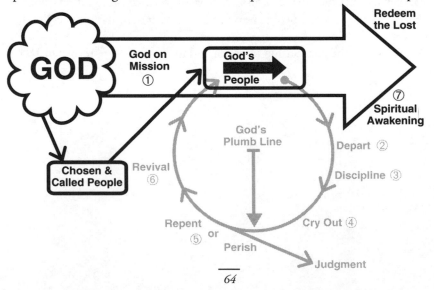

redeem a lost world. When God has a people rightly related to Him, spiritual awakening of a lost world is a natural and expected response. In this chapter we will focus on God's ideal plan for redemption.

♦ PHASE 1: God is on mission to redeem a lost world. God calls His people into a relationship with Him, and He accomplishes His work through them.

♦ PHASE 7: God exalts His Son Jesus in His people and draws the lost to saving faith in Him.

CREATED PERFECT FOR A LOVE RELATIONSHIP

God wanted a people with whom He could fellowship, so He created Adam in His own image, in His own likeness. His creation was perfect (Gen. 1:26–27, 31). He then created Eve from one of Adam's ribs. God loved His human creations and provided everything they needed in the Garden of Eden. Before sin entered into the world, the relationship of man and woman with God was beautiful and pure. God would come, in the cool of the evening or the early morning, and seek out fellowship with Adam and Eve. Nothing separated them: no shame, no guilt, no fear, no despair, no depression. They had a pure fellowship and love for each other.

God's desire was that men and women would choose to walk with Him and grow in a love relationship that would last for eternity. His primary command for us is that we love Him with our total being (Mark 12:29–30). This relationship is eternal. According to Jesus: "'This is eternal life, that they may know You, the only true God, and Jesus Christ whom You have sent'" (John 17:3). Our goal in life is to come to know God and His Son Jesus. This knowledge comes from experiencing God in a love relationship. God's primary goal for a person in this life is that he or she come to know God in a personal way. This pure and intimate love relationship in time prepares us for an eternity in His presence. Time is our opportunity to get to know Him.

A BROKEN RELATIONSHIP

From the very beginning, God gave His creation the choice of life and death. Sin, disobedience, and rebellion against God's commands carried severe penalties. Adam and Eve had a choice between (1) life in perfect fellowship with a loving Creator or (2) death for disobedience. Sadly, they chose to disobey God and suffer the consequences of their sin (Gen. 3). They broke their beautiful relationship with God.

Adam and Eve chose to walk independently of God and His commands. The consequence of their sin was death. Ever since then people have chosen to sin. At some point we have all chosen to rebel against God's rule. According to the Scriptures, this broken relationship means we are "dead in trespasses and sins . . . without Christ . . . having no hope and without God in the world" (Eph. 2:1, 12). Because of sin, we are dead. We are separated from God and without hope. That is just what we deserve. Our choices to sin bring us into slavery to sin.

GOD PROVIDES REDEMPTION

The Bible speaks of our need to be redeemed or ransomed from this spiritual death. A price must be paid to satisfy the wages of sin. "For the wages of sin is death, but the gift of God is eternal life in Christ Jesus our Lord" (Rom. 6:23). The good news of the gospel is that God has provided the way to life. He has provided for our redemption through Jesus Christ.

God loves His creations. It is not His desire that any perish. He wants all people to come to repentance (2 Pet. 3:9). So God sent His own Son Jesus to pay the death penalty for our sin. Jesus paid the price for our ransom or redemption. He did this so that we might be saved, so that we might have life (John 3:16).

When God saves us, He brings us back to a perfect love relationship. The diagram below shows this process. (1) You choose to sin. (2) You are dead in sin. (3) Christ paid the ransom for your sin by His death on the cross. (4) When you repent of your sin and place your faith in Him, (5) He forgives you and restores you to a right love relationship with God.

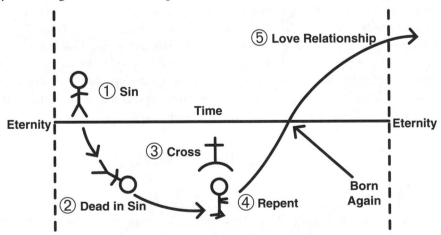

GOD CALLS A PEOPLE TO WORK WITH HIM

God's plan for redemption did not begin with the coming of Jesus to earth. Many see a promise of Jesus' victory over Satan in Genesis 3:15. About the woman's offspring, God said to the serpent, "He shall bruise your head" The seriousness of sin also is made clear. God described severe consequences for the serpent, woman, and man because of their sin (Gen. 3:14–19).

In Genesis 12 God began to reveal His plan to redeem the world. He called Abram (later changed to Abraham) to become involved in His eternal purposes:

> Now the LORD had said to Abram: "Get out of your country, From your family And from your father's house, To a land that I will show you. I will make you a great nation; I will bless you And make your name great; And you shall be a blessing. I will bless those who bless you, And I will curse him who curses you; And in you all the families of the earth shall be blessed." (Gen. 12:1–3)

> The LORD appeared to Abram and said to him, "I am Almighty God; walk before Me and be blameless. . . . And I will establish My covenant between Me and you and your descendants after you in their generations, for an everlasting covenant, to be God to you and your descendants after you." (Gen. 17:1, 7)

> "Abraham shall surely become a great and mighty nation, and all the nations of the earth shall be blessed in him? For I have known him, in order that he may command his children and his household after him, that they keep the way of the LORD, to do righteousness and justice." (Gen. 18:18–19)

The real focus of these Scriptures is not on Abraham but on God and His activity. God chooses to work through people, but the focus is always on God and what He does. In the call of Abraham, God was setting in motion His plan to redeem a whole world—all the nations and peoples of the earth. The only reason He came to Abraham was because He wanted to do it through him. God asked Abraham to follow Him, to be blameless, and to teach his children to obey God and do what is right and just. God kept his promises to Abraham and made his descendants a nation.

> Moses went up to God, and the LORD called to him from the mountain, saying, "Thus you shall say to . . . the children of Israel: 'You have seen what I did to the Egyptians, and how I bore you on eagles' wings and brought you to Myself. Now therefore, if you will indeed obey My voice and keep My covenant, then you shall be a special treasure to Me above all people . . . And you shall be to Me a kingdom of priests and a holy nation.'" (Exod. 19:3–6)

We usually think that God brought Israel into the promised land. God said, "'I . . . brought you to Myself.'" That is what made them special. He brought them to a relationship with Himself where they would be His special treasure, a kingdom of priests, and a holy nation. Israel was chosen by God for a purpose.

> "You are a holy people to the LORD your God; the LORD your God has chosen you to be a people for Himself, a special treasure above all the peoples on the face of the earth. The LORD did not set His love on you nor choose you because you were more in number than any other people, for you were the least of all peoples; but because the LORD loves you, and because He would keep the oath which He swore to your fathers, the LORD has brought you out with a mighty hand, and redeemed you from the house of bondage . . . Therefore know that the LORD your God, He is God, the faithful God who keeps covenant and mercy for a thousand generations with those who love Him and keep His commandments." (Deut. 7:6–9)

God chose Israel to be His special people because of His love and to keep His promise to Abraham. God asked the people to obey Him, not just to obey laws and commands. He asked them to keep the covenant relationship of love with Him.

A CONTINUED CALL IN A NEW COVENANT

God had called Israel to a royal priesthood. God intended to work through them to draw a world to Himself. By the time Jesus came to provide for our forgiveness, Israel had departed from God once again. Many were caught up in religious activity, but they had departed from the relationship with God. The religious leaders were so disoriented to God that they did not even recognize Him when He came to them (Luke 19:41–44). In fact, they killed Him.

In Christ, God established a new covenant with a new Israel—the church. This new relationship was based on faith, not on keeping the law. God chose and called out a new people (both Jews and Gentiles), who responded to His offer of salvation through faith in His Son. God said through Peter, "You are a chosen generation, a royal priesthood, a holy nation, His own special people, that you may proclaim the praises of Him who called you out of darkness into His marvelous light" (1 Pet. 2:9).

God said the church is a chosen generation, a royal priesthood, a holy nation, and a special people belonging to God. God chose His people in mercy and love. His purpose for them was that they declare His praises to people living in spiritual darkness. His purpose for the church was to continue what He began with Israel. God wants to redeem a lost world.

Chosen Generation. As God's people, we are chosen to be God's special treasures. We are special because we are related to Him. We belong to Him. We are not our own. We belong to another, but what a wonderful privilege we have to belong to the family of the Almighty God. Because we belong to Him, He deserves and expects our obedience for His purposes to redeem our generation.

Royal Priesthood. God did not say that they were a kingdom with a priesthood—a select few that can relate to Him. He said, "You are . . . a royal priesthood." Every single believer is a priest unto God. *Royal* means each one has direct access to the King of Kings and is a part of the royal family by adoption. The role of the priest was primarily to bring a word from God to the people. The priest also represented the people before God. We have that assignment and privilege: represent God to humanity and humanity to God. Each priest functions in the midst of the church—a priesthood of believers.

Holy Nation. Not only are we a kingdom of priests, but we are to be a holy nation. The word *holy* means "set apart for God's exclusive use." We are to be separated from the common and separated from the ways of the world. We are different than the world. We are to reflect God, His nature and His ways. We are commanded to be holy as He is holy and "abstain from fleshly lusts . . . having your conduct honorable among the Gentiles, that . . . they may, by your good works which they observe, glorify God in the day of visitation" (1 Pet. 2:11–12).

WORKERS TOGETHER WITH GOD

God has a people, and He is at work through His people to accomplish His redemptive work. His goal is to exalt Jesus and draw a lost world to faith in Christ. This is summarized in phases 1 and 7 of God's pattern. In 2 Corinthians Paul described this worker relationship with God:

> All things are of God, who has reconciled us to Himself through Jesus Christ, and has given us the ministry of reconciliation, that is, that God was in Christ reconciling the world to Himself . . . and has committed to us the word of reconciliation. Now then, we are ambassadors for Christ, as though God were pleading through us: we implore you on Christ's behalf, be reconciled to God. (2 Cor. 5:18–20)

Reconciled means "restored to a right relationship." God is the One reconciling the world to Himself through Christ. Yet, He has given the ministry and message of reconciliation to the church. In that ministry we are Christ's ambassadors and God's fellow workers (2 Cor. 6:1). Our motivation for this work is the love of Christ—He compels us by His love.

God is the One who is on a redemptive mission. The mission is His. In His love He has chosen the church to work together with Him in His mission. The mission is not one we can accomplish—we can do nothing apart from Him (John 15:5). God does the work through us. When God works through us, however, we will bear much fruit for the Kingdom—fruit that will last (John 15:8, 16). With God at work through His church, the church will accomplish greater things than Jesus did in His earthly ministry. He said, "'He who believes in Me, the works that I do he will do also; and greater works than these he will do, because I go to My Father'" (John 14:12).

When humanity sinned and broke fellowship with God, God began to prepare a people through which He would work to redeem a lost world. He provided for redemption through the death of His Son. Now, when God has a people rightly related to Him, He can work in mighty ways to significantly impact a lost world. When that happens spiritual awakening is happening. Spiritual awakening is a natural by-product of churches being rightly related to God.

A TESTIMONY OF GOD'S GRACE: THE ASBURY REVIVAL

In 1970 college campuses across the United States were filled with strife and protests. Yet at that time, the campuses of Asbury College and Asbury Theological Seminary in Wilmore, Kentucky, experienced a fresh encounter with God. During the college's regular chapel service on Tuesday, February 3, God brought a fresh wind of His Spirit across the students. The testimonies, singing, confessing of sin, and praying that began that Tuesday morning continued uninterrupted for 185 hours and ended about 3:00 A.M. Wednesday morning over a week later.

When a God-sent revival breaks out during a time of spiritual hunger, like the days of 1970, it cannot be contained. The testimonies of those present began to spread the refining fires of repentance and revival, first to the adjacent seminary then to churches and campuses across the nation. The Asbury Revival illustrates the way God uses a person's testimony of a divine encounter to stir the hearts of other believers.

The Asbury dean felt led to guide a time of testimony that Tuesday morning. He began by sharing his own testimony of faith and then encouraged others to share theirs.

One senior shocked the audience by confessing, "I'm not believing that I'm standing here telling you what God has done for me. I've wasted my time in college up to now, but Christ has met me and I'm different. Last night the Holy Spirit flooded in and filled my life. Now, for the first time ever, I am excited about being a Christian! I wouldn't want to go back to the emptiness of yesterday for anything."

The testimonies became real, fervent, up-to-date reports of God's activity. Toward the end of the chapel service, an invitation was opened for students who wanted to come to the altar for prayer and renewal of their commitment to Christ. A flood of students responded. Then came confessions of theft, cheating, resentment, jealousy, lust, worldly attitudes, prejudice, pride, hatred, and a variety of other sins. Students sought forgiveness. Broken relationships were reconciled. Some made restitution for sins committed. Many in the auditorium had an awesome sense of God's presence.

Word about the revival began to spread by phone, news reports, and word of mouth. Before long, visitors began to arrive to experience the revival firsthand. They carried the testimony of God's activity back to their churches and campuses, where revival often followed. Witnessing teams of students carried the testimony to churches and 130 colleges, seminaries, and Bible schools across the nation.

The Holy Spirit broke down church, denominational, and racial barriers. In some cases whole towns were swept up in the revival. In the high school in South Pittsburg, Tennessee, five hundred of the seven hundred students made commitments to Jesus Christ. People responded to God's call to missions and church-related vocations. By the end of 1970, the testimony of God's mighty activity had been shared across North America and on four other continents of the world.

After the Asbury Revival, many anticipated that God was in the process of sending another great awakening. Though the revival was widespread, it was short-lived. One possible reason for this short life is that the revival was primarily experience-oriented rather than Word-centered. Experience and emotional response to God can only carry you so far. The deep and long-lasting revivals in history have been Word-centered revivals. As people return to God and His plumb line, lives, churches, cities, and whole nations have experienced deep and lasting change.[1]

SUMMARY

- ◆ God's desire was that men and women would choose to walk with Him and grow in a love relationship that would last for eternity.
- ◆ Time is our opportunity to get to know Him.
- ◆ The good news of the gospel is that God has provided the way to life. He has provided for our redemption through Jesus Christ.
- ◆ God chooses to work through people, but the focus is always on God and what He does.
- ◆ God chose and called out a new people (both Jews and Gentiles), who responded to His offer of salvation through faith in His Son.

- His purpose for them was that they declare His praises to people living in spiritual darkness.
- His goal is to exalt Jesus and draw a lost world to faith in Christ.
- God is the One reconciling the world to Himself through Christ. Yet, He has given the ministry and message of reconciliation to the church.
- When God works through us, however, we will bear much fruit for the Kingdom—fruit that will last (John 15:8, 16).
- Spiritual awakening is a natural by-product of churches being rightly related to God.

ENCOUNTERING GOD IN PRAYER

- Spend some time working on your relationship with God today. Adam and Eve walked with God in the garden in the cool of the day. Plan for and take some time walking and talking with the Lord. Don't plan on anything but enjoying His company. He takes pleasure in fellowship with you.
- Ask God to guide you in evaluating the "fruit" of your life and that of your church. Does the fruit bring glory to your heavenly Father? Do others know you are His disciples by the fruit you bear? How much fruit are you bearing for the Kingdom? How lasting is the fruit you are bearing? What does this indicate about how well you are abiding in Him? Talk to the Lord about your love relationship and any improvement He may desire.

ENCOUNTERING GOD WITH OTHERS

As you have opportunity in a small group, consider these discussion questions for chapter 8:

1. What does "redemption" mean?

2. What does "reconciliation" mean?

3. What does "dead in sin" mean?

4. What does "workers together with God" mean?

5. What makes the people of God special? Are the members of our church living in the joy, wonder, and awe of being God's chosen and treasured possessions? How?

6. What does a church do to function as a royal priesthood? How faithfully is our church practicing our priesthood before God?

7. How faithfully are we declaring God's praises to the world in darkness? Are we shining brightly as the "light of the world"?

8. What are we doing as a church body to represent one another's spiritual needs to God?

9. How separate are we from the world and its ways? What evidence can we give that we are holy and set apart for God's service?

10. Do we act as a church like we can do nothing apart from God? Why do you think we do or do not?

11. How can the response of a lost world be an indicator of our church's relationship with God?

CHAPTER 9

GOD'S PEOPLE TEND TO DEPART FROM HIM

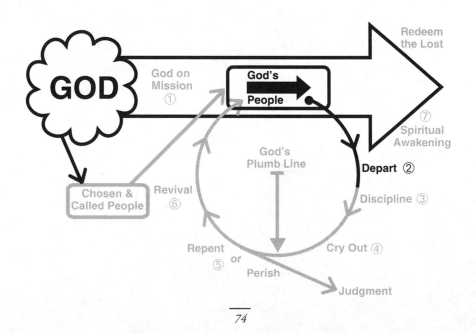

♦ PHASE 2: God's people tend to depart from Him, turning to substitutes for His presence, His purposes, and His ways.

God created us and called us into a love relationship with Him. He has called us to be on mission with Him in redeeming a lost world. Without God, that is an impossible mission. With God, however, all things are possible. In the Book of Deuteronomy, God explained that His requirements for His people were not too difficult.

> "This commandment which I command you today is not too mysterious for you, nor is it far off. It is not in heaven, that you should say, 'Who will ascend into heaven for us and bring it to us, that we may hear it and do it?' Nor is it beyond the sea, that you should say, 'Who will go over the sea for us and bring it to us, that we may hear it and do it?' But the word is very near you, in your mouth and in your heart, that you may do it.
> "See, I have set before you today life and good, death and evil, in that I command you today to love the LORD your God, to walk in His ways, and to keep His commandments, His statutes, and His judgments, that you may live and multiply; and the LORD your God will bless you in the land which you go to possess." (Deut. 30:11–16)

In this passage God asks you to do three things: (1) love Him; (2) walk in His ways; and (3) keep His commands, decrees, and laws. More than anything else, God wants you to love Him. He wants you to do things His way rather than your own way or the world's way. God wants you to obey Him, but His commands are not too difficult. His will is not hidden so that you have to have some religious specialist find and explain His word to you. His word and will are in you. As a Christian, God's Holy Spirit is present *in you* to guide you and empower you in every act of obedience. As a church, you are the body with Christ as your Head. God has done everything possible to see to it that you will obey Him, follow Him, and participate with Him in His redemptive mission.

A SHIFT OF THE HEART

God "has blessed us with every spiritual blessing" (Eph. 1:3). "His divine power has given to us all things that pertain to life and godliness" (2 Pet. 1:3). God has done great things for us, yet we still tend to depart from Him. How do you move away from God? How does a church move away from God? God explains: "'If your heart turns away and you are not obedient, and if you are drawn away to bow down to other gods and worship them'" (Deut. 30:17, NIV).

Moving away from God does not begin with wrong activity. It begins with a radical shift in your heart. Departing from God follows a downward course. It begins with a shift of your heart away from Him. You do not love Him like you used to love Him. That may be such a gradual shift that you do not realize it is happening until you are a long way from Him. Once your heart has shifted, you do not obey Him. You choose not to keep His commands thinking "this is not all that bad" or "God doesn't really care if I don't do this." Next, you turn to substitutes for Him and you "bow down to other gods and worship them." Here is a summary of how a person, a family, a church, a denomination, or even a nation can depart from God.

DEPARTING FROM GOD

1. *The heart shifts away from loving God fully.*
2. *The will no longer chooses to obey God.*
3. *The life turns or is drawn away to follow substitutes for God's presence, purposes, and ways.*

God knew that His people would tend to depart from Him, so He gave them a stern warning.

> "But if your heart turns away . . . I announce to you today that you shall surely perish; you shall not prolong your days . . . I call heaven and earth as witnesses today against you, that I have set before you life and death, blessing and cursing; therefore choose life, that both you and your descendants may live; that you may love the LORD your God, that you may obey His voice, and that you may cling to Him, for He is your life." (Deut. 30:17–20)

This passage was a warning to God's people. In love He wanted them to choose life and prosperity, not death and destruction. God gave only two options. There is no compromise. God wants a love relationship with you and with His people. You are to love Him with all your heart. With your will, choose to obey Him fully. And with your life, cling to Him. This Scripture doesn't promise that the Lord will give you life. The Lord *is* your life! He wants to take up residence in you and live through you.

Some people may object, "But that is Old Testament." They have a tendency to think that God changed in the New Testament and no longer brings consequences on His people for sin. Look, however, at what Jesus Himself had to say to the church at Ephesus: "'I have this against you, that you have left your first love. Remember therefore from where you have fallen; repent and do the first works, or else I will come to you quickly and remove your lampstand [church, Rev. 1:20] from its place—unless you repent'" (Rev. 2:4–5).

The departure of our heart from our first love for Christ is serious. In fact, it can be fatal for a church. Every week churches are dying and disbanding. One reason may be this: they have refused to repent and return to their first love for Christ. Then they are no longer of any use to the Lord. He will not let them remain and defame His name. Departing from God is serious. Therefore, spiritual leaders need to be like physicians. We need to be able to identify the heart shift so that we can deal with it like it is a fatal cancer that can destroy life. If a church has departed, the shepherd should not abandon the flock by going to another church. He should understand this is precisely why God put him there—to help guide them to return to God with all their heart. It may take time and be a painful process, but their lives are at stake.

TWO SIGNS OF A HEART SHIFT

1. Lack of obedience
2. Substitutes for God

LACK OF OBEDIENCE

In departing from God we follow a progression from a shift of the heart, to lack of obedience, to turning to substitutes for God. Usually by the time God gets our attention, we have been backsliding for a long time. Just like a divorce that begins when two people drift apart, so we don't jump away from God. We drift. It usually takes time—a period of neglect, carelessness, or rebellious choices. The symptoms may have been present in our lives or churches for a long time, but somehow we fail to pay attention until we are far away from Him. We just take small steps away from God. Then suddenly we realize we have departed and are far from Him.

How do you know if your heart has shifted as an individual or as a church? Two signs are clear indicators: (1) lack of obedience and (2) turning to substitutes for God. These are clear signs that your heart has turned. As a doctor looks for symptoms of the real problem, you can look for lack of obedience and substitutes for God as symptoms of a problem with your love for God. Let's identify some of the indications that your heart has departed from the Lord. First, notice the clear connection Jesus made between obedience and love in the following verses:

♦ "'If you love Me, keep My commandments'" (John 14:15).
♦ "'He who has My commandments and keeps them, it is he who loves Me'" (John 14:21).
♦ "'If anyone loves Me, he will keep My word . . . He who does not love Me does not keep My words'" (John 14:23–24).

Do you see the connection between the heart and obedience? Jesus says it is spiritually impossible to love Him and not obey Him. The problem is not obedience; the problem is love. If you do not obey, it is because your heart has shifted. Love will always obey. But, we protest strongly and say, "Lord, it's not that I don't love you, it's that I'm having difficulty obeying you."

God would say, "If you are having difficulty obeying Me, it is because you do not love Me." If you do not understand that, you will always be trying to get right with God. You will try to reform your behavior and you will fail. Like the Leaning Tower of Pisa. You can try to straighten out the walls, but the repairs will be short-lived if you don't fix the faulty foundation. We tend to treat the symptoms instead of the cause. Do you know how to solve the problem of disobedience? Return to your first love for God. If you want to correct your disobedience, begin with your heart. If you return to your first love, a love relationship with God, you will resolve the obedience problems in your life. "Walk in the Spirit, and you shall not fulfill the lust of the flesh" (Gal. 5:16).

Is there something God asks of you that you have done without any question, but now you question it? When Christ gives a command in His Word and you start to argue with Him, you give evidence that your heart has shifted. Are there things Christ has commanded that you or those in your church no longer choose to obey? Look over the brief list below to see how well your church measures up to obedience in these few areas.

♦ *Do you love one another as Christ loves you?* "A new commandment I give to you, that you love one another; as I have loved you'" (John 13:34).

♦ *Do you forgive others so that you may be forgiven?* "'Whenever you stand praying, if you have anything against anyone, forgive him, that your Father in heaven may also forgive you your trespasses'" (Mark 11:25).

♦ *Are you known as a people that pray?* "'It is written, "My house is a house of prayer"'" (Luke 19:46).

♦ *Do you tithe and practice justice, mercy, and faith?* "'Woe to you . . . hypocrites! For you pay tithe . . . and have neglected the weightier matters of the law: justice and mercy and faith. These you ought to have done, without leaving the others undone'" (Matt. 23:23).

♦ *Are you actively going to make disciples of the nations, even those around your community? Are you teaching them to practice all Christ has commanded?*

"'Go therefore and make disciples of all the nations, baptizing them . . . [and] teaching them to observe all things that I have commanded you'" (Matt. 28:19–20).

♦ *Are you witnessing about Christ to the world in power of His Spirit?* "'You shall receive power when the Holy Spirit has come upon you; and you shall be witnesses to Me in Jerusalem, and in all Judea and Samaria, and to the end of the earth'" (Acts 1:8).

♦ *Are you displaying unity with other believers in your church, with other churches, and with Christians in other denominations?* "'May they be brought to complete unity to let the world know that you sent me and have loved them even as you have loved me'" (John 17:23, NIV).

Based on these few commands of the Lord, would you say that your church is obeying all that Jesus commanded? If you see that your church is no longer obeying the commands of the Lord, this is one clear sign that you have departed from God. A church may sincerely seek the will of God. A great number of members clearly sense a direction from God. Some in the church, however, may raise such a storm of protest that they decide not to do what God directed. This would indicate that the heart of the church had begun to shift. The next time the church senses God's directions, they may choose again not to obey. The heart of the church has begun to harden. "Beware, brethren, lest there be in any of you an evil heart of unbelief in departing from the living God; but exhort one another daily, while it is called 'Today,' lest any of you be hardened through the deceitfulness of sin" (Heb. 3:12–13).

As a spiritual physician, we can identify the departed heart of a person or a church when we see that they no longer obey. Another sign of a departed heart is turning to substitutes for God. Is it possible we would ever turn away from God after all He has done for us? Israel did.

CRACKED CISTERNS INSTEAD OF LIVING WATER

Read about Israel's departure in Jeremiah 2:2–13 below and listen to the broken heart of God as He describes the way His people left Him.

"What injustice have your fathers found in Me, That they have gone far from Me, Have followed idols, And have become idolaters? Neither did they say, 'Where is the LORD . . .' I brought you into a bountiful country, To eat its fruit and its goodness. But when you entered, you defiled My land And made My heritage an abomination. The priests did not say, 'Where is the LORD?' And those who handle the law did not know Me; The rulers also transgressed against Me; The prophets prophesied by Baal, And walked after things that do not profit.

"Therefore I will yet bring charges against you," says the LORD . . .
"see if there has been such a thing. Has a nation changed its gods, Which
are not gods? But My people have changed their Glory For what does not
profit. Be astonished, O heavens, at this, And be horribly afraid; Be very
desolate," says the LORD. "For My people have committed two evils: They
have forsaken Me, the fountain of living waters, And hewn themselves cisterns—broken cisterns that can hold no water." (Jer. 2:5–13)

God has created us with a big emptiness that only He can fill. Yet, He is
the living water. He is like a well that springs up out of the ground, flowing
with fresh water that gives life. He alone is able to fill us completely with life
when He fills us with Himself. Life is a Person—"'The Lord . . . is your life'"
(Deut. 30:20). Jesus said, "'I am . . . the life'" (John 14:6). Even today we commit two sins: we forsake Him—the living water—and try to come up with
substitutes (broken cisterns/containers) for Him. The tragedy is that our substitutes are cracked. They cannot provide life, and they cannot hold any life
from other sources.

THE WOMAN AT THE WELL

On a trip through Samaria, Jesus stopped to rest at Jacob's well near the town
of Sychar. A woman came to draw water, and Jesus asked her for a drink. Jesus
knew that the woman had looked for fullness of life in substitutes for God. He
led her into a discussion of living water. Watch in the following passage for two
ways the woman had turned to substitutes for God.

> Jesus answered and said to her, "If you knew the gift of God, and who
> it is who says to you, 'Give Me a drink,' you would have asked Him, and
> He would have given you living water. . . . Whoever drinks of this water
> will thirst again, but whoever drinks of the water that I shall give him will
> never thirst. But the water that I shall give him will become in him a foun-
> tain of water springing up into everlasting life."
> The woman said to Him, "Sir, give me this water, that I may not
> thirst, nor come here to draw."
> Jesus said to her, "Go, call your husband, and come here."
> The woman answered and said, "I have no husband."
> Jesus said to her, "You have well said, 'I have no husband,' for you
> have had five husbands, and the one whom you now have is not your hus-
> band; in that you spoke truly."
> The woman said to Him, "Sir, I perceive that You are a prophet. Our
> fathers worshiped on this mountain, and you Jews say that in Jerusalem is
> the place where one ought to worship."

Jesus said to her, "Woman, believe Me, the hour is coming when you will neither on this mountain, nor in Jerusalem, worship the Father . . . But the hour is coming, and now is, when the true worshipers will worship the Father in spirit and truth; for the Father is seeking such to worship Him." (John 4:10–23)

The Samaritan woman tried to find a husband who could fill up the void in her life. That is a job too big for any human. When one husband couldn't meet her deepest needs, she looked for another. By the time she met Jesus she was working on number six in a sexual relationship outside of marriage. She was looking for love in the wrong places.

People can become substitutes for God. Sexual relationships can become a substitute for a love relationship with God. Neither can satisfy the spiritual thirst for the Living Water. That is a thirst that only Jesus can satisfy.

The Samaritan woman also discussed religious worship with Jesus. Did you notice that the focus of her question was not on God? She was concerned about the place of worship. She was concerned about external things. Apparently, worship for her was just a set of traditional religious activities. Worship was not a vital relationship with God.

Religious activity and tradition can become a substitute for a relationship with God. We can exchange a vital relationship with a living Lord for a set of religious activities. We can be very busy going through the motions of religion and never experience life in Him.

IDOLS OF THE HEART

The Bible is filled with examples of people who chose substitutes for God. Throughout history God's people have tended to turn to substitutes for their relationship with Him. Don't think that you are not vulnerable as well. Anytime we turn to anyone or anything when we should turn to God, we make that person or thing an idol. An idol is anything we substitute for God. It does not have to be an image you set up in your home to worship. The Scriptures also describe idols of the heart.

"These men have set up their idols in their hearts, and put before them that which causes them to stumble into iniquity. . . . Therefore say to the house of Israel, 'Thus says the Lord GOD: "Repent, turn away from your idols, and turn your faces away from all your abominations."'" (Ezek. 14:3, 6)

The people had set up idols in their hearts and before their faces. By setting up idols they had deserted God. Their hearts had shifted. So God was planning to recapture the hearts of His people (Ezek. 14:5). Isn't it sad to think that, after all God had done for Israel, He had to work to win back their love? Could that be true of us? After all God has done for us in Christ, is it possible that we, too, have set up idols in our hearts?

COMMON IDOLS

In the story of the woman at the well, we saw some common idols. People, sexual relationships, and even religious activity can be idols. Let's look at some of the more common "idols" or substitutes for God: "Of this you can be sure: No immoral, impure or greedy person—such a man is an idolater—has any inheritance in the kingdom of Christ and of God" (Eph. 5:5, NIV).

According to God's Word, sexual immorality, impurity, and greed are idols of the heart. Each of these could be a one-time act, or they could be a regular practice or attitude of life. The regular practice or attitude is the sin that is idolatry. In each of these sins a person gives his heart to something other than God. A person who practices these sins has departed from God. Read about some more idols:

> Thus says the LORD: "Cursed is the man who trusts in man And makes flesh his strength, Whose heart departs from the LORD." (Jer. 17:5)

> "These people draw near to Me with their mouth, And honor Me with their lips, But their heart is far from Me. And in vain they worship Me, Teaching as doctrines the commandments of men." (Matt. 15:8–9)

> "No one can serve two masters; for either he will hate the one and love the other, or else he will be loyal to the one and despise the other. You cannot serve God and mammon." (Matt. 6:24)

> "He who loves father or mother more than Me is not worthy of Me. And he who loves son or daughter more than Me is not worthy of Me." (Matt. 10:37)

> "If anyone desires to come after Me, let him deny himself, and take up his cross daily, and follow Me. For whoever desires to save his life will lose it, but whoever loses his life for My sake will save it." (Luke 9:23–24)

> "You search the Scriptures, for in them you think you have eternal life; and these are they which testify of Me. But you are not willing to come to Me that you may have life." (John 5:39–40)

> Do not love the world or anything in the world. If anyone loves the world, the love of the Father is not in him. For everything in the world—the cravings of sinful man, the lust of his eyes and the boasting of what he has and does—comes not from the Father but from the world. (1 John 2:15–16, NIV)

Let's look at a summary list of idols that we can turn to:

♦ sexual immorality (Eph. 5:5)
♦ impurity (Eph. 5:5)
♦ greed (Eph. 5:5)
♦ trusting in man/flesh or the help of others (Jer. 17:5)
♦ ritual worship and following the teachings of man (Matt. 15:8–9)
♦ love and devotion to mammon or money (Matt. 6:24)
♦ relationships with other people (Matt. 10:37)
♦ self (Luke 9:23–24)
♦ Bible study that doesn't go from head knowledge to Christ Himself (John 5:39–40)
♦ materialism, things of the world (1 John 2:15)
♦ career, job, or work ("what he . . . does") (1 John 2:16)

Do some of these (like Bible study) surprise you? People, things, or activities may be very good. However, if we allow anything to take the place of turning to God or our love of God, our heart has shifted. This is certainly not a complete list of things we can substitute for a love relationship with God. Could devotion to a hobby, to television, to community service, or even to church work become a substitute for a love relationship with God? Yes. Anything that captures your heart—your love—can be a substitute for God.

SUBSTITUTES FOR GOD

Every time a believer moves away from God, he or she puts a substitute in His place. When we no longer turn to God, we replace Him, His purposes, and His ways with something from the world. A major tragedy of the Christian community is that individuals and churches are filled with substitutes we have chosen for God. We have often substituted work, ritual or traditional religious activity, advertising, buildings, programs, relationships with others, or a love for the things of the world for a love relationship with God. Where we used to turn to Him, we now turn to someone or something else.

A pastor from the United States was in China talking with Christian leaders. One said, "Christians in China are praying for our Christian brothers and sisters in America. We believe we are handling our persecution better than you are handling your prosperity." Have we allowed our prosperity and materialism to become a substitute for God? Notice the danger God warns us about:

> "Beware that you do not forget the LORD your God by not keeping His commandments, His judgments, and His statutes which I command you today, lest—when you have eaten and are full, and have built beautiful houses and dwell in them; and when your herds and your flocks multiply,

and your silver and your gold are multiplied, and all that you have is multiplied; when your heart is lifted up, and you forget the LORD your God . . . then you say in your heart, 'My power and the might of my hand have gained me this wealth.'" (Deut. 8:11–17)

Ask yourself this question: "Is anything causing me to forget God?" This is a good way to discover things that have become substitutes for God. Think about prosperity or success. Pride in the heart exalts self and claims credit for wealth. Jesus said, "'Watch out! Be on your guard against all kinds of greed; a man's life does not consist in the abundance of his possessions'" (Luke 12:15, NIV). Material things are not the only substitutes we turn to in place of God. Look over the following three lists for some other possible substitutes:

SUBSTITUTES FOR GOD'S PRESENCE

♦ We may place our trust in methods, programs, or people to accomplish spiritual growth and church growth rather than trusting Him.
♦ We may substitute emotional hype, pageantry, entertainment, or ritual for the reality of His intimate presence in worship.
♦ We no longer have a quiet time with God in His word and in prayer.

SUBSTITUTES FOR GOD'S PURPOSES

♦ We may conduct baptism and the Lord's Supper as tradition or ritual when He intended them to be times of public testimony, remembrance of Him, personal examination, and renewal of fellowship with Him.
♦ We may spend much of our time and resources on selfish pleasures and ignore justice for the oppressed or meeting the needs of the poor.
♦ We may conduct "evangelistic" visits primarily to ask people to come to church for an attendance goal when God wants them to come to Him for redemption.

SUBSTITUTES FOR GOD'S WAYS

♦ We walk by sight, when God says walk by faith.
♦ We affirm self and give self first consideration, when God says deny self.
♦ We exalt self, when God says humble yourself.
♦ We try to save our life (hold on to what we have), when God says lose your life (give away what you have for the Kingdom sake).
♦ We try to manipulate people to serve, when God says pray for Him to call forth laborers.

God warns us about forgetting Him: "'If you by any means forget the LORD your God, and follow other gods, and serve them and worship them, I testify against you this day that you shall surely perish'" (Deut. 8:19). You may think that God's promise of destruction for following other gods is pretty severe. It is. That reveals how seriously God treats sin and rebellion. The Bible teaches that God is jealous of our love. He created us and deserves our love and life. In the next chapter we will look at the love of God that is revealed in His discipline of His people.

SUMMARY

♦ God wants you to obey Him, but His commands are not too difficult.

♦ With all that God has done for us, God's people still tend to depart from Him.

♦ Moving away from God does not begin with wrong activity. It begins with a radical shift in your heart.

♦ The Lord *is* your life! He wants to take up residence in you and live through you.

♦ Spiritual leaders need to be like physicians. We need to be able to identify the heart shift so that we can deal with it like it is a fatal cancer that can destroy life.

♦ In departing from God we follow a progression from a shift of the heart, to lack of obedience, to turning to substitutes for God.

♦ Lack of obedience and turning to substitutes for God are clear signs that your heart has turned.

♦ Jesus says that it is spiritually impossible to love Him and not obey Him.

♦ This may be a good way to determine things that have become substitutes for God—ask yourself if anything is causing you to forget God.

ENCOUNTERING GOD IN PRAYER

♦ If God evaluated your obedience record right now, what would He conclude about your love for Him? Ask the Holy Spirit to reveal ways you may be disobeying God. Start making a list of anything He brings to mind. Ask God to shed light on the quality of your love relationship with Him.

♦ Is God beginning to reveal some things in your life that have become heart idols or substitutes? Are there ways you have departed from Him for someone or something else? Have you given your passions or priorities to activities instead of God? Ask God to guide you in returning to Him.

Repent and put away any idols or practices He may call to your attention. Let Him recapture your heart.

ENCOUNTERING GOD WITH OTHERS

As you have opportunity in a small group, consider these discussion questions for chapter 9:

1. Why do we often allow our hearts to shift?

2. Do you think we can ever get out of the cycle of sin and repentance? Why or why not?

3. What difference should the presence of the Holy Spirit make in the life of a believer regarding his or her obedience?

4. How can we learn to identify a heart shift early in the cycle instead of waiting for God's discipline or judgment? What are some of the signs?

5. After reading Jeremiah 2:2–13 (pp. 79–80), how do you think God feels when His people choose to forsake Him?

6. What are some ways that many people are living life like the Woman at the Well?

7. How do idols of the heart affect our love relationship with God? What does God expect us to do with idols of the heart and why?

8. What are some ways our church may have turned to substitutes for God, His presence, His purposes, or His ways? What do you sense we may need to do to change our ways?

You may notice that we frequently will be studying passages from Deuteronomy. Don't discount these as "Old Testament" and therefore no longer valid for the Christian. I would remind you that Jesus quoted extensively from Deuteronomy as He taught the first disciples. These are the Scriptures to which He opened their minds (Luke 24:45) as He prepared the first church to carry out its role in His redemptive plan. Deuteronomy tells us much about God and how He relates to His people. Jesus saw great value in studying and memorizing Deuteronomy. We can gain great value from meeting God in its pages.

CHAPTER 10

GOD DISCIPLINES HIS PEOPLE IN LOVE

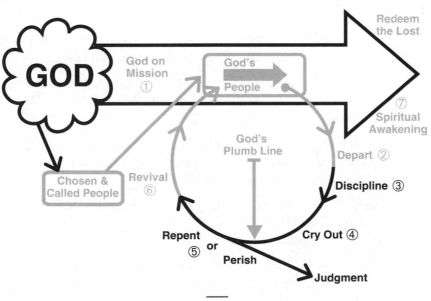

♦ PHASE 3: God disciplines His people out of His love for them.

♦ PHASE 4: God's people cry out to Him for help.

GOD'S NATURE

Many of God's people have lost their sense of the fear of God. We no longer believe that He disciplines and judges His people. Many think the God of judgment and wrath was the God we see in the Old Testament. They think of the God revealed in the New Testament as a God of love. Such thinking shows that a person does not know the Scripture or the God revealed in Scripture.

God said, "'I the Lord do not change'" (Mal. 3:8, NIV). "Jesus Christ [God] is the same yesterday and today and forever" (Heb. 13:8, NIV). We do not serve two Gods—one Old Testament and one New Testament God. The Lord is One. He doesn't change. Let's look together at the nature of our God. As you read the following Scriptures notice the words or phrases that tell you about God's nature.

> Jonah 4:2—"'I know that You are a gracious and merciful God, slow to anger and abundant in lovingkindness, One who relents from doing harm.'"

> 1 John 4:7–8—"Beloved, let us love one another, for love is of God; and everyone who loves is born of God and knows God. He who does not love does not know God, for God is love."

> Nehemiah 9:31—"'Nevertheless in Your great mercy You did not utterly consume them nor forsake them; For You are God, gracious and merciful.'"

> Jeremiah 9:24—"'I am the LORD, exercising lovingkindness, judgment, and righteousness in the earth. For in these I delight,' says the LORD."

> Psalm 51:4—"Against You, You only, have I sinned, And done this evil in Your sight—That You may be found just when You speak, And blameless when You judge."

> Romans 2:5—"In accordance with your hardness and your impenitent heart you are treasuring up for yourself wrath in the day of wrath and revelation of the righteous judgment of God."

> Psalm 78:38—"He, being full of compassion, forgave their iniquity, And did not destroy them. Yes, many a time He turned His anger away, And did not stir up all His wrath."

> Daniel 9:9—"'To the Lord our God belong mercy and forgiveness, though we have rebelled against Him.'"

Psalm 33:4–5—"The word of the LORD is right, And all His work is done in truth. He loves righteousness and justice; The earth is full of the goodness of the LORD."

Psalm 9:7–8—"The LORD shall endure forever; He has prepared His throne for judgment. He shall judge the world in righteousness, And He shall administer judgment for the peoples in uprightness."

Isaiah 5:16 —"The LORD of hosts shall be exalted in judgment, And God who is holy shall be hallowed in righteousness."

Isaiah 30:18—"The LORD will wait, that He may be gracious to you; And therefore He will be exalted, that He may have mercy on you. For the LORD is a God of justice; Blessed are all those who wait for Him."

God is beyond our understanding. Yet, He has revealed Himself in Scripture. He is perfect love. He forever convinced us of His love through the death of Jesus on the cross. He is kind, compassionate, patient, and slow to anger. God is also just. He never punishes the innocent. His judgments are always right and fair. Yet, He also is merciful. He seldom gives us the punishment we deserve. He forgives us when we repent and return to Him.

God also is holy and pure. He cannot simply tolerate our sin. Because of His holiness and justice, He must deal with our sin. He does get angry, and he sometimes displays His wrath on rebellious people. We need to develop a healthy fear of our holy God. When you enter His presence, you will sense His holiness. You also will see clearly the sin in your own life. When a church experiences genuine worship in His presence, they will realize any sin for which they may need forgiveness.

Read the following Scriptures and see what God takes pleasure in:

Ezekiel 18:23, 32—"'Do I have any pleasure at all that the wicked should die?' says the Lord GOD, 'and not that he should turn from his ways and live? . . . For I have no pleasure in the death of one who dies,' says the Lord GOD. 'Therefore turn and live!'"

2 Peter 3:9—"The Lord is not slack concerning His promise, as some count slackness, but is longsuffering toward us, not willing that any should perish but that all should come to repentance."

Don't we tend to think that God would delight in the death of the wicked? God does not delight in the death of anyone who needs to repent. He wants all people to repent and turn to Him.

GOD'S PURPOSE IN DISCIPLINE

God created and called out His people for a love relationship with Him. When God's people depart from that love relationship, He is grieved. He is brokenhearted over the shattered love relationship. He disciplines His people and invites them to return to Him. Phase Three in God's pattern for revival is that He disciplines His people in love. Notice what the writer of Hebrews tells us about God's discipline:

> "My son, do not despise the chastening of the LORD, Nor be discouraged when you are rebuked by Him; For whom the LORD loves He chastens, And scourges every son whom He receives." If you endure chastening, God deals with you as with sons; for what son is there whom a father does not chasten? But if you are without chastening . . . then you are illegitimate and not sons. Furthermore, we have had human fathers who corrected us, and we paid them respect. Shall we not much more readily be in subjection to the Father of spirits and live? For they indeed for a few days chastened us as seemed best to them, but He for our profit, that we may be partakers of His holiness. Now no chastening seems to be joyful for the present, but painful; nevertheless, afterward it yields the peaceable fruit of righteousness to those who have been trained by it. (Heb. 12:5–11)

God created His people for a love relationship. He knows that fullness of life is found only in that relationship. Thus, when we move out of a love relationship, God knows we are missing out on the life for which He created us. Because of His love, God disciplines His people when they depart from Him and sin. We need to feel the pain of the lost love relationship so we will return to Him.

Human parents discipline their children when they do wrong. Have you ever said, "This is for your own good" or "This is going to hurt me more than it is you"? Parents who love their children teach them to live correctly.

God loved us so much that He sent His Son Jesus to die on a cross for us. Our sin brought great pain to our heavenly Father. He loves us dearly. That is why He rebukes, disciplines, and punishes us as His children. We are disciplined as part of God's family, and anyone whom God does not discipline is not part of His family. God corrects His children for their own good. He wants us to share in His holiness. He wants us to reap righteousness and peace. Even though His discipline may be painful, we should submit to His correction and live! These words from Hebrews 12 (NIV) are intended to "encourage" you. Be encouraged when you are disciplined by God. That is a good sign that He loves you and has not given up on you.

There is another reason God disciplines us. He loves the lost world and wants to see lost people repent. When God's people depart from Him, His redemptive mission slows down. God has no Plan B in case the church fails to do its part in His mission. Thus, God disciplines us so we will return to Him in order that He can work mightily through us to redeem a lost world.

GOD'S DISCIPLINE AND JUDGMENTS

Someday soon Jesus is going to return to claim His own people and take them to heaven for eternity. At the end of history God will judge all people. "We shall all stand before the judgment seat of Christ. . . . So then each of us shall give account of himself to God" (Rom. 14:10, 12). The judgments in the end will be eternal. Our destiny in heaven or hell will be settled as God separates the "sheep" (his people) from the "goats" (those who do not belong to Him) (Matt. 25:31–46). In this chapter, we are not dealing with those eternal judgments, though our responses to God today will affect the outcome of those judgments.

Our focus in this chapter is on God's temporal judgments; these are judgments that occur in our lifetime on earth. These disciplines and judgments are intended to correct us or to punish us. Because God is loving and patient, His correction almost always comes first. Only after that fails to bring change does more severe punishment and the wrath of God come. God is sovereign, however. He can do what He pleases, but His judgments are always just, fair, and right. He will never give us greater punishment than we deserve. Thus:

- *Eternal judgments* are rulings that separate God's people to heaven and all others to hell for eternity.
- *Temporal judgments* are corrections and punishments that occur in this lifetime.

Temporal discipline and judgment in this life are of two types: remedial judgments and final judgments. Remedial judgments (or discipline) are intended by God to correct us. They are to guide us back to a right relationship with God. Final judgments come when God displays His wrath. He sometimes destroys or removes life in punishment. When final judgment comes, no opportunity for repentance is left; time for repentance is past. Final judgments usually come after prolonged periods of sin without repentance. Sometimes, however, God uses a final judgment because of His serious opposition to sin. He uses final judgments at other times because the sin could have great influence in others if He did not deal severely with the sin.

- *Remedial judgment* is discipline or judgment intended to correct us and point us back to a right relationship with God.
- *Final judgment* is judgment or punishment which ends life or usefulness because of prolonged rebellion or severe sin.

Lets look at an example of each from the Bible.

FINAL JUDGMENT ON ANANIAS AND SAPPHIRA

Ananias, with Sapphira his wife, sold a possession. And he kept back part of the proceeds, his wife also being aware of it, and brought a certain part and laid it at the apostles' feet. But Peter said, "Ananias, why has Satan filled your heart to lie to the Holy Spirit and keep back part of the price of the land for yourself? While it remained, was it not your own? And after it was sold, was it not in your own control? Why have you conceived this thing in your heart? You have not lied to men but to God."

Then Ananias, hearing these words, fell down and breathed his last. So great fear came upon all those who heard these things. . . . About three hours later . . . his wife came in, not knowing what had happened. And Peter answered her, "Tell me whether you sold the land for so much?"

She said, "Yes, for so much."

Then Peter said to her, "How is it that you have agreed together to test the Spirit of the Lord? Look, the feet of those who have buried your husband are at the door, and they will carry you out." Then immediately she fell down at his feet and breathed her last. . . . So great fear came upon all the church and upon all who heard these things." (Acts 5:1–11)

The church was young. God knew that a wicked influence of deceit could corrupt the entire redemptive work He intended for the church. Because their sin could have such a broad and lasting influence, God executed a righteous and final judgment on them. God is sovereign and can do what He chooses, for we all deserve death because of our sin. However, God more frequently uses remedial judgment to call His people to return.

REMEDIAL JUDGMENT ON THE IMMORAL MAN AT CORINTH

It is actually reported that there is sexual immorality among you . . . that a man has his father's wife! And you are puffed up, and have not rather mourned, that he who has done this deed might be taken away from among you. . . . In the name of our Lord Jesus Christ, when you are gathered together, along with my spirit, with the power of our Lord Jesus Christ, deliver such a one to Satan for the destruction of the flesh, that his spirit may be saved in the day of the Lord Jesus. Your glorying is not good. Do you not know that a little leaven leavens the whole lump? Therefore purge out the old leaven, that you may be a new lump . . . Therefore "put away from yourselves the evil person." (1 Cor 5:1–13)

The immoral man at Corinth experienced corrective discipline of God carried out by the church. In 2 Corinthians 2:5–11, Paul explains that the correction was effective. Paul asked the church to forgive the man, comfort him, and reaffirm their love for him. The church's correction by Paul also was effective. (See 2 Corinthians 7:8–13.)

In our study of revival, our focus is on God's remedial discipline or judgment. God's desire is to correct us so that we will return to Him. Look at the diagram on page 87. The word *judgment* at the bottom is a final judgment in this lifetime. God's desire for His people is that we will never reach that point. In the next chapter we will look at God's call for repentance.

TRUTHS ABOUT GOD'S JUDGMENTS

As we examine God's ways of discipline and judgment, several truths from Scripture are important to keep in mind.

♦ *Judgment should begin with the people of God.* "The time has come for judgment to begin at the house of God; and if it begins with us first, what will be the end of those who do not obey the gospel of God?" (1 Pet. 4:17).

♦ *Every deed, including hidden things, will be judged.* "God will bring every work into judgment, Including every secret thing, Whether good or evil" (Eccles. 12:14).

♦ *Jesus came to bring judgment.* "Jesus said, 'For judgment I have come into this world, that those who do not see may see, and that those who see may be made blind'" (John 9:39).

♦ *God's judgments always are right, true, and fair.* "'Even so, Lord God Almighty, true and righteous are Your judgments'" (Rev. 16:7).

God's discipline is progressive. It increases each time we do not respond.

"If you do not obey Me, and do not observe all these commandments . . . I also will do this to you . . . After all this, if you do not obey Me, then I will punish you seven times more for your sins. I will break the pride of your power . . . If you walk contrary to Me, and are not willing to obey Me, I will bring on you seven times more plagues, according to your sins. . . . If by these things you are not reformed by Me, but walk contrary to Me, then I also will walk contrary to you, and I will punish you yet seven times for your sins. . . . And after all this, if you do not obey Me, but walk contrary to Me, then I also will walk contrary to you in fury; and I, even I, will chastise you seven times for your sins. . . . I will destroy . . . I will lay your cities waste . . . I will bring the land to desolation . . . I will scatter you among the nations." (Lev. 26:14–33)

God is longsuffering and merciful in dealing with us. Yet, when the time comes that we refuse to repent, He will deal with His people. When He disciplines and judges us, He is right and justified in all that He does.

EXAMPLES OF GOD'S DISCIPLINES AND JUDGMENTS

The Scriptures are filled with examples of God's disciplines and judgments. Some are far more serious than others. As you have just read, His judgments usually are progressive. They get more severe the longer we refuse to respond. Some of the examples of discipline and judgment in Scriptures include the following:

♦ *Natural disasters:* earthquake, volcano, hurricane, tornado, flood, fire, drought, hail, famine, insect plague, and attack of wild animals.

♦ *Disease:* plague, wasting disease, fever, and leprosy.

♦ *Human conflict or trouble:* war, attack or defeat by an enemy, being taken into captivity or bondage, being ruled by those who hate, victim of crime, victim of immorality, bloodshed, increase in wickedness, broken human relationships, economic collapse.

Whenever these things happen, God may be using them to discipline or judge a people. Sometimes when God judges corporate groups such as nations, seemingly innocent people are hurt as well. But none of us is truly innocent. We all have sinned. God's judgments are not always limited to the wicked when He touches a nation. When He judged Judah during the times of Ezekiel the Lord said,

> "I will cut off both righteous and wicked from you, therefore My sword shall go out of its sheath against all flesh from south to north, that all flesh may know that I, the LORD, have drawn My sword out of its sheath; it shall not return anymore." Sigh therefore, son of man, with a breaking heart, and sigh with bitterness before their eyes. (Ezek. 21:4–6)

GOD JUDGED JUDAH FOR THEIR SIN

Israel departed from the Lord on numerous occasions. Because of the idolatry of Solomon in his later years, God divided the nation, taking ten tribes out from under the rule of Solomon's son. In 721 B.C. the Northern Kingdom of Israel was destroyed by Assyria. In 586 B.C. God used Babylon to destroy Jerusalem and carry the people of the Southern Kingdom into captivity (The Exile). God explained to the prophet Jeremiah what He had done.

> "For I earnestly exhorted your fathers in the day I brought them up out of the land of Egypt, until this day, rising early and exhorting, saying, 'Obey My voice.' Yet they did not obey or incline their ear, but everyone

followed the dictates of his evil heart; therefore I will bring upon them all the words of this covenant, which I commanded them to do, but which they have not done." (Jer. 11:7–8)

God wanted obedience from Israel. His first and foremost command was for them to love Him (Deut. 6:4–5). They had left the love relationship and did not obey Him or keep the covenant relationship. They followed their own evil ways. So God kept His oath to bring about "curses" in His judgment (Deut. 28:15). Notice He did not do this quickly. He spent hundreds of years trying to secure their obedience. This action was a final judgment.

WAYS GOD DISCIPLINES

God grieves to bring such a judgment, but at times He must. The "bad" things listed above like natural disasters, disease, human conflict, or trouble do not necessarily imply God's judgment. But spiritual leaders would do well to guide the people to seek the Lord anytime one occurs. If God is bringing discipline, the sooner we realize it, the sooner we can respond to the Lord and return to Him.

Throughout history these "bad" circumstances were seen as reasons to call an assembly of God's people for prayer. A murder or rape in town caused God's people to grieve over their failure to be salt and light in the community. A famine, plague, or natural disaster caused God's people to immediately stand before God to see if they were at fault because of sin. War was also seen as a possible judgment from God. (See the proclamations on pp. 209–212 as examples.)

God disciplines his people in various ways when they sin. He begins by bringing conviction of the sin. If people respond with a ready heart to repent, He does not have to discipline them. But when He must follow through with discipline people may face one or more of the following:

1. *God may refuse to hear their prayers.* "Your iniquities have separated you from your God; And your sins have hidden His face from you, So that He will not hear" (Isa. 59:2).

2. *God may withdraw the awareness of His presence.* "How long, O LORD? Will You forget me forever? How long will You hide Your face from me?" (Ps. 13:1).

3. *God may send a famine of hearing a word from the Lord.* "'Behold, the days are coming,' says the Lord GOD, 'That I will send a famine on the land, Not a famine of bread, Nor a thirst for water, But of hearing the words of the LORD. They shall wander from sea to sea, And from north to east; They shall run to and fro, seeking the word of the LORD, But shall not find it'" (Amos 8:11–12).

4. *God may remove the hedge of protection from us and those we love.* "'Let Me tell you what I will do to My vineyard [Israel]: I will take away its hedge, and it shall be burned; And break down its wall, and it shall be trampled down. I will lay it waste" (Isa. 5:5–6).

5. *God may allow us to reap the full consequences of our own sinful behavior.* God describes this late stage of judgment on sinful people: "God also gave them up to uncleanness, in the lusts of their hearts, to dishonor their bodies among themselves . . . God gave them up to vile passions . . . . God gave them over to a debased mind, to do those things which are not fitting; being filled with all unrighteousness, sexual immorality, wickedness, covetousness, maliciousness; full of envy, murder, strife, deceit, evil-mindedness; they are whisperers, backbiters, haters of God, violent, proud, boasters, inventors of evil things, disobedient to parents, undiscerning, untrustworthy, unloving, unforgiving, unmerciful" (Rom. 1:24–31).

6. *Finally, God may destroy or remove.* "'Your enemies will build an embankment around you, surround you and close you in on every side, and level you, and your children within you, to the ground; and they will not leave in you one stone upon another, because you did not know the time of your visitation'" (Luke 19:43–44).

God's desire is that we would respond to the conviction of the Holy Spirit. When we don't judge ourselves and repent, God judges us. His disciplines will increase until He gets our attention.

Phase Four in God's pattern for revival is this: God's people cry out to Him for help. This is God's purpose in discipline. He continues to increase the intensity of the discipline until we cry out to Him for help. Then He is able to call us to repent from our sinful ways.

WHEN GOD'S PATIENCE RUNS OUT

If we do not repent or respond to God, He will eventually deal with our stubbornness through more severe actions. He does have a limit on His patience. If we continue to refuse to respond, He may bring final judgments. Several final judgments are described in the New Testament.

Destruction of Jerusalem. Jesus prophesied the destruction of Jerusalem that took place in A.D. 70. This was a judgment on the Jews for rejecting God (Luke 19:41–44).

Ananias and Sapphira. Because of greed, Ananias and Sapphira lied to God about their giving. This planned lie could have infected the early church if not dealt with. God took their lives in a swift and final judgment because the redemption of the world was at stake (Acts 5:1–11).

Corinthian Christians. Paul rebuked the Corinthian church for not taking the Lord's Supper seriously. People were participating in an unworthy manner. They were sinning against the body and blood of Jesus. Paul said:

> He who eats and drinks in an unworthy manner eats and drinks judgment to himself, not discerning the Lord's body. For this reason many are weak and sick among you, and many sleep. For if we would judge ourselves, we would not be judged. But when we are judged, we are chastened by the Lord, that we may not be condemned with the world (1 Cor. 11:29–32).

Church at Ephesus. Some actually died (slept) because they refused to judge themselves properly. A warning of final judgment is given by the resurrected Christ to the church at Ephesus when He says, "'Repent and do the first works, or else I will come to you quickly and remove your lampstand [church] from its place—unless you repent'" (Rev. 2:5).

Some people have developed a theology that releases them from any personal accountability for sin once they are saved. They argue that God does not punish those who are redeemed and forgiven by the blood of Jesus. The examples above, with the exception of Jerusalem's destruction, all involved Christians and churches. Jesus has indeed paid the penalty for all sin—past, present, and future. Our eternal destiny is established when we are born again by His blood. However, our relationship with Him and our usefulness to His Kingdom purposes to redeem a world can be greatly affected by our sin. God does deal with believers who sin, and some of those consequences may be severe.

God is merciful and patient. He normally gives us many warnings and time to repent. If something "bad" happens to you, how can you know if it is God's discipline or not? By asking Him. He disciplines you on purpose to correct you. If He is disciplining you, He will let you know if you seek an answer. Check with God's people in your church for counsel. Spend time in God's Word and in prayer. If you sincerely seek a word about a "bad" circumstance and you hear nothing from God, you may assume it is not discipline.

SUMMARY

♦ We do not serve two Gods—one Old Testament and one New Testament God. The Lord is One. He doesn't change.

♦ He is perfect love. He forever convinced us of His love through the death of Jesus on the cross. He is kind, compassionate, patient, and slow to anger.

♦ God is also just. He never punishes the innocent. His judgments are always right and fair.

♦ When a church experiences genuine worship in His presence, they will realize any sin for which they may need forgiveness.

♦ When we move out of the relationship, God knows we are missing out on the life for which He created us. Because of His love God disciplines His people when they depart from Him and sin.

♦ When God's people depart from Him, His redemptive mission slows down. . . . Thus, God disciplines us so we will return to Him so He can work mightily through us to redeem a lost world.

♦ Temporal judgments are correction and punishment that occurs in this lifetime.

♦ Remedial judgment is discipline or judgment intended to correct us and point us back to a right relationship with God.

♦ Final judgment is judgment or punishment which ends life or usefulness because of prolonged rebellion or severe sin.

♦ God's desire is to correct us so that we will return to Him.

♦ Judgment should begin with the people of God.

♦ Every deed, including hidden things, will be judged.

♦ Jesus came to bring judgment.

♦ God's judgments always are right, true, and fair.

♦ God's discipline is progressive. It increases each time we do not respond.

♦ If God is bringing discipline, the sooner we realize it, the sooner we can respond to the Lord and return to Him.

ENCOUNTERING GOD IN PRAYER

Read back through the list of actions God may take to discipline or judge a person, family, or church. Are you experiencing any of these yourself? As a family? As a church? As a town or city? As a nation? If so, ask God if this is His discipline. If it is, repent of the sin He points out to you. Return to Him. If the discipline involves your church, city, or nation, pray that your leaders will identify the sin and call the people to return to the Lord.

ENCOUNTERING GOD WITH OTHERS

As you have opportunity in a small group, consider these discussion questions for chapter 10:

1. Why does God not take delight in the death of the wicked?

2. How is discipline a display of God's love?

3. Why do you think God brought final judgment on Ananias and Sapphira?

4. Why is God's discipline progressive—increasing in intensity?

5. How can a person know whether something bad is a discipline from God or not?

6. How is the story of Job an illustration of the fact that bad things are not always judgment or discipline? (See Job 1–2.)

7. How could a Christian distinguish between godly discipline and spiritual warfare? How important is it to know the difference?

8. In what ways, if any, do you sense our church is being (or has been) disciplined by God?

CHAPTER 11

GOD CALLS HIS PEOPLE TO REPENT

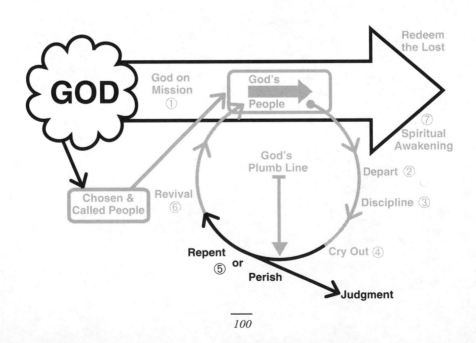

♦ PHASE 5: God calls His people to repent and return to Him or perish.

When we depart from the Lord, He disciplines us in love. We need to make the connection between our sin and what is happening to us. If we are experiencing God's discipline, the sooner we respond the better. The longer we delay, the more intense His discipline becomes. God deals with us more and more severely until He finally gets our attention. Then we cry out to Him for help. When we cry out to Him, He calls us to repent and return to Him: "'Return to Me, and I will return to you,' Says the LORD of hosts" (Mal. 3:7).

King Solomon was the wisest person to ever live. He understood that God's people would sin and depart from Him. As he dedicated the temple, Solomon asked God if He would forgive His people when they cried out to Him. Read Solomon's prayer:

> "If Your people Israel are defeated before an enemy because they have sinned against You . . . When the heavens are shut up and there is no rain because they have sinned against You . . . When there is famine in the land, pestilence or blight or mildew, locusts or grasshoppers; when their enemies besiege them in the land of their cities; whatever plague or whatever sickness there is . . . When they sin against You (for there is no one who does not sin), and You become angry with them and deliver them to the enemy, and they take them captive . . . yet when they come to themselves . . . and repent, and make supplication to You in the land of their captivity, saying, 'We have sinned, we have done wrong, and have committed wickedness'; and when they return to You with all their heart and with all their soul . . . and pray . . . then hear from heaven Your dwelling place their prayer and their supplications, and maintain their cause, and forgive Your people who have sinned against You." (2 Chron. 6:24, 26, 28, 36–39)

God disciplines His people when they sin against Him. Notice that the sin is against God. Solomon knew that God used disasters to punish and correct His people. God used things such as drought, famine, plague, blight, mildew, insect plagues, military defeat, and captivity to discipline His people. Solomon's question of God was this: *Lord, if You punish Your people because of their sin and they turn their hearts back to You, will you forgive them?*

GOD'S PROMISE FOR REVIVAL

God answered Solomon's prayer in this way: "'When I shut up heaven and there is no rain, or command the locusts to devour the land, or send pestilence among My people, if My people who are called by My name will humble themselves, and pray and seek My face, and turn from their wicked ways, then I will hear from heaven, and will forgive their sin and heal their land'" (2 Chron. 7:13–14).

God answered, *Yes! If I punish my people and they return to Me, I will forgive them and heal their land.* In this passage God identified four requirements for revival: humble yourselves, pray, seek God's face, and turn from your wicked ways.

FOUR REQUIREMENTS FOR REVIVAL

1. *Humble yourselves*
2. *Pray*
3. *Seek God's face*
4. *Turn from your wicked ways*

God wants His people to return to the love relationship with Him. He wants His people to spend time with Him in prayer. He wants them to seek His presence (His face). He wants them to repent of their wicked ways. Then He will forgive and heal!

LOOKING FOR SYMPTOMS OF SPIRITUAL ILLNESS

When you go to a doctor with an illness, she examines you, looking for symptoms of the illness. Once she sees what the illness is doing to you, she often knows what the cause is. Then she knows how to treat it.

Suppose, for instance, that your son has a fever and complains of an earache. You take him to the doctor, who finds that his temperature is 102 degrees. His white blood count is high. His right ear is red. Everything else seems to be okay. These symptoms are not the primary problem. An ear infection is the problem. The doctor could prescribe aspirin for the fever and the earache, but aspirin would not solve the problem. Your son needs an antibiotic to kill the infection.

In a similar way, we can observe symptoms of a spiritual illness. The symptoms are not the primary problem. We have already identified three symptoms of spiritual sickness:

1. God's discipline indicates a sin problem.

2. Turning to or accepting substitutes for God, His presence, purposes, or ways indicates a spiritual problem.

3. Lack of obedience or disobedience to the clear will of God in His Word indicates a problem.

These all indicate that our heart has shifted, that our love relationship with God is not right. Once you see the symptoms in your life, family, church, community, or nation, you need to cry out to God for help. You cannot fix the problem by yourself. The good news is that God has the help you need. In fact, by the time you respond to His call, He already has everything planned and in place for revival. When God took Israel into captivity because of their sin, He sent a message through Jeremiah. God took the initiative to call His people back to Him:

> "Thus says the LORD of hosts, the God of Israel, to all who were carried away captive, whom I have caused to be carried away from Jerusalem to Babylon: . . . I know the thoughts that I think toward you, says the LORD, thoughts of peace and not of evil, to give you a future and a hope. Then you will call upon Me and go and pray to Me, and I will listen to you. And you will seek Me and find Me, when you search for Me with all your heart. I will be found by you, says the LORD, and I will bring you back from your captivity; I will gather you from all the nations and from all the places where I have driven you, says the LORD, and I will bring you to the place from which I cause you to be carried away captive." (Jer. 29:4, 11–14)

Even when He brought great disaster on His people, God had all the plans in place to bring them back to Him. He was ready to prosper them and give them hope. God was standing ready for their call to Him in prayer. When they began to seek Him, He would respond to their plea.

GOD'S REQUIREMENTS FOR REPENTANCE

God calls His people to repent or perish (Rev. 2:5). Sin is very serious, and we must treat it as we would a serious wound. In Jeremiah 6, God describes the condition of the nation. The people were very sinful and the leaders treated the sin as if it were not serious at all.

> "From the least of them even to the greatest of them, Everyone is given to covetousness; And from the prophet even to the priest, Everyone deals falsely. They have also healed the hurt of My people slightly, Saying, 'Peace, peace!' When there is no peace. Were they ashamed when they had committed abomination? No! They were not at all ashamed; Nor did they know how to blush. . . ." Thus says the LORD: "Stand in the ways and see, And ask for the old paths, where the good way is, And walk in it; Then you will find rest for your souls." (Jer. 6:13–16)

God does not let us set the conditions of repentance. Repentance is not being sorry that you got caught. It is not just feeling sorrow for your sin. Repentance is not just taking an action to get away from God's wrath. The word *repent* indicates a turning away from our sin and a returning to the love relationship with God with our whole heart. Sorrow is not enough. Reforming our behavior for a while is not enough. Returning to some religious activity is not enough. God wants us to love Him with all our heart. When we return to the love relationship with Him, our lifestyle will reflect the change. According to Scripture, repentance must come before forgiveness.

> He [John the Baptist] went into all the region around the Jordan, preaching a baptism of repentance for the remission of sins . . . Then he said to the multitudes that came out to be baptized by him, "Brood of vipers! Who warned you to flee from the wrath to come? Therefore bear fruits worthy of repentance." (Luke 3:3, 7–8)

The fruit of repentance is a changed lifestyle. Confession of sin is not enough. Confession is merely agreeing with God about our sin. That is a first step, but it is not repentance. Sorrow for sin is not enough, either. "For godly sorrow produces repentance leading to salvation, not to be regretted; but the sorrow of the world produces death" (2 Cor. 7:10). A broken heart over our sin leads us to repent.

Our heart and lifestyle will change in a way that shows we have repented. Paul explained how new life in Christ reflects repentance: "'I have been crucified with Christ; it is no longer I who live, but Christ lives in me; and the life which I now live in the flesh I live by faith in the Son of God, who loved me and gave Himself for me'" (Gal. 2:20).

Once we die to self, Christ takes up residence in our lives. He becomes our life. He lives through us. That is how we show genuine repentance: We let Christ live through us.

Repentance for God's people—individuals and churches—involves a three-fold process of change.

1. *When we repent, our mind changes.* The first change required is a change of mind. We must agree with God about the truth. This is confession. We must agree that what we have done is wrong. If we want to argue with God about whether we have done wrong, we haven't repented yet. If we try to give God excuses to justify ourselves, we haven't repented yet. We must come to the place like David did where he said, "I acknowledge my transgressions . . . Against You, You only, have I sinned, And done this evil in Your sight" (Ps. 51:3–4).

2. *When we repent, our heart changes.* We must see how we have broken the heart of our heavenly Father because of our sin. Do you realize that Jesus had to die on the cross in order to forgive your sins? Instead of enjoying our sinful ways, we must come to the place that we grieve over our sin. David said, "The sacrifices of God are a broken spirit, a broken and contrite heart—These, O God, You will not despise" (Ps. 51:17). We begin our departure from God

when we have a shift of our heart—when we leave our first love. Repentance requires that we return to our first love. We must have a change of heart. Once we have returned to loving the Lord, we will be prepared to obey Him as well. But the change of heart will precede lasting obedience.

3. *When we repent, our will and actions change.* Repentance requires a turning away from the sin. It requires a change of lifestyle. Too often we try to walk as close to the world as possible without sinning. We flirt with temptation when we should flee from it. Repentance requires a radical putting away of the sin—radical surgery. You must get rid of any idol of the heart, tear down any stronghold, and remove yourself from tempting situations. That requires a change of your will. If you desire to change your will, God will enable you to do so, "for it is God who works in you both to will and to do for His good pleasure" (Phil. 2:13). Once you have allowed God to change your will, you must go on and allow Him to change your actions as well. When you begin to live life as God intends, you have repented.

CORPORATE REPENTANCE

Whenever people depart from God and sin, repentance is required. This not only includes individuals but also:

+ families who sin
+ committees who sin
+ cities who sin
+ churches who sin
+ businesses who sin
+ nations who sin
+ denominations who sin
+ Christian organizations who sin

All sin is serious. It cannot be dealt with lightly. God condemned the spiritual leaders of Judah because they dressed the wound (sin and rebellion) of His people as if it were not serious (Jer. 6:14). We cannot just forget about sin or hide it. Corporate (group) repentance is required for corporate sin. Without repentance the right relationship and fellowship with God will not be restored. Read the following messages of the risen Christ to the five churches in Revelation 2–3, and look for a common response that Christ called for.

"To the angel of the church of Ephesus write . . .

'I have this against you, that you have left your first love. Remember therefore from where you have fallen; repent and do the first works, or else I will come to you quickly and remove your lampstand from its place—unless you repent.'" (Rev. 2:1, 4–5)

"To the angel of the church in Pergamos write . . .

'I have a few things against you, because you have there those who hold the doctrine of Balaam, who taught Balak to put a stumbling block before the children of Israel, to eat things sacrificed to idols, and to commit sexual immorality. Thus you also have those who hold the doctrine of the Nicolaitans, which thing I hate. Repent, or else I will come to you quickly and will fight against them with the sword of My mouth.'" (Rev. 2:12, 14–16)

"To the angel of the church in Thyatira write . . .

'I have a few things against you, because you allow that woman Jezebel, who calls herself a prophetess, to teach and seduce My servants to commit sexual immorality and eat things sacrificed to idols. And I gave her time to repent of her sexual immorality, and she did not repent. Indeed I will cast her into a sickbed, and those who commit adultery with her into great tribulation, unless they repent of their deeds. I will kill her children with death, and all the churches shall know that I am He who searches the minds and hearts. And I will give to each one of you according to your works.'" (Rev. 2:18, 20–23)

"To the angel of the church in Sardis write . . .

'I know your works, that you have a name that you are alive, but you are dead. Be watchful, and strengthen the things which remain, that are ready to die, for I have not found your works perfect before God. Remember therefore how you have received and heard; hold fast and repent. Therefore if you will not watch, I will come upon you as a thief, and you will not know what hour I will come upon you.'" (Rev. 3:1–3)

"To the angel of the church of the Laodiceans write . . .

'I know your works, that you are neither cold nor hot. I could wish you were cold or hot. So then, because you are lukewarm, and neither cold nor hot, I will vomit you out of My mouth. Because you say, "I am rich, have become wealthy, and have need of nothing"—and do not know that you are wretched, miserable, poor, blind, and naked—I counsel you to buy from Me gold refined in the fire, that you may be rich; and white garments, that you may be clothed, that the shame of your nakedness may not be revealed; and anoint your eyes with eye salve, that you may see. As many as I love, I rebuke and chasten. Therefore be zealous and repent. Behold, I stand at the door and knock. If anyone hears My voice and opens the door, I will come in to him and dine with him, and he with Me.'" (Rev. 3:14–20)

An angel was a messenger. Some have considered these angels in Revelation 2–3 to be the pastors of the churches—messengers of God to His people.

Whether or not these are pastors, the messages were intended for the churches. All five of these messages include a call to repentance. Churches can sin, and God calls churches to repent. Have you ever been in a church that repented of anything? Many do not. The refusal to repent, however, can be fatal to churches as well as individuals. How does a church or other religious group repent?

Second Chronicles 7:14 was spoken by God to His people. This was a promise for corporate repentance. For revival to come and the land to be healed, God's people must first humble themselves. Pride may be the first and greatest barrier to revival. Because of our pride, churches do not want to admit that they have done anything wrong. They certainly don't want to do it publicly. If cover-ups can get a politician in trouble, how do you think God responds when His people try to cover up their sin? He tells us: "He who covers his sins will not prosper, But whoever confesses and forsakes them will have mercy" (Prov. 28:13). This applies to churches and Christian groups. We must first turn from our pride and humble ourselves before God.

After humility comes prayer and seeking God's face—communicating with God and seeking His presence. Hiding from God is no good. Trying to run from Him or avoid Him cannot help. We must seek Him, return to Him, come near to Him, and talk with Him. God said to Judah, "'Come now, and let us reason together . . . Though your sins are like scarlet, They shall be as white as snow; Though they are red like crimson, They shall be as wool'" (Isa. 1:18).

First we must humble ourselves, pray, and seek His face. Then we must turn from our wicked ways. Repentance, as we have already studied, requires a change in mind, heart, will, and actions. Repentance will result in a changed lifestyle. A church must agree with God about the nature of its sin. We must demonstrate a broken and contrite heart with a wholehearted desire to return to the Lord. Just like an individual, a repentant church must turn away from the sin. This may require the tearing down of some "idols," changing the way we do things, getting rid of traditions, selling property or material things, or making restitution for wrongs committed. Saying, "We'll just try to do better next time" is not sufficient. Repentance requires actions in the present, not a promise for the future.

A TESTIMONY OF GOD'S GRACE: A CHURCH REPENTED OF PRAYERLESSNESS

In April 1994, a small rural church in Tennessee had a special emphasis on prayer. After a two-hour study, time was given for members of the body to share what God had been saying to them. The bivocational pastor stood and confessed, "I have not been a man of prayer, and I have not led you to be a people of prayer. I need to ask you to forgive me."

The conference leader first asked the pastor to pray publicly, confessing his sin to the Lord and seeking God's forgiveness. Then the members of the congregation expressed their forgiveness to their pastor. Then the leader asked the group, "As I have been teaching tonight, how many of you sensed conviction by the Holy Spirit that you have not been a people of prayer or a house of prayer?" Everyone raised their hands. Then he asked, "Is prayerlessness a sin?" They all agreed that it was. That was corporate confession of sin.

The leader then asked if the church wanted to repent of its prayerlessness and experience God's forgiveness. They were all ready to get right with the Lord. The Holy Spirit had prepared them by revealing their sin, changing their mind about the nature of prayerlessness, and giving them a deep grief for sinning against the Lord. As a body, they were ready to repent with a whole heart. They stood before the Lord to acknowledge their sin, and their pastor led in a corporate prayer of confession. He prayed for God's forgiveness, and He asked the Lord to enable them to become a people of prayer.

Having come that far in the process of repentance, the conference leader called for them to bear the fruit of repentance by going to a time of corporate prayer. Small groups gathered across the worship center to pray until God was finished with them.

At the time of our writing this book, God has done a special work of grace at this church in Walter Hill, Tennessee. Following their corporate repentance in 1994, the people began to take prayer seriously. They worked on developing their personal prayer lives. They made time for prayer in classes and worship times. They called special prayer meetings from time to time. During this time their pastor resigned. They made prayer a major element in seeking a new pastor.

In the spring of 1995 they called Darryl Whaley to be their new pastor. God already had given Darryl a burden for prayer and a burden to lead a church to be a house of prayer. When God put pastor and people together, His presence and power began to be revealed. Inactive church members began to return. Members began to deal ruthlessly with sin. New people began to respond in the community. In a single week recently, six people made public professions of faith in Christ. People's lives began to change in such a way that the Methodist pastor in nearby Lascassas was calling it the "Walter Hill Revival" and praying it would spread to his community.

Corporate repentance need not be complicated or a long, drawn-out process. It doesn't have to be a negative issue, either. In fact, repentance "is one of the most positive experiences a church can have. Jesus preached, "'Repent, for the kingdom of heaven is at hand'" (Matt. 4:17). When a church repents, all the power, presence, and resources of God are standing right next to the members, ready to pour out revival on a repentant people.

SUMMARY

♦ When we cry out to Him, God calls us to repent and return to Him: "'Return to Me, and I will return to you,' Says the LORD of hosts" (Mal. 3:7).

♦ Once you see the symptoms of sin in your life, family, church, community, or nation, you need to cry out to God for help. You cannot fix the problem by yourself.

♦ Sin is very serious, and we must treat it as we would a serious wound.

♦ Repentance is not being sorry that you got caught. It is not just feeling sorrow for your sin. Repentance is not just taking an action to get away from God's wrath.

♦ This is how we show genuine repentance: We let Christ live through us.

♦ In confession, we must agree that what we have done is wrong.

♦ We must come to the place that we grieve over our sin.

♦ Once we have returned to loving the Lord, we will be prepared to obey Him as well.

♦ If you desire to change your will, God will enable you to do so, "for it is God who works in you both to will and to do for His good pleasure" (Phil. 2:13).

♦ Corporate (group) repentance is required for corporate sin.

♦ The refusal to repent can be fatal to churches as well as individuals.

♦ "He who covers his sins will not prosper, But whoever confesses and forsakes them will have mercy" (Prov. 28:13).

♦ When repentance has occurred, the fruit of repentance will be seen in the changed lifestyle.

ENCOUNTERING GOD IN PRAYER

♦ Is God disciplining you? Your family? Your church? Your town or city? Your nation? Hear His voice. Open the door and invite Him in for fellowship (Rev. 3:20).

♦ Ask God if there are any idols of the heart that must be put away.

♦ If you have sensed God is convicting you of sin, ask Him to guide you through a change of mind, heart, will, and actions. Pray through David's prayer of repentance in Psalm 51. Repent and return to your love relationship with the Lord. What fruit of repentance does He want you to show?

♦ Do you sense a need for revival? Have you seen symptoms of a spiritual problem in your life, family, church, city, or nation? God already has everything in place to bring about revival. He is waiting on the response of His people. Spend some time responding to Him right now.

ENCOUNTERING GOD WITH OTHERS

As you have opportunity in a small group, consider these discussion questions for chapter 11. Ask God to guide your thinking as you prayerfully consider the following questions.

1. Can you identify a time when your church disobeyed what God wanted?

2. Can you pinpoint ways your church has departed from God and turned to substitutes for Him?

3. Has your church dealt with known sin in the church in the way God commands?

4. Has your church sinned in a way that requires restitution? Perhaps to a former pastor or staff member or in some transaction?

5. Did your church grow out of a church split? Have you been reconciled with your brothers and sisters in Christ or is there still bitterness and hard feelings between you?

CHAPTER 12

GOD REVIVES HIS REPENTANT PEOPLE

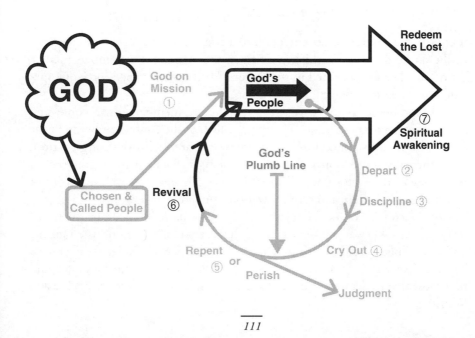

- PHASE 6: God revives His repentant people by restoring them to a right relationship with Himself.

- PHASE 7: God exalts His Son Jesus in His people and draws the lost to saving faith in Him.

A REFINER'S FIRE

When God comes in revival, He comes as a refiner's fire.

> "The Lord, whom you seek, Will suddenly come to His temple, Even the Messenger of the covenant, In whom you delight. Behold, He is coming," Says the LORD of hosts. "But who can endure the day of His coming? And who can stand when He appears? For He is like a refiner's fire And like launderer's soap. . . . And I will come near you for judgment; I will be a swift witness Against sorcerers, Against adulterers, Against perjurers, Against those who exploit wage earners and widows and orphans, And against those who turn away an alien—Because they do not fear Me," Says the LORD of hosts. (Mal. 3:1–2, 5)

A refiner's fire burns away all the impurities to leave pure metal. When God comes, He, too, burns away all the impurities and waste. Responding to God's presence produces holiness in churches and in the lives of believers.

SINS OF THE NATION IN THE CHURCH

A church in a southern state entered into a two-week series of revival meetings in the spring of 1994. At the beginning of the services, the members made a list of sins they knew existed in the nation. Their list contained forty-one specific sins. Then they prayed for the nation.

As God began to deal with sin in the church, members began confessing sin and seeking forgiveness and cleansing. Much of the confession began in the prayer room and with counselors. Some was shared with the congregation, when there was a need for corporate confession or when a person could share a testimony of the victory over sin that God had given. The refining work of God began to go deep, and services were continued for five weeks.

At the conclusion of the revival services, the pastor pulled out the list of forty-one sins. He was amazed to realize that every one of the sins listed for the nation had been confessed to by church members. Months later the church began to experience some of the joys and fruits of revival, but the pastor said that those five weeks were some of the most painful experiences of his life and ministry.

REVIVAL IS LIKE JUDGMENT DAY

When God comes into the midst of His people as a refiner's fire, the process of revival may be very painful to individuals and churches. Usually when we are praying for revival, what we really want are the fruits of revival—the joy, the closeness to God, the conversion of sinners, and so forth. But before we can experience the fruits of revival, we must be "baptized with fire."

When Jesus came preaching repentance, John said He would baptize with the Holy Spirit and fire (Luke 3:16–17). People either came to Jesus or fought against Him. God exposes the attitude of the heart when He comes in revival. You cannot be neutral. Once you hear what God wants you to do, you must do it. You must either obey Him or suffer the consequences of rebellion. Individuals and churches cannot continue to do business as usual when God is calling them to revival and to be part of a spiritual awakening in the land. Conditions are sad when God comes to His very own people and they refuse to respond to Him. Notice what happened in Jeremiah's day:

> "Why has this people slidden back, Jerusalem, in a perpetual backsliding? They hold fast to deceit, They refuse to return. I listened and heard, But they do not speak aright. No man repented of his wickedness, Saying, 'What have I done?' Everyone turned to his own course . . . But My people do not know the judgment of the LORD." (Jer. 8:5–7)

God came to His people (not to the pagan nations of the world), and here is what He found:

♦ They had turned away from Him.
♦ No one repents of wickedness.
♦ They cling to deceit.
♦ Everyone does whatever he wants.
♦ They refuse to return.
♦ They do not know God's judgments (requirements).
♦ They do not say what is right.

Do any of these kinds of behavior sound familiar to you? Even among God's people? The reason is found in Malachai 3:18, where God said, "'You will again see the distinction between the righteous and the wicked, between those who serve God and those who do not'" (NIV). When God comes, He causes a division between those who will follow Him and those who will not. Do not be surprised if people in your church oppose efforts at revival. According to Scripture, "'This is the condemnation, that the light has come into the world, and men loved darkness rather than light, because their deeds were evil. For everyone practicing evil hates the light and does not come to the light, lest his deeds should be exposed. But he who does the truth comes to the light, that his deeds may be clearly seen, that they have been done in God'" (John 3:19–21).

Many do not like the light because it will expose their evil deeds. Others, however, are ready to come to the light, deal with their sin, and find cleansing and forgiveness. In spite of the fact that some will refuse to come into the light, churches need revival, and that begins with repentance.

POSSIBLE OBJECTIONS TO REVIVAL

Not everyone will respond positively to a message that calls for repentance. Scripture reveals the sin and rebelliousness of people. Here are some responses you may observe from people when a call to repentance is preached:

1. *Some discount the truth from the Old Testament, saying, "God is not like that anymore."* God, however, does not change. God of the Old Testament is the same God of the New Testament. The Scriptures from Genesis to Revelation reveal Him and the ways He relates to His people. God says, "'I am the LORD, I do not change'" (Mal. 3:6). James 1:17 says that "the Father of the heavenly lights [the Creator] . . . does not change" (NIV). Jesus and the writers of the New Testament relied heavily upon the Old Testament for instruction. The New Testament church did not have any Scriptures other than the Old Testament for most of its history. Remember: "All Scripture is given by inspiration of God, and is profitable for doctrine, for reproof, for correction, for instruction in righteousness, that the man of God may be complete, thoroughly equipped for every good work" (2 Tim. 3:16–17).

2. *Some are offended to think of God as a God of discipline and judgment.* They choose to focus only on God's love and mercy. They try to exert "positive thinking," hoping to bring about a positive result. They will argue that the past should be forgotten and never mentioned. Sin is "swept under the rug." In Scripture God condemned those who went about saying, "Peace, peace" when there was no peace. In the middle of a sinful church, some will say, "We are a great church. Nothing is wrong." The writer of Proverbs tells us, "He who covers his sins will not prosper, But whoever confesses and forsakes them will have mercy" (Prov. 28:13). When known sin exists in a church and the Holy Spirit brings conviction, it is the work of a false prophet who says "Peace, peace, everything is wonderful."

3. *Some refuse to deal openly with sin in the church (past sins as well as present ones).* In order to protect the church's or a person's reputation, they will disobey the clear teaching of God on how to deal with the issue. They prefer to forget about the past and move forward. Open sin that we harbor or refuse to deal with

in God's way is a sure way to shut down God's activity in a church. If we regard iniquity in our heart, God refuses even to hear our prayers (Ps. 66:18).

Such a light treatment of sin can lead to open rebellion on the part of others. Sin can spread like a fast-growing cancer if not severely dealt with in repentance. Sometimes God requires that sin be dealt with openly in a congregation. To cover up such sins is corporate rebellion on the part of a church.

4. *Some choose to rely on human wisdom and reason even when it is in direct opposition to God's Word.* They may be very vocal and forceful. They may present their case in such a way that they say, "Anyone who disagrees with me is a fool." They may argue against God's ways even when confronted with a clear word from Scripture. They may try to redefine evil and call it good or say that it is no longer sinful. Do not allow such a person to intimidate you or your church from following what God says in His Word. A church and its leaders need to fear God and not fear men. "Let God be true but every man a liar" (Rom. 3:4).

REVIVAL IS GOD'S WORK

God is the One who revives His repentant people. It is an act of the Sovereign God. We cannot cause a revival to take place. We cannot force God to act. We cannot "pray it down." He brings revival under His conditions and on His timetable. Yet, He wants us revived more than we do. In fact, He is the One who causes us to want to be revived. We come to Him at His invitation. God initiates revival and He brings it to pass when His people have met His conditions.

God said, "'Return to Me, and I will return to you'" (Mal. 3:7). How can you know when revival has come? The way to know if you have returned is to see if God has returned to you. If you are still missing out on His presence and power, you have not yet met God's requirements. Your return (repentance) is not complete. When you experience God personally or corporately, you will never be the same. If you are still the same, whatever you have done, you have not encountered God. At a time like this, you need to go to God and ask Him what you still need to do in repentance.

He is waiting for you to draw near to Him. Repentance and revival, however, are not just a reform of behavior. Revival has not taken place unless a change of character has occurred, not unless a change of heart has taken place. But God even helps with the change of heart: "'Then I will give them a heart to know Me, that I am the LORD; and they shall be My people, and I will be their God, for they shall return to Me with their whole heart'" (Jer. 24:7).

When your love for the Lord compels you to obey Him and when your heart's desire is to please Him, revival has occurred. That is the indication that the love relationship has been restored.

Read the following verses from Ezekiel 36 and watch for the things God said He was going to do to revive and restore His people. You may want to underline the things God said He would do:

"'Thus says the Lord GOD: "I do not do this for your sake, O house of Israel, but for My holy name's sake, which you have profaned among the nations wherever you went. And I will sanctify My great name, which has been profaned among the nations, which you have profaned in their midst; and the nations shall know that I am the LORD," says the Lord GOD, "when I am hallowed in you before their eyes. For I will take you from among the nations, gather you out of all countries, and bring you into your own land. Then I will sprinkle clean water on you, and you shall be clean; I will cleanse you from all your filthiness and from all your idols. I will give you a new heart and put a new spirit within you; I will take the heart of stone out of your flesh and give you a heart of flesh. I will put My Spirit within you and cause you to walk in My statutes, and you will keep My judgments and do them. Then you shall dwell in the land that I gave to your fathers; you shall be My people, and I will be your God. I will deliver you from all your uncleannesses. I will call for the grain and multiply it, and bring no famine upon you. And I will multiply the fruit of your trees and the increase of your fields, so that you need never again bear the reproach of famine among the nations. Then you will remember your evil ways and your deeds that were not good; and you will loathe yourselves in your own sight, for your iniquities and your abominations. Not for your sake do I do this," says the Lord GOD, "let it be known to you. Be ashamed and confounded for your own ways, O house of Israel!"

"'Thus says the Lord GOD: "On the day that I cleanse you from all your iniquities, I will also enable you to dwell in the cities, and the ruins shall be rebuilt. The desolate land shall be tilled instead of lying desolate in the sight of all who pass by. So they will say, 'This land that was desolate has become like the garden of Eden; and the wasted, desolate, and ruined cities are now fortified and inhabited.' Then the nations which are left all around you shall know that I, the LORD, have rebuilt the ruined places and planted what was desolate. I, the LORD, have spoken it, and I will do it."'" (Ezek. 36:22–36)

As you read through Ezekiel 36, you should have found that these are some of the things God does when He brings revival:

1. He shows us the holiness of His name

2. He sprinkles us with clean water and makes us clean.

3. He cleanses us from all impurities and all substitutes (idols).

4. He removes our stony heart and gives a tender heart of flesh.

5. He puts a new spirit in us—His Spirit—and moves us to obey Him.

6. He saves us from all our uncleanness.

7. He restores what was taken away during His discipline and judgment.

8. He removes our disgrace.

9. He causes us to remember our evil ways and wicked deeds and despise ourselves for our detestable practices.

10. He cleanses us from all our sins.

11. He resettles and rebuilds our ruined places.

WHAT DOES REVIVAL LOOK LIKE?

Some people have a stereotyped idea of what revival will look like when it comes. Here are three examples:

1. *Some see revival as a well-planned series of services.* After much prayer and personal preparation, God's people gather to hear anointed preaching. Under that preaching, conviction comes and people respond with broken and contrite hearts and return to the Lord.

2. *Others think that revival cannot be planned.* They think revival is only a spontaneous response to God's presence and holiness. During a service, with no advanced warning, the Holy Spirit brings deep conviction of sin, and "everything breaks loose" as people get right with God.

3. *Someone else may say, "Our church is not the same as we used to be.* We love each other and we love the Lord. People are seeking to obey every command. We are united with one heart and spirit. But it didn't used to be that way. I just can't explain what happened. Somehow, over the past two years our church has changed."

Which of the above is genuine revival? They all may be evidence of revival. The essence of revival is that God's people have returned to Him and He has returned to His people. We could diagram revival in this way:

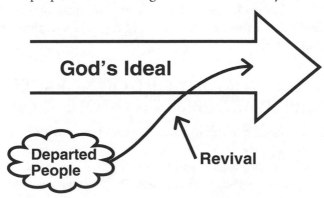

God has a standard for His people to function in a right relationship with Him. When they are living as He intended, spiritual awakening is a natural by-product. Before revival, a departed people are away from God and His ideal for them. They have departed from God's presence, His purposes, and His ways. Revival occurs when God calls His people to repent and return to Him and they do. When the people have returned and are rightly related to God, revival has occurred. However, that can happen in a multitude of ways. In fact, God can cause each experience of revival to be different. He doesn't want us looking for a program, a method, or a set pattern. He wants us looking to Him.

This means that one church may begin a process of returning to the Lord. Under the regular preaching and teaching of God's Word, the people—out of love for their Lord—hear God's call and return one step at a time. It is a gradual process. But over a period of time they have moved from where they once were to where God intended them to be. That is revival. You could call it renewal or use some other term, but they have returned.

This also means that the people of another church could be going about their normal religious activity. Then one day they face a crisis or they are confronted with a truth in such a way that God grips His people with conviction of sin. In a deeply emotional time, people flood the altar. There is weeping, praying, and public confession of sin. In a short period of time, God accomplishes what many thought could never happen. This might be a time when God had been calling, but He faced resistance. Then in His sovereign choice, He decides to deal deeply with sin in a quick blast of His Spirit. This, too, is revival if the people have returned to a right relationship to the Lord.

As we studied the revivals in Scripture, we saw that God also worked on scheduled days and times for covenant renewal. He can send genuine revival to a people who have sincerely sought Him in prayer and who join in a scheduled time to examine themselves and return to the Lord.

As you anticipate that God is working to send revival to the people where you fellowship or serve, don't lock God into working in only one way. He is Sovereign. Let Him work anyway He chooses. The fruits of revival can be the same regardless of whether you came back to the Lord over time or in a significant event of revival.

A TESTIMONY OF GOD'S GRACE: REVIVAL IN BROWNWOOD, TEXAS

Coggin Avenue was a fairly traditional Baptist church in Brownwood, Texas. Not many years ago, the church was in a state of spiritual need. Several pastors left under difficult circumstances and after short tenures. Broken relationships were common among the members. Sexual immorality was present in the church, even among some of the leaders. The church had almost no evangelistic impact on the community, and spiritual apathy was commonplace.

John Avant went to pastor this congregation in the middle of this spiritual deadness. After a year and a half of hard work, John sat in the truck of a key leader and wept. He cried out to the Lord and said, "God, I can't do anything with these people." He finally had reached the end of himself. And that was what God was waiting for so He could get the glory for what followed.

Gradually people began to develop a hunger for the Lord. Over three hundred went through a study of *Experiencing God: Knowing and Doing the Will of God.* They began to have a different intimacy with the Lord. John led the church in a study of *Fresh Encounter: God's Pattern for Revival and Spiritual Awakening.* People began to deal with sin in their lives, but nothing on a dramatic scale. Further information on other available church study materials can be obtained from Marketing Planning Department, Baptist Sunday School Board, MSN 135 egm, 127 9th Avenue N., Nashville, TN 37234. Then God began to reveal His presence and power among the people.

A godly man in the church ran for election as police chief on the platform "Revival is coming to Brownwood, and I want to be a part of it as your police chief." He won the election. A prominent citizen in town had left his wife and was contemplating suicide. God took hold of his life and turned him around. He was reconciled with his wife and fell in love with the Lord. God began to work through him to see others come to Christ. Some marriages were restored, and the church began to see the power of God manifest.

One member decided to quit selling pornography, alcohol, and lottery tickets in his convenience stores because of God's conviction. Everyone was amazed when his business actually increased. People didn't have to wait in line for lottery tickets, and his stores were faster.

Then John was introduced to Fernando, a Hispanic young man who had been a drug addict and was an ex-convict. Fernando had been saved, and he returned to his hometown with a burden to minister to the gang kids. He already had begun to see a response. Lives were changing. Kids who were formerly dropping out of school were now making good grades. Even the principals of the high school and junior high took notice.

John introduced Fernando to the members of Coggin Avenue. They were asked to help fund his ministry to gang kids. The only concern was that the charismatic church in town was already supporting his ministry. Not many Baptist churches jointly sponsor ministry with charismatics. After hearing the testimonies of some of the kids, the church overwhelmingly voted to sponsor his work. When word got to the charismatic church, denominational barriers in town began to fall. Pastors from a variety of denominations began meeting together to pray for revival in their town.

On January 22, 1995, God's Spirit brought great conviction of sin at the end of Coggin Avenue's 8:30 A.M. service. People came to the altar weeping and getting right with God. They began to openly confess sin and seek forgiveness. Relationships were reconciled. On that day, twenty-two people made public decisions for Christ. That evening they had a joint meeting (already planned) between Coggin Avenue and their Hispanic mission. They were baptizing some black kids that had come to know Christ through Fernando's ministry. By the end of the service, blacks, whites, and Hispanics were weeping and praying together. Racial barriers began to fall.

At least two other churches nearby were affected by God's Spirit in unusual ways that same day. Churches from other denominations were beginning to see times of revival and renewal as well. The charismatic pastor said to John, "We have a group in our church studying *Experiencing God.* It is led by a Presbyterian, filled with charismatics, and has a Church of Christ pastor in attendance, and they are studying Baptist materials. That's got to be revival!"

By mid-February, a deep time of confession of sin broke out on the campus of Howard Payne University in Brownwood. Testimonies from that experience have sparked similar movements of God's Spirit on dozens of other college and seminary campuses across the country. Many are praying that this is just the forerunner of revival and a mighty spiritual awakening that God so desires to send across our land.[1]

SUMMARY

♦ When God comes in revival, He comes as a refiner's fire.

♦ Responding to God's presence produces holiness in churches and the lives of believers.

♦ "Revival Is Like Judgment Day."

♦ Individuals and churches cannot continue to do business as usual when God is calling them to revival and to be part of an awakening in the land.

♦ Not everyone will respond positively to a message that calls for repentance.

♦ God is the One who revives His repentant people. It is an act of a Sovereign God.

♦ The way to know if you have returned is to see if God has returned to you.

♦ The essence of revival is that God's people have returned to Him and He has returned to His people.

♦ Don't lock God into working in only one way. He is Sovereign. Let Him work anyway He chooses.

ENCOUNTERING GOD IN PRAYER

◆ Ask the Lord to encourage you to remain faithful in pursuing revival until He returns with revival to your church.

◆ Pray for a willingness on the part of church members to join together in repenting and returning to the Lord.

◆ Ask the Lord to reveal anything in your life that might be a hindrance to revival.

◆ Pray for the various denominations in your community that God would send revival on all of them. Pray that pastors and leaders would begin praying together for revival.

ENCOUNTERING GOD WITH OTHERS

As you have opportunity in a small group, consider these discussion questions for chapter 12:

1. How does God get glory for Himself through the church?

2. How should we respond to people in our church who scorn and ridicule a call to revival?

3. What are some of the greatest barriers to revival?

4. What are some aspects of the revival process that would be difficult for individuals and churches?

5. What are the benefits of going through God's revival process?

6. How can we know when revival has taken place?

7. What are some ways that we can do a better job of praying for revival individually and as a church?

8. What is the best evidence that repentance has taken place? Why?

9. Why should the testimony of revival in Brownwood, Texas, be seen as only one of many ways God may send revival? What are some other ways revival might come to God's people?

PART III

Spiritual Leadership in Times of Revival and Awakening

CHAPTER 13

The Role of a Spiritual Leader

Serving as a leader of God's people is a very special privilege and a great responsibility. Though every believer has direct access and accountability to God, a spiritual leader carries much responsibility for the condition of God's people. He is also judged more severely if he leads God's people astray (James 3). Spiritual leadership is not limited to pastors, though pastors have an important function in guiding God's people to follow the Lord. Spiritual leaders may include parents, church staff, deacons or elders, teachers, board or committee chairpersons, denominational leaders, heads of para-church ministries, and others. Anytime you have an assignment from God that places you in a teaching or leadership position over other believers, you have a role in providing spiritual leadership to that group.

According to God's pattern for revival, God works through leaders to call the people back to Himself. If our nation and our churches can be so far from the Lord that we no longer reveal His holiness or His power, something is wrong. In part, the problem may be with leaders who are not guiding the people to return. What is a spiritual leader from God's perspective?

KING OR SERVANT?

When God established a people for Himself, He called on Moses to lead His people. Moses was known and referred to as "the servant of the Lord" (Deut. 34:5). Moses was the servant, and God was King and Ruler. After Moses died, Joshua was selected to be His servant, and he, too, was known as "the servant of the Lord" (Josh. 24:29). During the period of the Judges, God chose servants to guide the people to return to the Lord and follow Him. One day, however, Israel made a very significant departure from the Lord's pattern for leadership:

> All the elders of Israel gathered together and came to Samuel at Ramah, and said to him, "Look, you are old, and your sons do not walk in your ways. Now make us a king to judge us like all the nations."
>
> But the thing displeased Samuel when they said, "Give us a king to judge us." So Samuel prayed to the LORD. And the LORD said to Samuel, "Heed the voice of the people in all that they say to you; for they have not rejected you, but they have rejected Me, that I should not reign over them. According to all the works which they have done since the day that I brought them up out of Egypt, even to this day—with which they have forsaken Me and served other gods—so they are doing to you also. Now therefore, heed their voice. However, you shall solemnly forewarn them, and show them the behavior of the king who will reign over them." (1 Sam. 8:4–9)

Did you notice what the people wanted? They wanted a human ruler like all the nations around them. They wanted to be like the world. In turning to a human to rule (reign) over them, they were rejecting God's sovereign rule. Samuel gave the people God's warning that the king would take the very best of everything they had. They would be bound to serve the king and meet his needs. "Nevertheless the people refused to obey the voice of Samuel; and they said, 'No, but we will have a king over us, that we also may be like all the nations, and that our king may judge us and go out before us and fight our battles'" (1 Sam. 8:19–20).

We see many similarities today. The reason the people of the world are so strong on leadership is because they do not acknowledge God as their leader. So they set up their own leader. They also write books on leadership to teach people how to lead. Leaders turn to those books for help because they are not turning to God for direction. They have turned to a substitute for God. Human leaders become the substitute for God, and their methods become a substitute for God's ways.

Tragically, much of the Christian community has turned to the world for its direction. We take the books of the world on leadership and incorporate them into our books for Christian leaders. Now we have Christian leaders trying to follow or copy the substitutes rather than follow God. We are disoriented. On the one hand, we know God is our Ruler and Leader. But we have all these books that tell pastors and other church leaders how to be leaders. By following the way of the world, the pastor may function more like a chief executive officer or a chairman of the board instead of constantly pointing the people to the Lord for leadership. Churches contribute to the problem by seeking leaders who have the qualities they would look for in their businesses. We "hire" them to "go out and fight our battles for us."

As an example, look at what we are doing with the term *vision*. We look for a leader with vision. We want to know what his vision is for our church. We have visioning conferences and do our best demographic research to determine what our vision ought to be. We look at the trends in the world to help guide our vision. We develop vision statements to guide our churches.

Yes, the Scripture does say, "Where there is no vision, the people perish" (Prov. 29:18, KJV). But the "vision" described there is a "divine communication." God's people are not supposed to function on the vision of a leader or on the joint vision of the church. They function based on revelation. God reveals Himself and what He is doing so we can be involved in His work. God's people are then called to obey.

God may reveal what He has in mind to the pastor or other church leaders. But once He does, their job as leaders is to guide the people to follow the Lord, not their leadership. Jesus did a wonderful job of giving us vision statements for leadership, evangelism, and discipleship. But we decide to develop our own substitutes for what God has already revealed. Jesus told us what kind of leader was acceptable in His kingdom:

> "You know that the rulers of the Gentiles lord it over them, and those who are great exercise authority over them. Yet it shall not be so among you; but whoever desires to become great among you, let him be your servant. And whoever desires to be first among you, let him be your slave—just as the Son of Man did not come to be served, but to serve, and to give His life a ransom for many." (Matt. 20:25–28)

God's chosen leaders don't function like the world. They don't rule as dictators or autocrats based on position or personal influence. God's leaders are called to be servants, even slaves. They are first servants of God and then servants to God's people. Jesus gave us a model of One who provided spiritual leadership by being a servant rather than demanding a following like a human ruler.

CHRIST AS OUR LEADER

In redemption God put His people back the way they ought to be. He put His Son Jesus Christ as head over the church (His body). He is to be the Leader and Ruler of His people. Now, the Living Christ, through the Spirit of God and in the presence of the Father, guides His church to be on mission with Him. But we run into the same problem Israel encountered. We know that Christ is to be our leader, but we want a man to lead us. And we want him to function with the qualities of a chief executive officer.

God looks for a person whose heart is right toward Him and who will look to Him for leadership. God looks for a person who will point the people to Him for leadership. Then, as they together listen attentively to the Lord, Christ is able to guide His church to be anything He intends the local congregation to be. He empowers His people to do all He guides them to do, and a watching world sees an exalted Christ and is drawn to Him.

POINTING THE PEOPLE TO GOD

Certain leaders of God's people are remembered for the way they guided God's people to follow Him. Others are remembered for leading God's people astray. Moses, Joshua, Samuel, and David guided God's people to follow Him. Let's look at one occasion from each of these leaders. Pay attention to how each leader pointed the people to the Lord.

MOSES

[Moses said:] "Hear, O Israel: The LORD our God, the LORD is one! You shall love the LORD your God with all your heart, with all your soul, and with all your strength. And these words which I command you today shall be in your heart. You shall teach them diligently to your children, and shall talk of them when you sit in your house, when you walk by the way, when you lie down, and when you rise up. . . . So it shall be, when the LORD your God brings you into the land of which He swore to your fathers . . . —when you have eaten and are full—then beware, lest you forget the LORD who brought you out of the land of Egypt, from the house of bondage." (Deut. 6:4–12)

JOSHUA

[Joshua said]: "Fear the LORD, serve Him in sincerity and in truth, and put away the gods which your fathers served . . . Serve the LORD! And if it seems evil to you to serve the LORD, choose for yourselves this day whom you will serve . . . But as for me and my house, we will serve the LORD." So the people answered and said: "Far be it from us that we should forsake the LORD to serve other gods." (Josh. 24:14–16)

SAMUEL

Samuel said to the people, "Do not fear. You have done all this wickedness; yet do not turn aside from following the LORD, but serve the LORD with all your heart. And do not turn aside; for then you would go after empty things which cannot profit or deliver, for they are nothing. For the LORD will not forsake His people, for His great name's sake, because it has pleased the LORD to make you His people. Moreover, as for me, far be it from me that I should sin against the LORD in ceasing to pray for you; but I will teach you the good and the right way. Only fear the LORD, and serve Him in truth with all your heart; for consider what great things He has done for you." (1 Sam. 12:20–24)

DAVID

David first delivered this psalm into the hand of Asaph and his brethren, to thank the LORD:

Oh, give thanks to the LORD!
Call upon His name;
Make known His deeds among the peoples!
Sing to Him, sing psalms to Him;
Talk of all His wondrous works!
Glory in His holy name;
Let the hearts of those rejoice who seek the LORD!
Seek the LORD and His strength;
Seek His face evermore! (1 Chron. 16:7–11)

EARLY CHRISTIAN LEADERS

When we get to the New Testament we see the early church with servant leaders who pointed the people to the resurrected Lord. They saw themselves as "servants" and "bond-slaves" of Jesus Christ. They saw themselves as servants of the churches. The apostles knew that God was their leader, so they devoted themselves to prayer and the Scriptures (Acts 6). They constantly turned to God in prayer and in His Word for directions. They saw God as their Leader, Ruler, and King.

AS GOES THE LEADER . . .

In the Old Testament God's response toward His people was often determined by the life of the leader. Here are some examples:

♦ When Israel built and worshiped a golden calf, God was prepared to destroy them. Moses begged God not to bring this disaster on the people. God punished but did not utterly destroy the people because of His leader, Moses (Exod. 32).

♦ During David's reign, a three-year famine plagued the land. David sought the Lord's perspective. God said it was because King Saul had broken the covenant Israel had with the Gibeonites by trying to annihilate them (Josh. 9). Saul's sin brought disaster even after his death. David, in behalf of the nation, owned the sins of Saul and sought to be reconciled with the Gibeonites. "After that God heeded the prayer for the land" (2 Sam. 21:14).

♦ David decided to take a census of his fighting men against the counsel of Joab. David recognized his sin and asked God for forgiveness, but God first brought a plague on the land that cost the lives of seventy thousand (2 Sam. 24).

♦ Because of their rebellion against God, Israel fell to the Assyrians. Hezekiah, King of Judah, came humbly to the Lord in prayer in behalf of the people of Judah. God sent an angel that destroyed 185,000 Assyrian soldiers and Jerusalem was spared (2 Kings 18–19).

♦ After Hezekiah, Manasseh became king. He was very wicked. The people also had sinned, but Manasseh crossed over God's line of grace. God said, "'Because Manasseh king of Judah has done these abominations (he has acted more wickedly than all the Amorites who were before him, and has also made Judah sin with his idols), therefore thus says the LORD God of Israel: "Behold, I am bringing such calamity upon Jerusalem and Judah, that whoever hears of it, both his ears will tingle"'" (2 Kings 21:10–12).

♦ After God had determined to bring destruction on Jerusalem and Judah, Josiah led the people back to the Lord (2 Chron. 34). Because of Josiah's humility and responsiveness to God, God promised not to bring the disaster during his lifetime. "All his days they did not depart from following the LORD God of their fathers" (2 Chron. 34:33). The significant point in this experience is that God decided to spare that generation after Josiah humbled himself and *before* the people repented. Often the people followed the Lord as long as the leader followed the Lord.

JUDGED MORE STRICTLY

Spiritual leadership carries with it a great accountability to God. In New Testament times, a problem arose when people sought to be spiritual leaders for reasons other than a call of God. James warned, "Not many of you should presume to be teachers, my brothers, because you know that we who teach will be judged more strictly" (James 3:1, NIV). James went on to explain to spiritual leaders how powerful the tongue is. Like the little rudder that can direct a large ship, the tongue of a spiritual leader can influence the direction of a church for right or wrong.

Pastors have been given a great responsibility for the spiritual welfare of the believers entrusted to them. They are given a stewardship over these believers. Paul gave some sober counsel to leaders: "It is required that those who have been given a trust must prove faithful. . . . It is the Lord who judges me. . . . He will bring to light what is hidden in darkness and will expose the motives of men's hearts" (1 Cor. 4:2, 4–5, NIV).

Jesus said, "'Everyone to whom much is given, from him much will be required; and to whom much has been committed, of him they will ask the more'" (Luke 12:48). The spiritual leader must have a holy life and a pure heart before God. Leadership of God's people may mean the difference between revival or judgment.

Spiritual leaders of God's people have the wonderful privilege of being a fellow worker with God in His kingdom. They also have an awesome responsibility and accountability to God for those He has entrusted to their leadership. Throughout the Scriptures, when God's people departed from Him, God sought out spiritual leaders to guide the people back to a right relationship with Him. The future of God's people often depended on the response of the leaders.

SPIRITUAL PHYSICIAN

One role of a spiritual leader is to be a spiritual physician. Pastors or other leaders need to let God work through them to reveal the spiritual needs and to guide God's people to spiritual health. When the people had forsaken God, God said, "'I sought for a man among them who would make a wall, and stand in the gap before Me on behalf of the land, that I should not destroy it; but I found no one. Therefore I have poured out My indignation on them; I have consumed them with the fire of My wrath'" (Ezek. 22:30–31).

In this case God did not find a spiritual leader willing to stand in the gap before God on behalf of the land. So God brought destruction on the land with the fall of Jerusalem to the Babylonians in 587 B.C. In other cases a spiritual leader responded and the people were spared.

Moses is a good example. After Israel was miraculously delivered from Egypt, Moses went up on the mountain to receive the Law. While he was gone, Aaron and the people rebelled against the Lord and built a golden calf to worship. God said to Moses, "'Let Me alone, that My wrath may burn hot against them and I may consume them. And I will make of you a great nation'" (Exod. 32:10).

Moses could have been selfish and agreed with God. Then he would have become the father of the nation. But Moses demonstrated the character of a true spiritual leader when he unselfishly prayed for Israel: "LORD, why does Your wrath burn hot against Your people whom You have brought out of the land of Egypt with great power and with a mighty hand? Why should the Egyptians speak, and say, 'He brought them out to harm them, to kill them in the mountains, and to consume them from the face of the earth'? Turn from Your fierce wrath, and relent from this harm to Your people." (Exod. 32:11–12)

God heard Moses' plea on behalf of the people, and "the LORD relented from the harm which He said He would do to His people" (Exod. 32:14). After the spies brought back a majority report against entering the promised land, the people again rebelled against the Lord. God determined to destroy the people, and Moses prayed for God to spare the people (Num. 14). A spiritual leader must be prepared to unselfishly stand in the gap before the Lord on behalf of the people—even when the people are sinful and rebellious. When the people of God are sin-sick, the spiritual character of a leader is put to the test. God never gave Moses permission to leave the people when they were so rebellious. The people need spiritual leadership at those times more than at any other. This role for a spiritual leader is seen clearly as the living Lord addressed the pastors (messengers) of the churches in Asia Minor (Rom. 2–3).

SPIRITUAL LEADERSHIP IN TIMES OF CRISIS

Many spiritual leaders have looked to the world and to human books to discover what kind of leader they ought to be. The world cannot give you the necessary counsel. You need to allow God to mold and shape you into the instrument He can use to care for His people in times of spiritual crisis. God will always be at work preparing your character for any assignment He intends to give you. Only God knows what the future holds. He says: "'I know the thoughts that I think toward you,' says the LORD, 'thoughts of peace and not of evil, to give you a future and a hope. Then you will call upon Me and go and pray to Me, and I will listen to you. And you will seek Me and find Me, when you search for Me with all your heart'" (Jer. 29:11–13).

The crises we face in our churches, in our nation, and in the world today will require God-prepared, Christ-centered, Holy Spirit-empowered people of prayer. Spiritual leaders must seek God with all their hearts. They must truly be God-centered.

These are unique times when God is working mightily worldwide. He is breaking down barriers to the spread of the gospel—political barriers, language barriers, and even technological barriers. We are witnessing the beginnings of one of God's greatest moves in bringing a lost world to Him. Casual leadership will not be sufficient. Human-centered leadership will fail you. Only God has the counsel for the kind of leader He needs for these important days. These are extraordinary times.

♦ Are you willing to let God make you into the kind of leader He needs in times of crisis?

♦ Will you take that direction from God through the Scriptures?

♦ Will you surrender your agenda to guide your people to follow God's agenda?

♦ Are you willing to stand in the gap before God and intercede for a rebellious people?

♦ Are you willing to submit to the refiner's fire for personal cleansing and purification?

A TESTIMONY OF GOD'S GRACE: A REVIVED PASTOR AND A REVIVED CHURCH

Lonnie was pastor of a relatively small church in Ohio. Because of problems and frustrations, he had written his letter of resignation and prepared a résumé to return to engineering. Later that week he attended a statewide conference, where God met him through the Scriptures and godly counsel. Lonnie said, "I spent the next three days on my face, weeping before the Lord." God began to deal with Lonnie and the kind of pastoral leadership he had provided. Over and over he was confessing that God was right and seeking forgiveness.

God dealt with Lonnie on two particular issues. One was Lonnie's approach to church growth. He was studying and trying to apply the latest principles and methods of church growth. But during his time before the Lord, God impacted him with Matthew 16:18. Jesus said He would build His church and the gates of hell would not prevail against it. Lonnie sensed Jesus saying to him, "Lonnie, you have had my church long enough. I want it back." Lonnie agreed, wept before the Lord, and gave up trying to build Christ's church himself. He asked Christ to build His church any way He wanted to—with or without the pastor's help.

Lonnie claimed to be a very evangelistic pastor. He preached evangelistic messages and witnessed to people door-to-door. Neither of those things was wrong, but . . . As Lonnie prayed, God turned his thoughts to John 10. Lonnie read about the Good Shepherd and how He took care of His sheep. Again, the Lord confronted Lonnie as he prayed by asking, "What are you doing as the shepherd of my sheep in your church?" Lonnie confessed he was going after new sheep. Then the Lord broke him when He said, "Lonnie, you haven't taken care of the sheep I gave you. Why do you think I would give you any new sheep?"

Lonnie surrendered his life to the Good Shepherd and pledged to drop anything he was doing when God showed him ways to care for the needs of the members of his church. Then he sensed God saying, "Lonnie, you take care of my sheep. When they are healthy, well-fed, and contented, I will work through them to produce new sheep."

That three days of returning to the Lord had a radical impact on Lonnie, his family, and his church. Lonnie began to guide his family to an intimate relationship with the Lord, and God reconciled him with a wayward son. His daughter saw God begin to work through her at her high school. Moreover, Lonnie's wife took some big steps of faith as she came to know God's guidance and power to provide in a fresh new way.

As this revived pastor began guiding God's people (sheep) back to the Lord, God began to change things in the church. During the following eight months, the church began to see and know the power of God.

- One member was delivered from an addiction to pornography and reconciled with his family.

- Ten couples whose marriages were headed for divorce were reconciled, and the church did not see a divorce during the following year.

- God added a lay leader to the church and led the church to begin ministries at a high-crime apartment community. The chief of police reported that calls to 911 from that area decreased by 30 percent.

- The lay leader then quit his job in obedience and faith so he could do the Lord's work full-time. When the church began praying, God provided eighteen thousand dollars in the next two weeks to provide for this work. Twelve thousand dollars came to this Baptist church from a Brethren church that said, "We believe God wants us to have a part in the apartment ministry." The church was amazed at what God did.

- God led them to begin work with Russian emigrants. Then God called a Russian-speaking college professor to work with them. He, too, sensed a need to quit his job, and God has provided. This beginning led to the establishment of a foreign-mission partnership with a city in Russia.

- When Lonnie reported on God's activity eight months after his personal revival, he said, "Our people are experiencing the mighty power and presence of God, and they can't help telling people about it. Last Sunday we had seven professions of faith, and I only knew one of them."

Since that report in 1992, God has brought the Hillcrest Church to a spirit of unity and love most Christians have never seen before. God continues to display His mighty hand through that church; they are touching the world for Christ's sake. Jesus began to demonstrate what He could do to build His church when He has a people who will return to following Him. But God began His work by reviving a discouraged and self-centered pastor, transforming him into a spiritual leader who points the sheep to follow the Good Shepherd Jesus.

SUMMARY

♦ Serving as a leader of God's people is a very special privilege and a great responsibility.

♦ God works through leaders to call the people back to Him.

♦ In turning to a human to rule (reign) over them, Israel was rejecting God's sovereign rule.

♦ The world is strong on leadership because worldly people do not acknowledge God as their leader.

♦ Much of the Christian community has turned to the world for its direction.

♦ Many of today's Christian leaders try to follow or copy the substitutes rather than follow God.

♦ God's chosen leaders don't function like the world. They don't rule as dictators or autocrats based on position or personal influence.

♦ God's leaders are called to be servants, even slaves.

♦ God put His Son Jesus Christ as head over the church. He is to be the Leader and Ruler of His people.

♦ God looks for a person whose heart is right toward Him and who will look to Him for leadership.

♦ The apostles constantly turned to God in prayer and to His Word for direction. They saw God as their Leader, Ruler, and King.

♦ God decided to spare that generation after Josiah humbled himself and *before* the people repented!

♦ The role as a spiritual leader calls for a holy life and a pure heart before God.

♦ A spiritual leader must be prepared to stand in the gap before the Lord on behalf of the people, even when the people are sinful and rebellious.

♦ The crises we face in our churches, in our nation, and in the world today requires God-prepared, Christ-centered, Holy Spirit-empowered people of prayer.

ENCOUNTERING GOD IN PRAYER

If you are a spiritual leader, God may have been speaking to you in very specific ways. He may have been dealing with you in some specific areas. Take some time, perhaps an extended period of time, responding to the Lord in the areas where He is speaking.

- ◆ If God has revealed that you have turned to substitutes, repent and return to Him.
- ◆ Ask God to purify your life in such a way that you will be a useful vessel in His work.
- ◆ Surrender your own agenda for revival to Him and pray that He will begin by thoroughly reviving your own heart.
- ◆ Pray that God will be glorified in all that He does through you.

ENCOUNTERING GOD WITH OTHERS

As you have opportunity in a small group, consider these discussion questions for chapter 13:

1. How did Israel turn from the Lord and to a substitute for Him when they asked for a king?

2. In what ways have Christian churches and leaders become like Israel in looking for a human leader rather than to the Lord?

3. What is God looking for in a spiritual leader?

4. How does a spiritual leader guide a church or group to follow Christ?

5. What are the essential roles of a spiritual leader in the midst of God's people?

6. How important to a leader are prayer and study of the Scripture? Why? (See Acts 6.)

7. What correlation do you see in Scripture between the life and actions of a leader and God's response to the people?

8. Where do you sense God wants to begin revival in your life or church? How will that affect your praying?

CHAPTER 14

QUALITIES OF A SPIRITUAL LEADER

In Matthew 10, Jesus gave instructions to His twelve disciples to prepare them for the mission He was about to send them on. This was an inauguration time for the leaders to whom God was going to entrust the future of His Kingdom's work. He gave those twelve men guidelines on the cost of spiritual leadership for those critical days. Those instructions are just as powerful and relevant today as they were two thousand years ago. Here are fourteen qualities of the spiritual leaders God is calling on for His redemptive mission in our day.

1. A SENSE OF URGENCY

The context for chapter 10 is found in the last verses of Matthew 9.

> Jesus went about all the cities and villages, teaching in their synagogues, preaching the gospel of the kingdom, and healing every sickness and every disease among the people. But when He saw the multitudes, He was moved with compassion for them, because they were weary and scattered, like

sheep having no shepherd. Then He said to His disciples, "The harvest truly is plentiful, but the laborers are few." (Matt. 9:35–37)

Jesus expressed a sense of urgency over the condition of God's people. Spiritual leaders of today must have a God-like sense of urgency. The leader who is going to be walking about with our Lord today will catch the sense of urgency on the heart of the Lord. Jesus was burdened and had compassion for God's people "because they were weary and scattered, like sheep having no shepherd." This was the desperate condition to which Jesus sent the Twelve on mission.

2. A PERSON OF GENUINE AND INTENSE PRAYER

When faced with such a severe need, Jesus told these leaders to pray: "'Therefore pray the Lord of the harvest to send out laborers into His harvest'" (Matt. 9:38). In times of crisis a spiritual leader must be a person of genuine, intense, God-called prayer. He must be an intercessor who knows what it means to labor before God in prayer for the people. Even though you may not know what to pray for, the Holy Spirit has been given the assignment to guide your praying according to the will of God as He intercedes with us (Rom. 8:26–27). Prayer must become the first priority of a leader's work strategy. A leader must also know how to pray for laborers.

A church in Alaska was studying our course *Experiencing God: Knowing and Doing the Will of God.* The pastor became convicted that the church had forced and manipulated people to take positions of leadership to which God had not called them. He knew the church could not function as a healthy body of Christ unless it was arranged the way Christ the Head wanted it. One Sunday the pastor preached on the need for God-called leaders in the church. For his invitation the pastor asked every leader in the church to pray during the week about their positions of leadership. He asked all leaders who did not sense God had called them to their leadership positions to turn in their resignations the following week. Then the church would pray that God would call forth the laborers that He wanted in place.

The next Sunday every leader in the church resigned with the exception of two Sunday school teachers. With clear guidelines in Scripture, they began to pray with confidence that God would call forth laborers. Within two weeks every position in the church was filled by people who sensed God wanted them to serve there.

This kind of bold action required great faith and confidence in the One who said, "'Pray the Lord of the harvest to send out laborers into His harvest'" (Matt. 9:38). Spiritual leaders of today must be people with prayer as a primary work strategy who trust in a God who answers prayer.

3. UNCONDITIONAL RELATIONSHIP TO JESUS AS LORD

Jesus "had called His twelve disciples to Him" (Matt. 10:1). They were called to be disciples—to become like Him in an intimate relationship to Him. "He who calls you is faithful, who also will do it" (1 Thess. 5:24). The One who calls you is faithful to accomplish His work through those He calls. Spiritual leaders must be in an intimate love relationship with Jesus as the Sovereign Lord of their lives.

4. AWARENESS OF ACCOUNTABILITY TO GOD

You did not choose God as your master. He chose you as His servant. As a God-called leader you have an accountability to God for your leadership. Your number-one accountability is to the God who called you. Spiritual leaders must not be swayed by every wind of opinion or pressure group that comes along.

Too many leaders today watch to see which way the opinion is running in the followers before they are willing to take a stand. That kind of leadership will never do in times of crisis. Like Paul, you must see yourself as a bondslave to Jesus Christ with a high level of accountability to Him. You must choose to please God rather than men.

5. CLEAR DEMONSTRATION OF SPIRITUAL AUTHORITY

In Matthew 10, Jesus commissioned these spiritual leaders and sent them out. "He gave them power over unclean spirits, to cast them out, and to heal all kinds of sickness and all kinds of disease. . . . 'Heal the sick, cleanse the lepers, raise the dead, cast out demons. Freely you have received, freely give'" (Matt. 10:1, 8).

Spiritual authority comes from Christ, who has the full measure of God within Him. He has taken up residence within a believer to work through him (Col. 2:9–10). Christ is the One with power and authority who will be at work through spiritual leaders.

The term "spiritual authority" has been so abused in our day. Do not misunderstand. A spiritual leader will go forth in humility. He does not work in his own power or authority or in the authority that comes with a position. A spiritual leader goes forth in the power and authority of Christ, who is present in and at work through the leader.

As a spiritual leader, you have an incredible dimension of the Father's presence to undergird and strengthen you in everything you do. No crisis will get out of the control of the heavenly Father. You will be able to stand in the middle of any crisis, understanding that God has given a dimension of His power and authority that will flow through you. That power and authority will be evident to all those around you. Therefore, in humility and servanthood you can trust God to work through you. You do not need to pressure God's people to follow.

6. ABSOLUTE FAITH, TRUST, AND CONFIDENCE IN GOD

Jesus explained to the disciples that they had a whole different set of resources than they had known previously: "'Provide neither gold nor silver nor copper in your money belts, nor bag for your journey, nor two tunics, nor sandals, nor staffs; for a worker is worthy of his food'" (Matt. 10:9–10).

They would not have to worry about their provisions. A spiritual leader must have an incredible faith, trust, and confidence in God and in His provision. The God who sends you is also the God who will provide for you. The lifestyle of a spiritual leader will have confidence like that of Paul: "God is able to make all grace abound toward you, that you, always having all sufficiency in all things, may have an abundance for every good work" (2 Cor. 9:8). You dare not go into the crises of your world without that kind of confidence in the God you serve. A God-called leader need never be tentative, hopeless, or despairing in the middle of crisis. He like David will say, "He only is my rock and my salvation; he is my defence; I shall not be greatly moved" (Ps. 62:2).

7. GOD-GIVEN SENSE OF DIRECTION

When God sends out leaders, He directs them in His ways. He sends them on His terms. He also makes them aware of the awesome consequences of their own actions as well as the actions of those to whom they are sent.

"Do not go into the way of the Gentiles, and do not enter a city of the Samaritans. But go rather to the lost sheep of the house of Israel. And as you go, preach, saying, 'The kingdom of heaven is at hand. . . .'

Now whatever city or town you enter, inquire who in it is worthy, and stay there till you go out. And when you go into a household, greet it. If the household is worthy, let your peace come upon it. But if it is not worthy, let your peace return to you. And whoever will not receive you nor hear your words, when you depart from that house or city, shake off the dust from your feet. Assuredly, I say to you, it will be more tolerable for the land of Sodom and Gomorrah in the day of judgment than for that city! Behold, I send you out as sheep in the midst of wolves. Therefore be wise as serpents and harmless as doves." (Matt. 10:5–7, 11–16)

A spiritual leader is under no misconception of what is involved in his mission with Christ. Jesus warned the disciples they would face great distress as they went on mission for Him. As you follow God's directions, you need to have a God-given sense that God has sent you; that He knows where you will be going; that He knows what you will experience; and that He will be present to guide, direct, and enable you to complete your mission.

8. CLEARLY COMMITTED TO THE COST INVOLVED

Jesus explained the cost of following Him:

> "But beware of men, for they will deliver you up to councils and scourge you in their synagogues. You will be brought before governors and kings for My sake, as a testimony to them and to the Gentiles. But when they deliver you up, do not worry about how or what you should speak. For it will be given to you in that hour what you should speak; for it is not you who speak, but the Spirit of your Father who speaks in you.
>
> "Now brother will deliver up brother to death, and a father his child; and children will rise up against parents and cause them to be put to death. And you will be hated by all for My name's sake. But he who endures to the end will be saved. When they persecute you in this city, flee to another. For assuredly, I say to you, you will not have gone through the cities of Israel before the Son of Man comes." (Matt. 10:17–23)

Yet, His disciples did not need to worry beforehand about what to do. Jesus knew the times that were coming. He was orienting these leaders to be prepared for the things to come. He reminded them that the Holy Spirit would be present through those difficult circumstances to guide them clearly.

You must be very aware that there is a great cost in being a spiritual leader. You may not win any popularity contests. You must not try to please men, but rather deliver the message from God. Do not back away from obedience just because the cost is high. Keep in mind that the Holy Spirit is provided by God to give you all the resources you need at the very time you need them—even in the face of severe opposition. You need to understand that calling a people to repent will almost always bring some opposition. Sometimes that opposition is significant and relentless.

9. ABSOLUTELY GOD-ORIENTED

Jesus wanted these leaders to be God-oriented. They did not need to be afraid of others; they were of great value to God. God knew about the most intimate parts of their lives. God would vindicate the ones He had chosen:

"There is nothing covered that will not be revealed, and hidden that will not be known. Whatever I tell you in the dark, speak in the light; and what you hear in the ear, preach on the housetops. And do not fear those who kill the body but cannot kill the soul. But rather fear Him who is able to destroy both soul and body in hell. Are not two sparrows sold for a copper coin? And not one of them falls to the ground apart from your Father's will. But the very hairs of your head are all numbered. Do not fear therefore; you are of more value than many sparrows." (Matt. 10:26–31)

God will be very intimate with you as His leader. Nothing will escape His knowledge. The God who controls all of history will take care of you. You need never be afraid of men or the opinions of men. They can only kill your body. The One you are to fear is God. You need a healthy fear of Him. He is the One who determines your eternal destiny.

10. A SERVANT LIFE PATTERNED AFTER THE LORD JESUS

Jesus told His disciples to pattern their lives after Him. He was their Master. They were servants to Him. A spiritual leader will function in the ways of the Kingdom. "'A disciple is not above his teacher, nor a servant above his master. It is enough for a disciple that he be like his teacher, and a servant like his master. If they have called the master of the house Beelzebub, how much more will they call those of his household! Therefore do not fear them'" (Matt. 10:24–26).

You must pattern your life after Jesus. He is your absolute Master. You are His servant. Your identity should not be with the world but with your Master. Do not develop your leadership style and qualities from the world. Don't go to the books of worldly men to determine how you should lead. Do not try to function in the world's ways. The Kingdom's guidelines and ways are very different. It will be enough to be like your Master. In order to pattern your life after Him, however, you must thoroughly study His life under the instruction of the Holy Spirit. You must seek His counsel for every decision and direction, as He lives out His life in you and through you.

A spiritual leader also will be one who shares in the ridicule and sufferings of His Lord. You do not have the option to pick and choose the things about Jesus that you are willing to follow. To be a spiritual leader in a time of crisis, you must be ready to share in His cross like Paul, who said, "I want to know Christ . . . and the fellowship of sharing in his sufferings, becoming like him in his death" (Phil. 3:10, NIV). Would you be willing to identify with the sufferings of Christ? You may need to pray through Isaiah 53 before you answer that question. Are you willing to suffer as He suffered?

This is the kind of requirement God had for spiritual leaders at the moment Jesus came the first time to bring redemption to the world. God did not spare Jesus. Many of those leaders also lost their lives following Jesus. Do you suppose the requirements would be any lower when the Lord is preparing to return and bring history to a close? We may be approaching that special time in history when a special dimension of spiritual leadership will be required.

11. AN OPEN WITNESS TO JESUS AS LORD

A spiritual leader will have an open witness to Jesus as Lord, especially in a world filled with people who do not believe that He is Lord. "'Whoever confesses Me before men, him I will also confess before My Father who is in heaven. But whoever denies Me before men, him I will also deny before My Father who is in heaven'" (Matt. 10:32–33).

This witness is not just saying words in favor of Jesus. A spiritual leader must have an authentic life in Christ before a watching world. You must display a lifestyle in which Christ openly displays Himself before a watching world. Paul had such a lifestyle. He said to the church at Corinth:

> I resolved to know nothing while I was with you except Jesus Christ and him crucified. . . . My message and my preaching were not with wise and persuasive words, but with a demonstration of the Spirit's power, so that your faith might not rest on men's wisdom, but on God's power. (1 Cor. 2:2, 4–5, NIV)

Could you describe your life and ministry as a "demonstration of the Spirit's power"? Or are you depending more on yourself, your wisdom, or your persuasive words? You must come to the place where the Christ who dwells in you is indeed your life. When your life on the outside reflects the Christ on the inside, your open witness to Christ is true. That is the kind of witness God uses to draw men and women to His Son for redemption.

12. WILLING TO RISK FOR THE KINGDOM

A spiritual leader will be a person willing to risk for the Kingdom. He will be unafraid of the opinions of men. He will be ready for spiritual warfare, regardless of its source.

> "Do not think that I came to bring peace on earth. I did not come to bring peace but a sword. For I have come to 'set a man against his father, a daughter against her mother, and a daughter-in-law against her mother-in-law'; and 'a man's enemies will be those of his own household.'" (Matt. 10:34–36)

Not everyone will be with you when you are following God. Your enemies may even be people in your own household. You must be ready in a time of crisis for a quality of spiritual warfare that may test every intimate relationship you have. Yet, you must be willing to risk with your eyes wide open to the possible conflict.

Jesus said, "'For judgment I have come into this world'" (John 9:39). Notice that when Jesus sends you out with a message like that, He does not bring peace but a sword. You will face spiritual warfare. Will you be willing to risk all, including your very life, to deliver that message obediently?

13. WHOLEHEARTED LOVE FOR GOD AND HIS SON JESUS

Jesus knew the world into which these leaders were going. He deliberately called them into the kind of lifestyle that would require a cross. He knew that the crosses for many of these leaders would require their very lives. Yet, He knew that the future of the Kingdom of God was going to rest on the quality of the love relationship these men had with Him. Jesus demanded absolute surrender to Him—nothing withheld.

> "He who loves father or mother more than Me is not worthy of Me. And he who loves son or daughter more than Me is not worthy of Me. And he who does not take his cross and follow after Me is not worthy of Me. He who finds his life will lose it, and he who loses his life for My sake will find it." (Matt. 10:37–39)

Jesus hid nothing from these leaders. For on them, as they guided God's people, would rest the redemption of the world in every generation until He returned. The call would be real. The power would be real. The authority would be real. His presence would be real. The enemy would be real. The demands would be real. The cross would be real.

In a time of crisis a spiritual leader will have a wholehearted love for God and His Son that exceeds all other affections. The quality of your love relationship will be uncontested by any other relationship in your life, including your love for your own life. That is the only love relationship that is worthy of Christ. The love of Christ will compel you to serve Him. But that love relationship will require a cross. The will of God is the cross. Self-will must be crucified in order to follow Him. Be careful that you do not turn aside from the will of God when the cross factor becomes real. This will be reflected in your total abandon to the will of God—no strings attached. And on that love relationship will rest your obedience to all He commands (John 14:21, 23–27; 15:1–17).

14. LIVES LIFE WITH UNMISTAKABLE IDENTITY WITH JESUS CHRIST

Jesus called the disciples to a clear and unmistakable identity with Him. They would be identified with Him. They would be in union with Him, taking on the nature, pattern, and lifestyle of their living Lord. They knew, however, that this would bring them into conflict with the prevailing attitudes and even the religious practices of their day. They also knew that He stood ready to reward the faithful servant. A day of accountability would come.

"He who receives you receives Me, and he who receives Me receives Him who sent Me. He who receives a prophet in the name of a prophet shall receive a prophet's reward. And he who receives a righteous man in the name of a righteous man shall receive a righteous man's reward. And whoever gives one of these little ones only a cup of cold water in the name of a disciple, assuredly, I say to you, he shall by no means lose his reward." (Matt. 10:40–42)

A spiritual leader will do everything with a clear anticipation of accountability before his Lord. The consuming passion of your heart should be to hear on that day, "Well done, good and faithful servant."

THE PATTERN IS CLEAR

We need this kind of spiritual leader in this day of spiritual crisis . God's pattern for spiritual leadership is clear. It is not hidden. The cost factors are not hidden. The resources of God are not hidden. The love relationship in not hidden. From the call, to the empowering, to the going out, to what you will encounter, to the identification with the pattern of Jesus, to the open witness, to the fact that the work will not be easy, God reveals His requirements for spiritual leadership in times of crisis. With all this in mind, you can know you have a message that means life and death to those who hear. The world awaits the messenger who comes with an authentic call and message that are demonstrated by the power and authority of the One who sent him. The message is this: "The kingdom of heaven is near."

SUMMARY

♦ The leader who is going to be walking about with our Lord today will catch the sense of urgency on the heart of the Lord.

♦ Spiritual leaders of today must be people with prayer as a primary work strategy who trust in a God who answers prayer.

♦ You must choose to please God rather than men.

♦ A spiritual leader will go forth in humility.

♦ A spiritual leader must have an incredible faith, trust, and confidence in God and in His provision.

♦ You must be very aware that there is a great cost in being a spiritual leader.

♦ A spiritual leader also will be one who shares in the ridicule and sufferings of His Lord.

♦ When your life on the outside reflects the Christ on the inside, your open witness to Christ is true.

♦ Will you be willing to risk all, including your very life, to deliver the message obediently?

♦ The quality of your love relationship will be uncontested by any other relationship in your life, including your love for your own life.

♦ The world awaits the messenger who comes with an authentic call and message that are demonstrated by the power and authority of the One who sent him.

QUALITIES OF A SPIRITUAL LEADER

1. *A sense of urgency (Matt. 9:35–37)*
2. *A person of genuine and intense prayer (Matt. 9:38)*
3. *Unconditional relationship to Jesus as Lord (Matt. 10:1)*
4. *Awareness of accountability to God (Matt. 10:1, 8)*
5. *Clear demonstration of spiritual authority (Matt. 10:1, 8)*
6. *Absolute faith, trust, and confidence in God (Matt. 10:9–10)*
7. *God-given sense of direction (Matt. 10:5–7, 11–16)*
8. *Clearly committed to the cost involved (Matt. 10:17–23)*
9. *Absolutely God-oriented (Matt. 10:26–31)*
10. *A servant life patterned after the Lord Jesus (Matt. 10:24–25)*
11. *An open witness to Jesus as Lord (Matt. 10:32–33)*
12. *Willing to risk for the Kingdom (Matt. 10:34–36)*
13. *Wholehearted love for God and His Son Jesus (Matt. 10:37–39)*
14. *Lives life with unmistakable identity with Jesus Christ (Matt. 10:40–42)*

ENCOUNTERING GOD IN PRAYER

♦ Consider this prayer for your life as a leader: *Lord, Whatever it costs me, I release my life to You to be a spiritual leader during these times of crisis. Do with me whatever you will. Amen.*

♦ Before the Lord, review the qualities and the costs of spiritual leadership that Jesus outlined for His disciples. Discuss with the Lord what He asks of you.

ENCOUNTERING GOD WITH OTHERS

As you have opportunity in a small group, consider these discussion questions for chapter 14:

1. What kind of a relationship will a spiritual leader have with Christ?

2. What are the strengths of being the kind of spiritual leader just described? Where do these strengths come from?

3. What are some of the costs a spiritual leader must be willing to pay?

4. What are some of the things a spiritual leader will do in obedience to the Lord's command?

CHAPTER 15

PERSONAL REVIVAL FOR SPIRITUAL LEADERS

In the Bible, revivals always were led by spiritual leaders. Revivals are intended to began at the top. If you are a spiritual leader of a family, a church, a denomination, or other group, our prayer is that you will experience a personal revival in preparation for leading others to return to the Lord. Perhaps God has already prepared your heart and life. Let this chapter point you to the Lord for fine-tuning your personal preparation so that you will be the kind of instrument and servant God can use in revival of His people.

ALLOW GOD TO SHAPE YOUR LIFE

Continually allow God to work in your own life. As God works in you, guide other church or group leaders to respond to the Lord. Biblical revivals began with the leadership and moved downward. You may want to consider some of the following suggestions.

♦ *Find a godly pastor or other leader that you respect for their spiritual maturity and spiritual consistency.* Put your life alongside him as a prayer partner and a counselor. Help each other as you lead your churches or groups to encounter God. God created us for mutual interdependence.

♦ *Work diligently on getting rid of any pride in your life.* The hour is late. Time is short. Live with a sense of urgency and humble yourself before God. Don't allow pride to keep you from any action that God calls for.

♦ *Determine on the front end of this experience that you are more interested in pleasing God than self or man.* If you struggle with that commitment, stay before God until He gives you that desire. "It is God who works in you both to will and to do for His good pleasure" (Phil. 2:13).

♦ *Surrender your will and every aspect of your life to God.* Ask Him to reveal any sin or impurity that is keeping you from usefulness. Ask God to make your life a "highway of holiness" over which others may travel in coming to the Lord (read carefully and prayerfully Isa. 35).

♦ *Take a personal prayer retreat.* Get away from the busy life of home and church to spend time with your heavenly Father. Jesus often did this. Focus on your love relationship with God. Let Him guide the agenda of your praying, because "the Spirit also helps in our weaknesses. For we do not know what we should pray for as we ought, but the Spirit Himself makes intercession for us with groanings which cannot be uttered. Now He who searches the hearts knows what the mind of the Spirit is, because He makes intercession for the saints according to the will of God" (Rom. 8:26–27).

♦ *Like Paul, ask people to pray for you at every opportunity.*

♦ *If you have not already done so, consider reading and studying* Experiencing God *(Blackaby and King).* This book may help you learn to hear God's voice more clearly. It may help you better understand ways to guide God's people into intimacy with God. God may even use it to enhance your personal love relationship with Him.

DO YOU NEED TO BE SET FREE FROM YOUR PAST?

Statistics from various sources indicate that anywhere from 60 to 80 percent of today's pastors grew up in a hurting home environment. God often uses the pain of that experience to sensitize a person to the hurts of others. However, unresolved pain from your past can become a spiritual stronghold that hinders effective ministry.

One prominent pastor shared how he grew up with an abusive stepfather. Home was often in chaos. Love and approval were based on conditions that could never quite be met. He seldom heard any word of encouragement or praise. Most frequently he heard words of criticism and condemnation.

Years later, in a very successful ministry, he reached a point of physical, emotional, and spiritual burnout. He described himself as a highly critical person. He was one who always had to be in control. He was very sensitive to any disagreement or constructive criticism and took such statements as a personal attack. He was a perfectionist and a workaholic. No matter how successful he was, he never felt any peace or satisfaction from his work. He always felt inferior to others. He was always trying to get people to love him, but he would never allow them to get too close. He was lonely and frustrated. He was constantly berating himself for not being good enough.

He was on the verge of quitting the ministry when some friends encouraged him to get help. In great humility and brokenness, he shared his life story with a small group of pastor friends from which he sought spiritual counsel. One of those men prayed with and for him and he was set free by God's grace.

Causes of Pain

A variety of problems in your past could be affecting your relationship with God and your ministry with God's people. We have seen individuals and leaders who have been in a sort of spiritual bondage because of physical, emotional, or sexual abuse in their childhood. Divorce, death of a parent, abandonment by a parent, or even a long-term serious illness can have a strong influence on a person.

If you grew up in an environment of abuse or great adversity, you may have a tendency to shrug it off and say, "I'm over that now." If, however, you have problems similar to those of the pastor described above, or if you have problems with most of your relationships, you may still be responding out of a painful past.

God's Love

Your heavenly Father wants to set you free from your past to become all He has planned for your life. Often God will allow such a person to "hit the bottom" because that person finally realizes he has no hope apart from Him. At that point, a person is in a wonderful condition where he can experience some of the fullest dimensions of God's love.

God's Solution

Certainly if you have sinned in your anger, developed a root of bitterness, abused others, governed your people harshly, or sinned in some other way, you are accountable for your actions. You have sinned. You need God's forgiveness. God calls for repentance in such cases. Your repentance needs to include a change of mind whereby you agree with God and say, "I'm guilty. I have sinned."

You need a change of heart whereby you are broken over the grief you have caused your heavenly Father. Here you come to the place of genuinely saying, "I'm sorry." You need a change of will whereby you determine that, because God is your helper, you will not live that way again. Then you need a change in your actions or behavior that demonstrates that you have changed. God's grace is more than adequate to enable you to change.

From God's side you need to first hear His conviction of sin. You need to experience His forgiveness and cleansing. You need to be made right with Him once again. Then you need the enabling power of His Spirit within you to help you live your life differently. You cannot do it alone. Getting right with God is a major process that is not complete when you say you are sorry. It continues until your repentance is complete and your love relationship with God is reestablished. You will know when God's fullness is being manifest through you.

HEALING TOO

If you have a painful past due to the sin of others, you probably need more than forgiveness. You may have a brokenness that needs to be mended. You also may need to be set free from any bondage that has kept you at a distance from experiencing God's unconditional love in personal and intimate ways.

Growing up in a hurtful home environment can leave some open wounds in adulthood that are tender or painful. It does not matter whether the problems at home were due to sin (like alcoholism) or due to unfortunate circumstances (like an invalid parent). You still may be affected by the dynamics of that time. Your pain may be expressed in your need to control everything and everyone around you. It might show up in a critical spirit or workaholism. God wants to heal you and set you free. Here are some steps you may want to take:

1. "Confess your faults one to another, and pray one for another, that ye may be healed. The effectual fervent prayer of a righteous man availeth much" (James 5:16, KJV). Sometimes you need the prayers of another to receive God's healing work in your life. God may require those prayers so you will not think that you somehow earned His favor. His love is freely given. Share with another trusted believer about your hurt and ask him or her to pray for you.

2. Allow God to demolish this spiritual stronghold. Recognize that God has given spiritual weapons to demolish strongholds like this one: "Though we live in the world, we do not wage war as the world does. The weapons we fight with . . . have divine power to demolish strongholds. We demolish arguments and every pretension that sets itself up against the knowledge of God, and we take captive every thought to make it obedient to Christ" (2 Cor. 10:3–5, NIV).

A believer with the power and authority of the indwelling Christ has divine weapons that can demolish this stronghold in your life. Watch for a person of faith who will pray for you. Share your need and ask him or her to pray. The prayer of a righteous person is very effective in the courts of God.

3. Put the past behind you. Paul talked to the Philippians about his past, but he determined not to let his past keep him from experiencing God's fullness. His goal was to know Christ and His power. So Paul said, "I do not count myself to have apprehended; but one thing I do, forgetting those things which are behind and reaching forward to those things which are ahead, I press toward the goal for the prize of the upward call of God in Christ Jesus" (Phil. 3:13–14).

God created you for eternity. He wants to work in the present to conform you to the image of His Son Jesus. The focus of your attention needs to be on Christ and eternity. When you focus on your painful past, you are facing the wrong direction, and your whole life will seem out of sorts. You need to repent (turn away from) your past and the pain or abuse you experienced. You need to turn toward God and eternity. Though you will not actually forget the past, you can treat it as dead and without influence in your present. Focus your attention on Jesus and allow God to remake you in His likeness. T. W. Hunt, author of *The Mind of Christ*, has said that you are not a product of your past. You are a product of your future and what you are becoming in Christ.

4. Receive your heavenly Father's love and healing. Often a person who has been abused in some way by a parent—especially a father—has trouble feeling close to God the Father. Though you may know intellectually that God's love is pure, safe, trustworthy, unconditional, and free, you may have trouble experiencing His love in that way. You may treat your heavenly Father like you do (or did) your earthly father. You may crave God's love and acceptance, yet keep Him at a distance for fear of getting hurt. You may work day and night trying to please Him but never feel like you have done enough. But God's love is not for sale.

To really *know* God's love you must experience it. God is standing ready to lavish His love on you. He just needs you to allow Him. To experience God's love, you need some uninterrupted time with your heavenly Father.

Go to a place where you can have an extended period alone with Him. Don't try to word some special prayer. God's love is entirely free. Nothing you can do will prompt God to love you—so don't *do* anything. Just spend time with your heavenly Father and open your life freely to receive all the love He wants to bestow. In a way that probably will be unique to you, He will be able to convince you of His love. He will bind up your brokenness. He will heal the hurts of your past. He will spiritually lift you into His lap and enfold His loving arms around you. Or He will spiritually take a walk and place His arm around your shoulder as a son or daughter. There, surrounded by His presence, you will begin to experience the life-giving dimensions of the unconditional love of the heavenly Father.

HEALING FOR THE SHEPHERDS

The above suggestions are not intended to be a rigid set of steps to go through. They describe a love relationship with an almighty God. He is the only One who can heal the brokenness or pain you may sense. Very likely, He will do His healing work through the prayers of other believers (James 5:16). This is not something you have to do on your own. Trust your loving Father. Ask Him to guide you to a fellow believer who can help.

We sense that God wants to heal the shepherds of His sheep, so He can cause His healing love to flow through them to His people. If you are a wounded shepherd, let God set you free from your past and heal the hurt or brokenness of your life. He is "the God and Father of our Lord Jesus Christ, the Father of mercies and God of all comfort, who comforts us in all our tribulation, that we may be able to comfort those who are in any trouble, with the comfort with which we ourselves are comforted by God" (2 Cor. 1:3–4).

A PLUMB LINE FOR SHEPHERDS

In a sense, pastors, church staff members, Sunday school teachers, deacons, elders, discipleship leaders, and other leaders in a church have a role in being a shepherd to the people they serve. The following passages describe the kind of shepherd God desires and the kind he despises. Reading about the reasons God liked or did not like spiritual leaders of the past should help you evaluate how He views your work as a spiritual leader.

Pray that God will help you see how you measure up to His plumb line for shepherds of His people. Read the following Scriptures related to shepherds. Use the questions after each passage to evaluate your role as a shepherd. If God reveals areas in which you have departed from His plumb line, repent and ask God to give you a heart like His for His people. Ask Him to enable you to be a shepherd that is pleasing to Him.

Plan on studying this plumb line at a time when you can retreat from interruptions and spend ample time with God. This may be your invitation for personal revival as a spiritual leader. If God does bring great conviction during this study, keep in mind that any call to repentance by God is an invitation to revival on the other side of the repentance. It is a clear demonstration of His love for you. Let God use this time with Him as a refiner's fire so that you may be a vessel of pure gold—one that is prepared for His service.

Take time to pray now before beginning to read and respond to the Scriptures and questions that follow.

> Numbers 27:16–17—"Let the LORD, the God of the spirits of all flesh, set a man over the congregation, who may go out before them and go in before them, who may lead them out and bring them in, that the congregation of the LORD may not be like sheep which have no shepherd."

♦ Are you guiding God's people to *be* what God wants them to be as His people?

> 1 Samuel 3:19, 21—So Samuel grew, and the LORD was with him and let none of his words fall to the ground. . . . Then the LORD appeared again in Shiloh. For the LORD revealed Himself to Samuel in Shiloh by the word of the LORD.

♦ Are you like faithful Samuel—you do not forget or fail to apply any of the words God speaks to you?

♦ Is God clearly speaking to you through His Word?

> Psalm 23:1–6 —The LORD is my shepherd;
> I shall not want.
> He makes me to lie down in green pastures;
> He leads me beside the still waters.
> He restores my soul;
> He leads me in the paths of righteousness
> For His name's sake.
> Yea, though I walk through the valley of the shadow of death,
> I will fear no evil;
> For You are with me;
> Your rod and Your staff, they comfort me.
> You prepare a table before me in the presence of my enemies;
> You anoint my head with oil;
> My cup runs over.
> Surely goodness and mercy shall follow me
> All the days of my life;
> And I will dwell in the house of the LORD
> Forever.

♦ Do you guide people to Christ and His Word in such a way that their hunger is satisfied with the bread of life and their thirst with the living water?

♦ Are you guiding them in paths of righteousness through the model of your own life? Have you modeled unrighteousness for them at any time?

♦ Do you help people find comfort in God even in the shadow of death?

♦ Are you guiding them into God's presence in such a way that He overflows their spiritual cup?

> Psalm 78:70–72—He also chose David His servant,
> And took him from the sheepfolds;
> From following the ewes that had young He brought him,
> To shepherd Jacob His people,
> And Israel His inheritance.
> So he shepherded them according to the integrity of his heart,
> And guided them by the skillfulness of his hands.

♦ Are you shepherding God's people with integrity of heart and with skillful hands?

> Isaiah 40:11—He will feed His flock like a shepherd;
> He will gather the lambs with His arm,
> And carry them in His bosom,
> And gently lead those who are with young.

♦ Do you love the people and gently lead them? Or do you have hard feelings toward them and treat them harshly?

> Isaiah 56:10–11—His watchmen are blind,
> They are all ignorant;
> They are all dumb dogs,
> They cannot bark;
> Sleeping, lying down, loving to slumber.
> Yes, they are greedy dogs
> Which never have enough.
> And they are shepherds
> Who cannot understand;
> They all look to their own way,
> Every one for his own gain,
> From his own territory.

♦ Are you a faithful watchman alerting God's people to any impending danger?

♦ Do you lack a knowledge of God's ways? Of God's requirements?

♦ Do you dream and sleep too much?

- Do you have a strong appetite for personal gain that is never satisfied?

- Have you turned to your own way?

  > Jeremiah 2:8—"The priests did not say, 'Where is the LORD?'
  > And those who handle the law did not know Me;
  > The rulers also transgressed against Me;
  > The prophets prophesied by Baal,
  > And walked after things that do not profit."

- Do you regularly ask, "Where is the Lord?" Do you seek His presence? His directions?

- Do you know God by experience in an intimate and personal way?

- Have you rebelled against God's leadership or lordship over you or over His people?

- Have you followed after worthless idols, especially idols of the heart?

  > Jeremiah 3:14—"Return, O backsliding children," says the LORD; "for I am married to you. I will take you, one from a city and two from a family, and I will bring you to Zion."

- Will you allow God to make you a shepherd after His own heart? Will you lead with knowledge and understanding of God, His purposes, and His ways?

  > Jeremiah 10:21—For the shepherds have become dull-hearted,
  > And have not sought the LORD;
  > Therefore they shall not prosper,
  > And all their flocks shall be scattered.

- Is prayer your primary planning strategy whereby you ask God for every direction and wait until He shows you?

- Is your flock failing to prosper? Are the people being scattered?

  > Jeremiah 12:10–11—"Many rulers have destroyed My vineyard,
  > They have trodden My portion underfoot;
  > They have made My pleasant portion a desolate wilderness.
  > They have made it desolate;
  > Desolate, it mourns to Me;
  > The whole land is made desolate,
  > Because no one takes it to heart."

- Have you done more to build up God's people or to tear them down? Are they stronger or weaker because of your leadership? Do you really care?

Jeremiah 23:1–4—"Woe to the shepherds who destroy and scatter the sheep of My pasture!" says the LORD. Therefore thus says the LORD God of Israel against the shepherds who feed My people: "You have scattered My flock, driven them away, and not attended to them. Behold, I will attend to you for the evil of your doings," says the LORD. "But I will gather the remnant of My flock out of all countries where I have driven them, and bring them back to their folds; and they shall be fruitful and increase. I will set up shepherds over them who will feed them; and they shall fear no more, nor be dismayed, nor shall they be lacking," says the LORD.

♦ Are you destroying or strengthening the sheep?

♦ Are you scattering or gathering the sheep?

♦ Are you driving the sheep away or are you bestowing care on them?

♦ Are any of your sheep afraid? Terrified? Missing?

♦ Are you taking care of the sheep God already has given you? (Healthy and contented sheep are fruitful and multiply.)

♦ Will you be a shepherd who feeds the sheep and one that is not feared?

> Jeremiah 25:34–36—"Wail, shepherds, and cry!
> Roll about in the ashes,
> You leaders of the flock!
> For the days of your slaughter and your dispersions are fulfilled;
> You shall fall like a precious vessel.
> And the shepherds will have no way to flee,
> Nor the leaders of the flock to escape.
> A voice of the cry of the shepherds,
> And a wailing of the leaders to the flock will be heard.
> For the LORD has plundered their pasture."

♦ Are you aware of your accountability to God for the sheep entrusted to you?

♦ Do you see how God punishes unfaithful shepherds?

♦ Do you fear God?

> Jeremiah 50:6–7—"My people have been lost sheep.
> Their shepherds have led them astray;
> They have turned them away on the mountains.
> They have gone from mountain to hill;
> They have forgotten their resting place.
> All who found them have devoured them;
> And their adversaries said, 'We have not offended,

Because they have sinned against the LORD, the habitation of justice,
The LORD, the hope of their fathers.'"

♦ Have you led the people astray? Have you guided them to do things that
are not part of God's purposes for His people? Have you led them to devote
their time to activities that distract from God's work?

♦ Have the people forgotten their mission?

♦ Have the people forgotten their resting place? Have they strayed from an
intimate and personal relationship with God?

♦ Are your sheep wandering from church to church with no firm resting
place?

♦ Are your sheep being devoured by enemies like crime, abuse, bankruptcy,
or sin's consequences?

Ezekiel 34:2–6—"Son of man, prophesy against the shepherds of Israel,
prophesy and say to them, 'Thus says the Lord GOD to the shepherds: "Woe
to the shepherds of Israel who feed themselves! Should not the shepherds
feed the flocks? You eat the fat and clothe yourselves with the wool; you
slaughter the fatlings, but you do not feed the flock. The weak you have
not strengthened, nor have you healed those who were sick, nor bound up
the broken, nor brought back what was driven away, nor sought what was
lost; but with force and cruelty you have ruled them. So they were scattered
because there was no shepherd; and they became food for all the beasts of
the field when they were scattered. My sheep wandered through all the
mountains, and on every high hill; yes, My flock was scattered over the
whole face of the earth, and no one was seeking or searching for them.""

♦ Are you more concerned about taking care of yourself than taking care of
God's sheep?

♦ Have you strengthened the weak? Healed the sick? Bound up the injured?

♦ Have you brought back the strays or searched for the lost? Or have you
said, "When they get right with the Lord, they will come back"?

♦ Have you ruled them harshly and brutally or tenderly?

♦ Are they being devoured by wild animals like divorce, adultery, greed,
materialism, envy, and strife? Or are they standing strong against the world?

Ezekiel 34:7–10—"Therefore, you shepherds, hear the word of the
LORD: 'as I live,' says the Lord GOD, 'surely because My flock became a
prey, and My flock became food for every beast of the field, because there

was no shepherd, nor did My shepherds search for My flock, but the shepherds fed themselves and did not feed My flock'—therefore, O shepherds, hear the word of the LORD! Thus says the Lord GOD: 'Behold, I am against the shepherds, and I will require My flock at their hand; I will cause them to cease feeding the sheep, and the shepherds shall feed themselves no more; for I will deliver My flock from their mouths, that they may no longer be food for them.'"

♦ Does God hold you accountable for the condition of His sheep?

♦ Has God ever been the source of resistance you have experienced?

♦ Have you experienced attempts to remove you from your leadership role? If so, could it be because of God's discipline?

♦ Are personal financial problems God's discipline for unfaithfulness?

Ezekiel 34:11–16—"For thus says the Lord GOD: 'Indeed I Myself will search for My sheep and seek them out. As a shepherd seeks out his flock on the day he is among his scattered sheep, so will I seek out My sheep and deliver them from all the places where they were scattered on a cloudy and dark day. And I will bring them out from the peoples and gather them from the countries, and will bring them to their own land; I will feed them on the mountains of Israel, in the valleys and in all the inhabited places of the country. I will feed them in good pasture, and their fold shall be on the high mountains of Israel. There they shall lie down in a good fold and feed in rich pasture on the mountains of Israel. "I will feed My flock, and I will make them lie down,' says the Lord GOD. 'I will seek what was lost and bring back what was driven away, bind up the broken and strengthen what was sick; but I will destroy the fat and the strong, and feed them in judgment.'"

♦ What kind of shepherd does God want for His sheep? What will a godly shepherd do for the flock?

Zechariah 10:2–3—For the idols speak delusion;
The diviners envision lies,
And tell false dreams;
They comfort in vain.
Therefore the people wend their way like sheep;
They are in trouble because there is no shepherd.
"My anger is kindled against the shepherds,
And I will punish the goatherds.
For the LORD of hosts will visit His flock,
The house of Judah,
And will make them as His royal horse in the battle."

- Have you allowed the people to be deceived by false teaching?

- Have they turned to false gods and come into bondage and oppression for their sins?

> Zechariah 11:16—"For indeed I will raise up a shepherd in the land who will not care for those who are cut off, nor seek the young, nor heal those that are broken, nor feed those that still stand. But he will eat the flesh of the fat and tear their hooves in pieces."

- Has God raised up an ungodly leader over your people to discipline and judge them for their sins?

> Mark 6:34—Jesus, when He came out, saw a great multitude and was moved with compassion for them, because they were like sheep not having a shepherd. So He began to teach them many things.

- Do you have compassion on the scattered sheep?

- Are you teaching them about the Kingdom and God's ways?

> Luke 15:4–7—"What man of you, having a hundred sheep, if he loses one of them, does not leave the ninety-nine in the wilderness, and go after the one which is lost until he finds it? And when he has found it, he lays it on his shoulders, rejoicing. And when he comes home, he calls together his friends and neighbors, saying to them, 'Rejoice with me, for I have found my sheep which was lost!' I say to you that likewise there will be more joy in heaven over one sinner who repents than over ninety-nine just persons who need no repentance."

- Are you willing to leave the sheep that are safe to go after the ones that have gone astray—the ones that are inactive?

- Have you shown any concern for the non-resident members in your church who may need to transfer to another flock so they can be cared for?

> John 10:2–5, 11–15—"But he who enters by the door is the shepherd of the sheep. To him the doorkeeper opens, and the sheep hear his voice; and he calls his own sheep by name and leads them out. And when he brings out his own sheep, he goes before them; and the sheep follow him, for they know his voice. Yet they will by no means follow a stranger, but will flee from him, for they do not know the voice of strangers." . . . "I am the good shepherd. The good shepherd gives His life for the sheep. But a hireling, he who is not the shepherd, one who does not own the sheep, sees the wolf coming and leaves the sheep and flees; and the wolf catches the sheep and scatters them. The hireling flees because he is a hireling and

does not care about the sheep. I am the good shepherd; and I know My sheep, and am known by My own. As the Father knows Me, even so I know the Father; and I lay down My life for the sheep."

♦ Do you love the sheep enough that you are willing to give your life away in service to them? Or do you run away when the going gets tough because you are just a hired hand working for the money?

The following Scriptures are especially directed to the pastors or overseers of the flock.

John 21:15—So when they had eaten breakfast, Jesus said to Simon Peter, "Simon, son of Jonah, do you love Me more than these?" He said to Him, "Yes, Lord; You know that I love You." He said to him, "Feed My lambs."

♦ Do you love Jesus? Are you feeding His lambs?

Acts 20:28–30—"Therefore take heed to yourselves and to all the flock, among which the Holy Spirit has made you overseers, to shepherd the church of God which He purchased with His own blood. For I know this, that after my departure savage wolves will come in among you, not sparing the flock. Also from among yourselves men will rise up, speaking perverse things, to draw away the disciples after themselves."

♦ Are you keeping watch over the flock and protecting them from the wild animals that destroy and the false teachers that lead astray?

1 Timothy 3:1–7—If a man desires the position of a bishop, he desires a good work. A bishop then must be blameless, the husband of one wife, temperate, sober-minded, of good behavior, hospitable, able to teach; not given to wine, not violent, not greedy for money, but gentle, not quarrelsome, not covetous; one who rules his own house well, having his children in submission with all reverence (for if a man does not know how to rule his own house, how will he take care of the church of God?); not a novice, lest being puffed up with pride he fall into the same condemnation as the devil. Moreover he must have a good testimony among those who are outside, lest he fall into reproach and the snare of the devil.

♦ Are you above reproach inside and outside the church? In public and in private? Do you have a good reputation with outsiders?

♦ Are you husband of one wife?

♦ Are you temperate, self-controlled, respectable, hospitable, able to teach, and not given to drunkenness?

- Are you gentle and not violent?

- Are you able to manage your own family? Do your children obey and respect you?

- Are you a mature convert?

Titus 1:6–11—If a man is blameless, the husband of one wife, having faithful children not accused of dissipation or insubordination. For a bishop must be blameless, as a steward of God, not self-willed, not quick-tempered, not given to wine, not violent, not greedy for money, but hospitable, a lover of what is good, sober-minded, just, holy, self-controlled, holding fast the faithful word as he has been taught, that he may be able, by sound doctrine, both to exhort and convict those who contradict. For there are many insubordinate, both idle talkers and deceivers, especially those of the circumcision, whose mouths must be stopped, who subvert whole households, teaching things which they ought not, for the sake of dishonest gain.

- Are you blameless?

- Are you bossy and overbearing?

- Are you patient or quick-tempered?

- Are you holy and disciplined?

- Are you able to encourage others with sound doctrine?

- Are you rebellious or a deceiver?

- Do you serve for the sake of dishonest gain?

1 Peter 5:1–7—The elders who are among you I exhort, I who am a fellow elder and a witness of the sufferings of Christ, and also a partaker of the glory that will be revealed: Shepherd the flock of God which is among you, serving as overseers, not by compulsion but willingly, not for dishonest gain but eagerly; nor as being lords over those entrusted to you, but being examples to the flock; and when the Chief Shepherd appears, you will receive the crown of glory that does not fade away. Likewise you younger people, submit yourselves to your elders. Yes, all of you be submissive to one another, and be clothed with humility, for "God resists the proud, But gives grace to the humble." Therefore humble yourselves under the mighty hand of God, that He may exalt you in due time, casting all your care upon Him, for He cares for you.

- Are you serving out of duty or love?

- Are you working more for money or the pleasure of service?

- Do you lead by your position and authority or by your example?

♦ Are you proud and arrogant or humble and submissive?

♦ Do you cast your burdens and anxiety on the Lord because He cares for you?

THE VINE AND BRANCHES

If you are like most shepherds of God's people, the plumb line may have left you feeling very inadequate as a spiritual leader. The truth of the matter is that you are inadequate apart from the Lord. The good news is that God has a remedy for that condition. Jesus said:

> "I am the true vine, and My Father is the vinedresser. Every branch in Me that does not bear fruit He takes away; and every branch that bears fruit He prunes, that it may bear more fruit. You are already clean because of the word which I have spoken to you. Abide in Me, and I in you. As the branch cannot bear fruit of itself, unless it abides in the vine, neither can you, unless you abide in Me. I am the vine, you are the branches. He who abides in Me, and I in him, bears much fruit; for without Me you can do nothing." (John 15:1–5)

Jesus said you can do *nothing* without Him. Yet, He has chosen you to abide in Him as a branch abides in a vine. When you have His life flowing through you, He bears much fruit through your life. God the Father may want to take some time right now to prune your life of things that may keep you from being the most fruitful. He may want to remove some things that are good in order to give you His best. Allow the Father to do all the pruning He desires, because the end result will be greater fruitfulness.

The Word that God may have just spoken to you through the plumb line may be an invitation to come to Him for cleansing. Let Him thoroughly cleanse your life of all impurities. "'If you abide in Me, and My words abide in you, you will ask what you desire, and it shall be done for you. By this My Father is glorified, that you bear much fruit; so you will be My disciples'" (John 15:7–8).

After reading the plumb line for shepherds, are there things you want to ask the Father to do so that He may be glorified in and through your life? Ask Him first to enable you to abide. Ask Him to teach you to let Christ's words abide in you. Then ask Him for the desires you have as a shepherd. "'As the Father loved Me, I also have loved you; abide in My love. If you keep My commandments, you will abide in My love, just as I have kept My Father's commandments and abide in His love. These things I have spoken to you, that My joy may remain in you, and that your joy may be full'" (John 15:9–11).

Jesus loves you with an eternal love. If you do as He commands, you will experience an abiding love from your heavenly Father. You will experience a fullness of joy!

"No longer do I call you servants, for a servant does not know what his master is doing; but I have called you friends, for all things that I heard from My Father I have made known to you. You did not choose Me, but I chose you and appointed you that you should go and bear fruit, and that your fruit should remain, that whatever you ask the Father in My name He may give you." (John 15:15–16)

As a shepherd of God's flock, you must remember that you did not choose Him. He chose you. He gave you an assignment. He is the One who enables you to bear fruit, and that fruit will last. Jesus has chosen you to be His friend if you obey His commands. This kind of abiding relationship with God leads to this promise: "'Whatever you ask the Father in My name He may give you'" (John 15:16). Don't let any failures of your past keep you from your future in Christ. Learn to abide. Experience His love, joy, and life flowing through you.

CHRIST'S YOKE

Perhaps you have served for some time as a shepherd of God's people. You may be weary and ready to give up. You may be longing for retirement or hoping a different job offer will come along. Jesus has another invitation for you that may be encouraging: "'Come to Me, all you who labor and are heavy laden, and I will give you rest. Take My yoke upon you and learn from Me, for I am gentle and lowly in heart, and you will find rest for your souls. For My yoke is easy and My burden is light'" (Matt. 11:28–30).

Are you weak and burdened down with the heavy load of your ministry for the Lord? This invitation is for you! Jesus has a yoke built for two. He is already going about His Father's work. His invitation is for you to get into the yoke with Him. Learn from Him. Learn His gentleness, lowliness, meekness, and humility. Put away any pride you may have about "your" ministry and join Him in His work. There you will find that the yoke is well fitted for you. The burden is light because He is carrying the greater load. You get to experience working with Him as He completes His work in God-sized dimensions. Get into His yoke!

SUMMARY

♦ In the Bible, revivals always were led by spiritual leaders. Revivals are intended to began at the top.

♦ Work diligently on getting rid of any pride in your life.

♦ Determine . . . that you are more interested in pleasing God than man.

♦ Surrender your will and every aspect of your life to God.

♦ A believer with the power and authority of the indwelling Christ has divine weapons that can demolish strongholds.

♦ When you focus on your painful past, you are facing the wrong direction, and your whole life will seem out of sorts. You need to repent.

♦ God wants to heal the shepherds of His sheep, so He can cause His healing love to flow through them to His people.

♦ Don't let any failures of your past keep you from your future in Christ. Learn to abide. Experience His love, joy, and life flowing through you.

♦ You get to experience working with Him as He completes His work in God-sized dimensions. Get into His yoke!

ENCOUNTERING GOD IN PRAYER

Jesus often went to a lonely place to pray. He went up onto a mountain or into a desert. Sometimes He rose early, while it was still dark, to pray—or prayed into the night. God may have revealed some things to you in this chapter to which He alone can guide you to respond. Look for some time to get alone with God. Stay with Him until He is through with you. Pray that revival would begin in your heart today.

ENCOUNTERING GOD WITH OTHERS

As you have opportunity in a small group, consider this activity and these discussion questions for chapter 15:

SPIRITUAL RESOURCES ACTIVITY

Read through Ephesians 1–3 and Colossians 1–2 and list every blessing or resource God has provided you. Begin making a list of all the blessings and spiritual resources God has given you or made available to you.

Together with others, enter a period of prayer. Spend some time in praise and thanksgiving. Agree with God that He has made available all the resources of heaven to accomplish His spiritual purposes through Christ in you and in His church. Be specific in your thanksgiving. Receive from Him the resources He already has provided.

DISCUSSION QUESTIONS:

1. What spiritual blessings has God given you?

2. What spiritual resources are available to you?

3. How can a spiritual leader live an "exchanged life" where Christ lives through him? What kind of difference would that make in your own ministry?

4. What are the things God desires from shepherds of His sheep?

5. What things does God despise in shepherds of His sheep?

6. How does God deal with unfaithful shepherds?

7. How has God been speaking to you about your spiritual leadership and how have you responded to Him? What is He saying about your family? Your class or committee? Your church? Your denomination? Other organizations?

8. How can you pray for other spiritual leaders? Take some time to do that right now. Pray for your own leaders and for each other.

CHAPTER 16

PREPARING THE WAY FOR THE LORD

When God sent His Son Jesus to earth, He sent John the Baptist to prepare the way for Him. John prepared for the coming of the Messiah—the Anointed One. When Jesus comes again to take His bride (the churches) to heaven for His wedding, the bride will have prepared herself.

> "Alleluia! For the Lord God Omnipotent reigns! Let us be glad and rejoice and give Him glory, for the marriage of the Lamb has come, and His wife has made herself ready." And to her it was granted to be arrayed in fine linen, clean and bright, for the fine linen is the righteous acts of the saints. (Rev. 19:6–8)

We, too, need to prepare ourselves for the coming of the Lord—for His coming in revival and awakening and for His coming to take His bride away.

The place for revival to begin is in your heart and life. Whether you are the pastor, an elder or deacon, or a member without elected responsibilities, you can allow God to prepare your own heart for revival. Sharing out of your own fresh encounter with God will be the very best preparation you can make.

Jesus often said that every word He spoke was not His but the Father's. For example, Jesus said: "'I have not spoken on My own authority; but the Father who sent Me gave Me a command, what I should say and what I should speak. And I know that His command is everlasting life. Therefore, whatever I speak, just as the Father has told Me, so I speak'" (John 12:49–50).

Is that your pattern of ministry? When Jesus said it, it was so. As a servant of Christ and as a spiritual leader, you need to be so intimate with God that when you speak, people know they have heard a Word from God. Your people don't need plain sermons or lessons; they need a Word from God.

PASTORS AND TEACHERS

You may need to spend time teaching your people how to respond to God as a corporate body. For instance, they need to know guidelines for confession—when it should be private and when it should be public. Members need to know how to confess moral failure without damaging others and without causing lustful or sinful thoughts to be aroused by the confession. They need to know how to share a life message about what God is doing in their lives in such a way that God gets glory.

Here is a list of things you may want to deal with in preparing your people for a fresh encounter with God:

♦ Preach on revivals in Scripture.

♦ Teach on fasting and prayer.

♦ Teach about confession and repentance.

♦ Discuss the need to quit clock watching. Time is required for returning to God. If God does not finish with us in an hour, we don't need to start making plans to leave.

♦ Explain how to prepare to meet God. In Exodus 19:9–15 Moses told people to spend three days cleaning up to prepare to meet God. People need clean hands and pure hearts to enter God's presence.

♦ Focus people's attention on the nature of God and how He works with His people.

♦ Help your people develop a sense of corporate identity. Preach about the corporate nature of the church. Emphasize the importance of the response of every member.

♦ Point people to an intimate, real, personal love relationship with God.

♦ Pray for the demolishing of strongholds due to bondage to the past (2 Cor. 10:3–5).

◆ Help people recognize the difference between spiritual warfare and God's discipline.

◆ Teach believers to deny self.

◆ Help them develop a servant heart for others.

◆ Teach them to fear God and to fear offending Him.

◆ Help them make an absolute surrender to the Lordship of Christ.

◆ Develop in your church a readiness to release everything to Him for reordering: resources, schedule, programs, positions of leadership, calendar of activities, conflicting involvement in secular pursuits, plans, goals, and so forth.

◆ Prepare for brokenness before restoration. Help them understand the process of moving toward spiritual health.

◆ Help your church look beyond the brokenness to the joy and fruits of revival.

PRAYING FOR REVIVAL

Do you remember God's four requirements for revival in 2 Chronicles 7:14? We humble ourselves, pray, and seek His face. Some people have noticed that united, visible, and extraordinary prayer has preceded every great revival in history. They have reached the conclusion that prayer is the secret to get God to act. Many pray, however, and never experience revival.

Prayer is not just a religious activity. Prayer is a relationship between a person and his God. But prayer alone does not cause revival to come. We pray because God has initiated a relationship with us. He invites us into His presence. When we pray, we enter into the throne room of the universe. There we come to know the heart and will of our heavenly Father. In His presence in prayer, we become aware of our sinful condition. We cry out to God with a broken and contrite heart, and He calls us to repent.

Prayer alone is *not* the key to revival. Humility is not enough. Seeking God's face in not enough, either. All these are important, but repentance is the ultimate requirement. Without repentance, no revival will take place. We must turn from our wicked ways. When we return to God, He has promised that He will return to us. He is a covenant-keeping God—He keeps His promises.

Prayer for revival is not a tool for manipulating God. It is not magic or just an activity to complete. Prayer is a relationship with God where we respond to Him, come near to Him, and find Him. Prayer that results in genuine repentance is our part of the process. Then God keeps His promises! Praying for revival is a place of preparation. As people enter His presence they cannot help being confronted with their sinfulness. That can lead to the repentance required for revival.

GATHER THE PEOPLE

Ask the Lord to give you guidance about how to call the people to come together. Because our church members have lost their sense of corporate identity, many do not sense any accountability to the call of a church on their lives. Yet, every member needs to be involved in returning to God. The sin of one or a few can have a continuing affect on the whole body. When one member is sick, the whole body is involved. A little leaven of sin can work its way through a whole church.

Emphasize the importance of coming together before God to respond to Him. Help the people understand that God Himself is issuing the call to return. People may be able to turn your invitation down. They should have greater difficulty turning down an invitation from the Lord. Remember, however, that God is the One who does the convincing. Your job is to bear witness to what you sense and trust that God will convince members to gather together to stand before His plumb line.

RECITE GOD'S ACTIVITY IN YOUR CHURCH.

In Deuteronomy 29, Moses gathered the people to renew their covenant with God. He began by reviewing the spiritual history of the nation to remind the people of God's faithfulness and His covenant love. Remembering the mighty activity of God in the past also strengthens faith for the present. Psalm 105 was used to help Israel remember God's activity with His people. This reciting of God's activity among His people in the past was a prominent part of the sacred assemblies (feast days) in Israel's history.

In Psalm 78, that history is recalled to remind God's people how seriously He treats their sin. The Psalmist said, "We will not hide them from their children, Telling to the generation to come the praises of the LORD, And His strength and His wonderful works that He has done" (Ps. 78:4).

In the revival under Ezra and Nehemiah, the leaders called the people to celebrate their past relationship with God and worship Him before they moved on to repentance. Nehemiah said, "'Do not sorrow, for the joy of the LORD is your strength'" (Neh. 8:10).

Do you remember the church at Ephesus in Revelation 2? They had left their first love. Christ commanded them, "'Remember therefore from where you have fallen'" (Rev. 2:5). These illustrations from Scripture are instructive for us. Remembering where we have been with God, remembering the "mountain-top" experiences, will better prepare us for repentance and revival.

Plan on a special service for your church to recite God's activity with His people in your church. Celebrate the things God did in the past. Allow those members who long for the "good old days" to tell the stories of what God did in the life of your church. Don't hide God's past activity from His people. Magnify it! Take time to praise and thank the Lord for all the things He has done.

Keep the focus on God's activity and not on human accomplishments. These are some things that may help you celebrate:

♦ Ask someone to read through or research your church's history and prepare a report on some of the things God has done.

♦ Report on missions started, people called into ministry, and significant salvation experiences.

♦ Remember God's guidance at crucial times of decision.

♦ Ask for testimonies of answered prayer where God did a special work in answer to prayer.

♦ Allow time for testimonies of ways people have seen God at work in the past in your church.

♦ Report on any significant revival experiences of the past.

♦ Invite testimonies of ways God has worked significantly in individual lives.

Help your congregation remember where they have been with God. This will prepare them for the next steps of returning to the Lord. This will also help orient a new generation and new members to what God has already been doing in this place and with this group of people.

IDENTIFY CORPORATE (CHURCH) SINS

Ask leaders and people to help identify anything that may be a corporate (church) sin. Help them understand that this is a positive process that can help restore health if needed. Ask leaders to help you identify any areas they believe the church has sinned or departed from God.

Collect a listing of these possible sins. As pastor, gather church leaders together. Pray together and discuss the issues that have surfaced. Compile a list of things the leaders believe are indeed sins of the church. You will want to deal with this list in a time of corporate worship. You might ask one or more leaders to read through the list of corporate sins. Call the church to confess (agree with God) their sins. Guide them in corporate prayer for repentance like that in Daniel 9, Ezra 9, or Nehemiah 9.

What are corporate sins? Any occasion the church has sinned by its action or lack of action is a corporate sin. Corporate sins might also include an individual sin that is common to a large number of your people (for example, the intermarriage dealt with by Ezra in Ezra 9–10 might be similar to a church with widespread sexual immorality or divorce). Churches need to deal with all sin for which they have not repented—including past sins as well as current ones. Examples of corporate sins might include such things as:

- participating in a church split
- adopting the ways of the world
- allowing an ungodly person (or persons) to "run off" an innocent pastor or staff person—especially if your church has a pattern of doing so
- choosing to do good things instead of the best things
- coming into being as a church, group, or denomination in a wrong or sinful way, such as a split, envy, controversy, or pride
- covering up sins of the past
- defaulting on a debt where you borrowed and did not repay
- disgracing God's name in the eyes of the community (for example, a leader or member experiences moral failure that became known in the community with no response by the church)
- failing to care for the needs of members, families, or couples
- failing to take a strong stand on God's standards for family and marriage and failing to support those needing help
- forcing agreement or compromise on a decision with no unity of mind, heart, or spirit
- isolating yourself from other believers, churches, denominations in your community or state—doing your own thing when they needed your help, encouragement, or leadership
- lacking faith when confronted with a God-sized assignment and deciding not to attempt it because of your limited resources
- leaving a field of ministry to take the easy road (like leaving the inner city for the suburbs rather than dealing with the problems of the people in the inner city)
- making a wrong decision contrary to God's guidance
- mistreating a pastor, staff member, or family member
- permitting controversy, strife, or dissension
- practicing prejudice or discrimination (for example, against the poor, blacks, ethnic groups, or hippies)
- refusing to follow God's commands related to church discipline of sinful members
- refusing to go after the stray members who have become inactive
- refusing to make adjustments to God because they "cost" too much

- shifting control of the church from Christ as Head of the church to anyone else: pastor, deacons, elders, board, or power block in church
- tolerating evil in the congregation
- trying to save your life rather than give it away in service and ministry
- selfishly using resources for personal comforts and not responding to the needy or missions opportunities

This is by no means a comprehensive list. Perhaps it has given you an idea of what we mean by corporate sin. Pay attention to the things God brings to the minds of your members. Take every suggestion very seriously.

IDENTIFY DEPARTURE MARKERS

Corporate sin may include some things that took place many years ago. A small, struggling, declining church, for instance, invited a guest speaker to talk about the new church planting work being done in the area. Two different members spoke to him later, and each said something like this: "Our pastor tried to lead us to start a new church in 1954, and we refused to do it. I believe God has been punishing us for that decision ever since."

Such an event may be a "departure marker." If your church members believe that your church has departed from God, ask them to try and identify these departure markers. Was there an event or decision that was the beginning of the departure? When and how did the first signs of departing from God begin to surface? What was happening during that time that may have been a cause of the departure? If something surfaces during this search, it may help you understand what you need to do to repent, to make restitution, and to be restored.

PREPARE FOR SPIRITUAL AWAKENING

When revival comes, a natural result that follows is spiritual awakening of lost people to saving faith in Christ. Our churches need to be prepared for spiritual awakening, too. However, you cannot wait for revival to come to prepare. You must be prepared in advance. Here are some suggestions you may want to consider as you help your church prepare for spiritual awakening.

- Provide extensive discipleship training at all levels of spiritual growth for your members. Remember that the Great Commission task is not complete until you have taught them to obey all that Christ has commanded (Matt. 28:19–20).
- Develop multiplying leaders who will be able to teach others. The task will be too big for a pastor and church staff. Every member of the body

needs to be equipped for the work of ministry, for building up the body (Eph. 4:11–13).

♦ Pray that the Lord of the harvest will thrust forth laborers into the harvest (Matt. 9:37–38). Now is the time to pray for leaders and prepare them for service. If you wait until the awakening comes, you will be behind schedule.

♦ Prepare witnesses and commitment counselors. People who are drawn to Christ in awakening will come asking the question, "What must I do to be saved?" People need to be trained to help them. This, however, should not be training to merely go through a prescribed plan or to lead a certain prayer. These witnesses and commitment counselors need to be spiritual physicians who can guide people to repent of their sins, place their faith and trust in Christ, and surrender to His absolute lordship in their lives.

♦ Train new Christian advocates to help new believers begin to grow and mature as disciples of Jesus Christ. *The Survival Kit for New Christians* is an example of a tool to help new Christians grow in their relationship with God.

♦ Prepare for an avalanche of ministry needs. Our world is filled with broken-ness. Families are broken and hurting. Often in awakening, the poor and needy are the ones most responsive to the gospel. People will be brought into the Kingdom and into your church who have all kinds of significant needs. You will need to help them realize the fact that the good news of the gospel is more than going to heaven when we die. They need to experience the healing power of Christ at work reconciling relationships, restoring families, healing the pains of the past, and setting them free from bondage to vices of all kinds.

Many will have tangible needs for food, clothing, jobs, health care, and housing. The model in the New Testament church is a model for your church. The members gave sacrificially to provide for the needs of others so that "there were no needy persons among them" (Acts 4:34, NIV).

♦ Prepare your people to make major adjustments. Any time God invites you to become involved with Him, you will have to make major adjust-ments in your life and church. You don't need to be fearful, just obedient. Prepare your church to accept any cost or adjustment involved in seeing the Kingdom come in the lives of the people in your community.

♦ Prepare to give God all the glory. A sure way to shut down revival and spiritual awakening is to claim God's glory for yourself or your church. Recognize that you cannot do what God does in revival and spiritual awakening. When God does it, magnify God in the eyes of His people. Declare His glory among the peoples. Do not claim any credit for yourself.

♦ Prepare yourself and God's people to let Him be in control. Another way to shut down what God is doing is to try to organize it or control it. As a spiritual leader, when revival starts you will be tempted to try and control or manage what is taking place. Let the Holy Spirit guide you moment by moment. Adjust your plans and agenda to what God is doing. Work on His time table, not your own. When God's Spirit is poured out on your people or community, forget your plans or agenda and adjust to what God is doing. If you don't know what to do next, ask for the counsel of other leaders in your church or from the body. God will speak to His body to guide it correctly. You can depend on Him.

LEADERS PREPARING TO LEAD

As you prepare for corporate times of renewal, keep these things in mind: If you have a tendency to think, "I'll call Henry Blackaby or _____ to get counsel for my situation," wait. Before you pick up the telephone, turn to the Lord in prayer. God wants to guide you and your church in revival. If you turn to man first, you are turning to substitutes for God. That could be an indication that you have departed from Him and will settle for a substitute. Do not, however, hesitate to seek God's counsel through other believers and particularly other leaders in your church. But let God be your first and primary source, not your last resort.

Seek the Wisdom of the Body. Every member of your congregation is a priest unto the Lord. Christ is Head of your church. He has direct access to every leader and member. Seek the counsel of other leaders about what they sense God is saying to your church or how He is guiding your church to respond to Him. The "eye" and the "ear" both need to be heard as the body seeks to know God's will (see 1 Cor. 12 and Rom. 12).

Trust God. What needs to take place in your church cannot happen unless God does it. Yes, a human response is required; but God is the One who initiates, guides, and completes His work. "Trust in the LORD with all your heart, And lean not on your own understanding; In all your ways acknowledge Him, And He shall direct your paths" (Prov. 3:5–6). Keep these other thoughts in mind:

In Revelation 2–3, Christ stands in the midst of His churches. He holds the stars (pastors) in His hand. He is present to help and guide the response of His people. Trust Him to be present and at work.

Trust God to enable you to do His work, to guide your leadership. You may feel like Moses and say to God, "I can't do this. Find someone else." The truth is, apart from Him you can't do anything, but with Him all things are possible. God is far more interested in bringing revival than you are. He will be present to fill you with His power and authority, working through you to accomplish what you cannot do (see Col. 1–2).

When you recognize and are overwhelmed by your weaknesses, remember the words of Paul: "'My grace is sufficient for you, for My strength is made perfect in weakness'" (2 Cor. 12:9).

Notice in Acts how the early church turned to God for every problem. Follow their model.

Remember that your job is faithfulness, not success. God is the One responsible for success, and He will measure success far differently than the world does.

Don't trust in a method, but depend on God. This ought to be good news to you. A method or program is not the answer to your needs. You do not have to know the right words to say or the right things to do. You just need God's presence and guidance. Obey Him each step of the way and you will find yourself and your church right in the middle of His activity and mighty power.

Don't substitute an outside leader for God's leadership in times of revival. At some point, God may guide you to include an outside leader. However, this may be far more appropriate after revival, when your church is prepared to be part of an evangelistic harvest.

Don't let what you believe about your people cancel what you believe about God. Preach to the valley of dry bones (Ezek. 37) and believe God to bring them back to life.

Don't be discouraged by the failure of others. Keep your eyes on God and not on the responses of the people.

Develop and display a spirit of humility. Your dependence on God and your humility will set the tone for the response of others. The first requirement of revival is to humble yourself (2 Chron. 7:14).

SUMMARY

- When Jesus comes again to take His bride (the churches) to heaven for His wedding, the bride will have prepared herself

- We, too, need to prepare ourselves for the coming of the Lord—for His coming in revival and awakening.

- Spend time teaching your people how to respond to God as a corporate body.

- Prayer is not just a religious activity. Prayer is a relationship between a person and his God.

♦ Prayer alone is *not* the key to revival . . . repentance is the ultimate requirement.

♦ Yet, every member needs to be involved in returning to God.

♦ Remembering where we have been with God, remembering the "mountain-top" experiences, will better prepare us for repentance and revival.

♦ Churches need to deal with all sin for which they have not repented—including past sins as well as current ones.

♦ Churches need to be prepared for spiritual awakening, too. However, you cannot wait for revival to come to prepare.

ENCOUNTERING GOD IN PRAYER

♦ Pray that God would prepare your own heart for revival.

♦ Ask the Lord to guide you and all spiritual leaders in your church to prepare His people for revival and awakening.

♦ Ask God to raise up the right leadership for these days of preparation.

♦ Ask the Lord to reveal the corporate sins of the church for which repentance and forgiveness is required.

ENCOUNTERING GOD WITH OTHERS

As you have opportunity in a small group, consider these discussion questions for chapter 16:

1. What are some of the most important ways our church needs to prepare for revival? For awakening?

2. How can reciting God's activity in our past set the stage for revival? (You may want to begin reciting some of these things in your small group.)

3. How is prayer related to revival?

CHAPTER 17

GUIDING GOD'S PEOPLE TO RETURN TO HIM

The time to guide God's people to return to Him starts the moment the Holy Spirit begins to bring conviction of sin, especially corporate sin. This will probably be an ongoing process. Like pealing layers from an onion, God will be working to cleanse one "layer" of sin away at a time until a person and church are thoroughly clean. Then a church and individuals should be encouraged to keep "short accounts" with the Lord. Daily times for personal cleansing should limit the need for dealing with sin as thoroughly as is probably needed today.

Obedience to the conviction of the Holy Spirit ought to be immediate. Regardless of the times you may have planned for revival experiences, leaders should be prepared to call for confession and repentance anytime they sense that God has brought the people under conviction for individual or corporate sin. This may mean canceling a sermon or class session and giving an invitation. It might mean calling a special service tomorrow night because of what you have just seen God do. If God decides to bring revival, let Him do it His way! Agree with your people that you will drop your agenda and adjust to God's agenda if He decides to bring revival. You do not have to wait. In fact, you should not wait. God's timing always will be correct.

NOT METHODS BUT A PERSON

One factor about Biblical times of revival ought to encourage you. None of those leaders had a manual on how to guide the people to return to the Lord. You don't need a manual, either. All you really need is the Lord. He can and will guide you in very practical ways to lead the people you serve to return to Him. He is the One most interested in their return. You don't need to look for methods or a program. They could become substitutes for God. Trust the Lord uniquely to guide you and His people to return.

"So," you may ask, "why did you write this book?" One advantage Biblical leaders had was that they grew up in the middle of a people that responded to the Lord as a corporate group. Today's Christians have lost the understanding of how a group responds to the Lord. We have written this book in an attempt to give you counsel that the Lord may help you. We also see in the Scriptures some emphases that may help you. Please read the following suggestions very prayerfully. Ask the Lord to guide you, to teach you, and to prepare you for leading His people. Don't do or try anything that He doesn't guide you to do.

MULTIPLE LOCAL LEADERSHIP

In Bible times, the king, governor, prophet, scribe, or priest led nations in revival. Often national revivals included two or more of these leaders. In Nineveh, the king led his city to repent. Jacob (as father) led his family to repent. We sense that the established leadership of a group needs to lead the group to respond. This is not a time to bring in an outside leader. Trust the Lord to guide you to lead His people. Multiple leadership is the primary model. Seldom did one person try to carry the burden alone.

Pastors may want to involve church staff or other leaders in the church to act as a leadership team for guiding a return to the Lord. The pastor should provide the primary leadership. He also should lead in discerning when and how to guide the church in repentance. A wise pastor, however, will listen carefully to every suggestion that may come from the Lord through other people. This may require pastor and people to pray intensely as they seek God's directions for their church.

MOBILIZE PRAYER

Because you need to be sensitive to the Spirit's leadership, you must always be in a Spirit of prayer. Make prayer a primary part of your work strategy. Like the apostles in Acts 6, devote yourself to prayer and the ministry of the Word.

> The twelve summoned the multitude of the disciples and said, "It is not desirable that we should leave the word of God and serve tables. Therefore,

brethren, seek out from among you seven men of good reputation, full of the Holy Spirit and wisdom, whom we may appoint over this business; but we will give ourselves continually to prayer and to the ministry of the word.' And the saying pleased the whole multitude. (Acts 6:2, 4)

Perhaps you cannot imagine asking your church to provide enough help to allow you to devote yourself to prayer and ministry of the Word. Some pastors would not dare suggest such a thing. However, something about the spiritual character of the apostles and the leadership of the Holy Spirit caused the whole church to be pleased with such a suggestion. So they chose seven men to help carry the load so their spiritual leaders could spend time with the Lord in prayer and in His Word.

Don't allow anything to rob you of your time with God. Revival is such a crucial need in the life of your church that you cannot afford to miss what God is wanting to do through you. Don't spend all your prayer time alone, however. You need to join with others in prayer. Jesus said, "'If two of you agree on earth concerning anything that they ask, it will be done for them by My Father in heaven. For where two or three are gathered together in My name, I am there in the midst of them'" (Matt. 18:19–20).

Jesus promised a greater authority to united prayer, and He promised a different dimension of experiencing His presence with other believers than a person will experience alone. Pray with other leaders in your church. Pray with and for other churches and Christian denominations or groups. Visit and pray with and for other pastors. Imagine the kind of unity that might develop in the Christian community if you were to say to other pastors, "We are praying for God's blessings on your church and ministry. How can we pray for you and your church?" One seemingly common factor in places where God is sending community-wide revivals is that pastors and groups are already meeting together across denominational lines to pray.

Prayer also should be a major emphasis in all you do as a church. God is interested in your being a "house of prayer for all nations" (Isa. 56:7). Consider some of the following suggestions to increase corporate praying and thus increase the frequency of encounters with God:

♦ Provide a prayer room with praying counselors available during your services. Train your people to respond immediately to God's conviction. Give them permission to get up at any time and move to the prayer room to do business with God. Prayer warriors can also use this place and time to undergird the work God is doing in the service itself.

♦ If you do not use a prayer room, you may encourage people to come to the altar to pray. This may give some of them a tangible way to respond to the Lord. It may give others a needed opportunity to humble themselves. Dealing with pride almost always requires a public response.

♦ Encourage small-group prayer. Whether in classes, special prayer meetings, or at other times, encourage members to pray together and for each other. Encourage them to pray for spiritual concerns, not just for physical problems. This is one place where love begins to flow when people take praying for each other seriously.

♦ Plan times of corporate prayer just as carefully as you do the music or sermon. Guide the church in praying together in worship. Ask the Lord to show you ways to train your people to pray effectively as a corporate body.

♦ Some churches offer opportunities for persons to seek out a person to pray with them about a specific problem or need. One pastor called these times "set-free services." Following his Wednesday evening service, he would extend an invitation to those who needed prayer to stay in the sanctuary. He encouraged mature disciples to stay and be available to pray with those who had burdens. The prayer persons would kneel around the front of the altar. Those seeking prayer would seek out one person, share his or her burden, and receive the prayers of this believer. The Scripture says, "The effective, fervent prayer of a righteous man avails much" (James 5:16). This church found this time of prayer to be life-changing for many. The pastor even realized that his counseling load dropped significantly after they began these weekly prayer times.

CLEAR THE CALENDAR OF COMPETITION

Activity, even religious activity, can crowd God out of people's lives. Members need to focus their attention on God and His call on their lives. Satan will be happy to use every distraction to keep Christians from dealing with the sin in their lives and churches. Do everything you can as a church to remove any activities that will distract your people from a fresh encounter with God.

A church in Austin, Texas, sensed that God was calling them to repent for a variety of sins. The church decided these actions were far too important to squeeze into a busy church schedule. The leaders decided to cancel all unrelated church programming for the summer months and devote time to prayer, fasting, and repentance.

They had two things on the calendar each week: Sunday morning services and a Wednesday evening church assembly. They spent Wednesday evenings standing before God's Word with a focus on one theme or subject each week. After a time of reading the Word and some brief exposition by the pastor, the people responded to God in prayer, confession, and repentance. They spent the entire summer returning to God.

God did some wonderful things in the lives of individuals and families and in the church. By summer's end the leaders sensed God was saying to them, "I'm not finished with you yet, but you may return to your regular schedule now."

That may seem like a radical adjustment. As church leaders, however, you will have to determine how important revival is for your church. It could be a matter of life and death as a church. There is a cost to pay for revival. Your church's willingness to make adjustments may be a good indication of how serious they are about genuine revival. You will be wise to clear the church calendar of conflicting events. Carefully pray for God's direction regarding your church schedule during times of returning to the Lord.

HOLD THE PLUMB LINE BEFORE THE PEOPLE

God's call to revival indicates that His people have departed and need to return. God's people, however, do not always realize they have departed so far from God's original standards. In our day God's Word serves as a plumb line to reveal God's ideal for the body of Christ (the churches) and for Christian living. As God's people clearly understand God's standards set forth in the Scripture, the Holy Spirit can bring conviction of sin. Godly sorrow over their sin should lead to repentance (2 Cor. 7:10).

♦ Use God's Word in services, Bible studies, hand-outs, and in other ways to set forth God's plumb line beside His people.

♦ Preach on a particular topic or theme that uses God's Word as a plumb line. Help the people measure themselves and the church by God's plumb line.

♦ Go beyond being Word-centered to being Christ-centered. The Word is not an end in itself. It points to a relationship with a Person (see John 5:39–40). The Word helps identify the places where a person may have departed from God. The next step is to go to God and seek to be restored to a right relationship with Him. Once a person is in a right relationship with God, he or she can seek God's help in reordering their behavior to be obedient to God's standards and commands.

RESPONDING TO GOD'S ACTIVITY IN A GROUP

One of the lessons you need to learn from the Lord is how to respond to God's activity in a group experience. Normally, we have not been taught how to respond when God interrupts our worship services, group activities, plans, or programs. This is a lesson God can and will teach you. You can depend on Him. He cares far more for your group than you do. If He wants to work in the midst of that group in a special way, He can and will enable you to respond appropriately. However, you must make some prior commitments in the way you function as a spiritual leader. You must give your plans and agenda to God. If He interrupts your group, cancel your agenda and see what God wants to do. If you have not decided beforehand to do this, you may fail to make the adjustment in the middle of a service when God tries to interrupt you and take over the agenda Himself.

We [Henry and Claude] were leading a conference together for 150 people. Small groups were just completing a sharing and prayer time. Henry was to speak next. A woman stood and explained that one of the women in her group needed us to pray for her. The woman had been abused as a young child, and now her father was at home dying from cancer. She was having trouble coming to terms with her father's death.

We have seen God bring dramatic emotional and spiritual healing to people such as that. We realized God wanted to do more than just share a prayer request with our group. We had to decide to pray briefly and go on with our teaching agenda or turn the session over to God. We had already agreed before the conference that if God ever interrupted us we would cancel our agenda and give Him freedom to work. That is what we did.

We knew that God had entrusted that woman's needs to this group, so we assumed that He also had placed in that group the people who could best minister to her. We asked those who could identify with her need to come and stand around her and pray with her. Eight or ten women came to minister to her in prayer. We then gave an invitation for others to come for prayer if they had deep needs that only God could meet. People led by God then came to pray with those who responded.

As God completed His work in a person's life, we gave him or her an opportunity to share with the group what God had done. Often the testimony would be used by God to invite someone with a similar problem to come to Him to be set free. For the rest of the hour we watched as God used members of that group to minister to other members who had needs. People who had been in spiritual bondage for decades found freedom in Christ. Others experienced the comfort, healing, and peace that only God can give. Some, for the first time in their lives, experienced (and felt) the unconditional love of a father—a heavenly Father. Those who were used by God in ministry to others experienced God working through them in dramatic ways they had never before experienced. We learned more about God in that hour through experience than we could have learned in a week of lectures.

Here are some suggestions for responding to God's activity in your group. Again, realize that God can guide you personally without these suggestions. That is what He did with us.

♦ Spend much time in developing your personal relationship with God so that you come to know the voice of God when He is speaking to you. You must always be right with God when you go to stand before His people. Any impurity in you could cost the whole group a fresh encounter with God.

♦ Before group sessions, take time to be sure all sins have been confessed and you have a clear conscience before God.

♦ Place your absolute trust in God to guide you when He wants to work in your group setting.

♦ Decide beforehand that you will cancel your agenda and give God freedom to move anytime He shows you that He wants to do a special work. When you see God at work in your group, that is your invitation as a leader to join Him.

♦ Watch for things like tears of joy or conviction, emotional or spiritual brokenness, the thrill of a newfound insight, or an urgency for prayer in response to a need. These things are sometimes seen only in a facial expression or quiet sigh. Determine whether you need to talk to the person with the group or privately. You must depend on the Holy Spirit for such guidance. Trust Him to guide you. Don't be afraid of making a mistake.

♦ Respond by asking a probing question like one of these: *Is something happening in your life right now that you would share with us? How can we pray for you? Would you share with us what God is doing in your life? What can we do to be of help to you?*

♦ If a person responds by sharing, then provide ministry based on the need. If he or she does not seem ready to respond, do not push or pressure the individual. Give God time to work in that person's life.

♦ When appropriate, invite members to share in ministry to each other. This may be to pray, to comfort, to counsel privately, or to rejoice with the person. When you do not feel equipped to deal with a problem that surfaces, ask the group if one of them feels led to help. You will be amazed at how God works to provide just the right person or persons to provide the needed ministry.

♦ When one person shares with the group, prayerfully consider what response would be appropriate. You need not respond after each person shares. However, you might:

—Ask him or her to pray aloud and respond to the Lord.

—Ask others with the same burden or sin to come and pray together.

—Invite those who want this person to pray for them about a similar matter.

—Ask others to come and pray for this person out of their personal victory.

—Invite those with common sin to stand and have people around them pray, or have one lead in prayer.

—Read a Scripture as a promise, instruction, or correction.

—Redefine sin as sin. There are no minor sins. Do not dismiss a lie as a "white lie." Do not dismiss adultery as an "affair."

—Encourage members to form accountability groups where they meet together for prayer and sharing to help each other in obedience.

♦ Give people the opportunity to testify to what God is doing. This is a very critical point. Often the testimony of one person may be used of God to help another person with an identical problem or challenge. This is also one of the best ways for people to experience God—by hearing testimony of His wonderful work in the life of another person. Do not hide God's glory from His people.

♦ When you do not sense a clear direction about what to do next, ask the group. Say something like this: "I do not have a clear sense of what we need to do next. Does anyone have a sense of what God would want us to do?"

♦ Continue on God's agenda until you sense He is finished with you.

We cannot give you directions for handling every situation. But we can speak from experience: When God wants to work in a group, He can and will give the guidance needed for that time. Your job is to recognize His voice or His activity and then do everything you sense He wants you to do. At the same time, trust Him to work through His body—the church. He has placed members in your group and gifted them to build up the body of Christ. Acknowledge and use all of the resources God has given your group.

GUIDING CORPORATE RESPONSES

During times of corporate worship, you will need to guide corporate responses to God. Follow the basic guideline that confession ought to include the people offended and those who are aware of the sin. Generally the circle of confession should be as large as the circle of offense. Public confession normally should be limited to public sin. Mutual confession, like that suggested in James 5:16, may be helpful for sin-weaknesses or besetting habits.

Remind members that confession is not the same as repentance. It is merely the beginning of a process of repentance. When appropriate, remind members of the need to be reconciled to offended persons and to make restitution when tangible damage has been done and it can be restored.

Claim and confess the sins of your fathers. If the church becomes aware of sins that occurred years ago but have never been dealt with, guide a time of confession for the sins of your fathers. See Daniel 9 for a sample prayer of confession for the sins of the fathers. In confessing their sins, you agree with God that what they did was wrong. Then you pledge to correct your ways and not go that way again.

Lists of corporate sins could be read and followed by prayers of confession led by spiritual leaders. A time of covenant renewal might follow. Then, seek God's direction on what to do with any idols or false gods that your church may have become aware of. Some other suggestions for corporate response include:

♦ Ask key people to stand, read, confess, or pray.

♦ Write sins on paper and nail them to a cross or burn them in a basket.

♦ Prepare and read a corporate written prayer and/or a written covenant.

♦ Provide for times of silent prayer.

♦ Provide for times of small- and large-group prayer.

♦ Offer times for simultaneous prayer.

♦ Invite persons to come for prayer at the altar.

♦ Allow members to request prayer and then immediately get an individual or group of others to pray for him or her. Utilize the members of the body.

♦ Don't prematurely assure people of forgiveness. Allow God to bring conviction until the person realizes God is the only hope of cleansing and forgiveness.

LEADING TIMES OF TESTIMONY
(Contributed by Bill Elliff, Pastor, Little Rock, Arkansas)

One of the primary ingredients for the spread of historic revivals has been an abundance of personal testimonies. The accounting of the work of God in individual hearts can prove a powerful tool in the hands of God to inspire, encourage, and convict others of their need.

Often pastors are fearful of testimony times for the following reasons:

♦ embarrassingly "dry" testimony times

♦ excessive long or emotional testimony times

♦ testimonies that step over certain lines of propriety

♦ non-specific, generalized testimonies that seem useless and unedifying

Testimony times can provide freedom for God to accomplish considerable good in the following ways:

♦ Give God the glory due Him as He has transformed lives.

♦ Help believers confirm and verbalize what God is doing in their lives.

♦ Allow specific testimonies to inspire, convict, encourage, teach, and train other believers.

♦ Grow the church through a fresh sense of the magnitude of corporate work God is doing in the body of Christ.

♦ Give the pastor an opportunity to identify and "preach" off certain primary themes that are repeatedly mentioned during testimonies.

♦ Provide a spiritual "thermometer" by giving the church leaders an increased understanding of where God is at work and by identifying primary areas of need.

♦ Give opportunity for public confession and corporate forgiveness when needed.

The following are hints on how to lead an effective testimony time. The average lay person may be just as fearful regarding these times as a pastor, often because of bad experiences in the past. Precluding these fears by proper explanation can pave the way for a fresh release of God's Spirit through His people in the body.

Pray! Spend time privately and publicly praying for:

♦ God to bring just the right people to share.

♦ protection from the enemy.

♦ wisdom, as the pastor, to know how to lead the time—particularly how to be sensitive to key points of conviction.

Take time to educate the congregation on how to give a testimony. The following model might be used.

1. Share how God is developing in each Christian a special Life Message that is peculiar to him or her. God is using all the experiences of their lives and their right responses to develop these truths in them. Learning to articulate and transparently communicate these truths to others is one of the great keys in usefulness for God's kingdom.

2. Describe how to share a Life Message (you may want to put these up on an overhead projector or in a simple handout).

   a. Share where God found you. Be specific regarding areas of sin, need, etc.

   b. Share what you were experiencing as a result of controlling your own life.

   c. Share what God said to you.

   d. Share how you responded. You may have responded negatively at first . . . be honest.

   e. Share what you are now experiencing as a result of obedience to God's truth. What benefits of obedience are you experiencing?

3. Describe simple ground rules.

   ♦ Be brief.

   ♦ Be specific.

   ♦ Be current.

   ♦ Bring all the glory to God.

   ♦ Don't reflect negatively on others.

   ♦ Use the term "moral failure" for any moral sins.

4. Invite the congregation to think of one area where God has been working in recent days (you may want to identify this as the past week, month, six months, etc.). Then ask members to turn to one other person and, using the above method, share a three-minute testimony.

5. Spend a moment in prayer. Let members ask God whether He wants them to share a public testimony. Invite those who feel so led to come and be seated on the front row. Indicate that you may or may not get to all those who came forward. This gives the pastor the discretion to chose those he feels led to call upon.

6. As they come, the pastor can stand by the microphone with those who are sharing. Feel free to interrupt and help them clarify or give further specifics if needed. Offer encouragement and love.

7. Lead in ministering to the person after he has shared.

   ♦ Give a word of encouragement or affirmation, if appropriate.

   ♦ If they have asked for the church's forgiveness, lead the church in corporately verbalizing "I forgive you!" to the individual.

   ♦ Invite people to give a hug or a word of encouragement or blessing to those testifying as they head back to their seats.

♦ If the testifier still has needs, burdens, etc., invite a group of people with concerned hearts to gather around that person or take them to a side room for prayer, encouragement, counsel, or other needed help.

8. Be sensitive not only to the person testifying, but to what God is saying to the church through the testimony. Remind the people that they are not spectators but participants in this time. God may be speaking directly to them about similar or related issues. When a similar testimony is repeated several times, see this as God speaking to the church.

9. Be sensitive to opportunities to "preach" based on the testimonies. Don't feel the need to say something after every testimony. If God brings to your mind key thoughts that will help crystallize and convict through the testimonies, seize the opportunity, perhaps even stopping for an invitation.

Other helpful hints include:

1. Don't worry about excesses. If someone seems to step over the line in some way, thank God publicly that people feel the freedom to share, then gently remind folks of the boundaries for the testimonies.

2. When people share things that should have been shared with another individual, ask them to go to that individual immediately if possible to clear their conscience.

3. Don't feel you must have everyone share. It is often better to stop on a significant note instead of "dragging it out." This leaves the congregation anxious to hear more from God. Inform those who did not get to share that there will be other opportunities and affirm that they have been obedient to God in being willing to share.

4. Remind the people often that every testimony is significant.

Although the above suggestions may seem mechanical, they have proven helpful to many in aiding the church to express the life of God. Trust God to use you in opening the way of blessing through this wonderful and biblical practice.

SUMMARY

♦ The time to guide God's people to return to Him starts the moment the Holy Spirit begins to bring conviction of sin, especially corporate sin.

♦ Obedience to the conviction of the Holy Spirit ought to be normally immediate.

♦ Be prepared to call for confession and repentance anytime you sense that God has brought the people under conviction for individual or corporate sin.

♦ You don't need a manual . . . all you need is the Lord.

♦ Trust the Lord uniquely to guide you and His people to return.

♦ Make prayer a primary part of your work strategy.

♦ Jesus promised a greater authority to united prayer, and He promised a different dimension of experiencing His presence with other believers than a person will experience alone.

♦ God's Word serves as a plumb line to reveal God's ideal for the body of Christ (the churches) and for Christian living.

♦ Remind members that confession is not the same as repentance.

♦ One of the primary ingredients for the spread of historic revivals has been an abundance of personal testimonies.

ENCOUNTERING GOD IN PRAYER

♦ Share with the Lord any feelings of inadequacy you may have. Thank Him for His presence in your life to guide you and prepare you.

♦ Ask the Lord to teach you experientially how to lead His people to return to Him.

♦ Seek His specific directions concerning when and how He might want you to guide the people to return.

♦ Give Him permission to interrupt you anytime He chooses.

ENCOUNTERING GOD WITH OTHERS

As you have opportunity in a small group, consider these discussion questions for chapter 17:

1. When is the best time to lead God's people to return to Him?

2. Why is there value in using multiple leaders in guiding a return to the Lord?

3. How can we give greater emphasis to prayer?

4. What are some ways of using God's Word as a plumb line for God's people? When and how does God want to speak His Word through us?

5. What are some of the most important factors in guiding a response to God's activity in a group?

6. How can testimony services be useful in spreading revival?

CHAPTER 18

WHEN REVIVAL COMES

When God restores His people, He takes them all the way back into the mainstream of His mighty movement in history. Spiritual awakening waits on revival in the hearts of His people. You will know revival has come when God returns to His people. There will be evidence. You will recognize:

♦ God's presence return
♦ new freedom
♦ new joy
♦ new peace
♦ true worship
♦ deep love for and faith in Jesus
♦ clean and clear conscience
♦ Christ-likeness
♦ reconciliation (among individuals, couples, families, groups, churches, denominations)

- holiness
- moral changes based on love for God, not just a reformed behavior
- the church advance, though "the gates of hell" try to prevail
- God's voice clearly speaking
- answered prayers
- power of the Spirit evident to all
- simple and authentic way of life, more like Jesus
- increased love for one another
- increased hunger and love for God's Word
- new burden for the lost

There may be much other evidence of genuine revival. Be attentive to ways God will reveal what He is doing in the midst of His people. When revival comes, a spiritual leader needs to proceed with great caution and much prayer to keep the revival from going astray. The following is a brief list of some words of counsel and caution to consider when revival comes.

1. *Watch out for problems that can hinder revival from continuing.* Potential problems include physical exhaustion, harmful publicity, organizing the response, wrong motives, pride rather than brokenness in testimonies, emotionalism instead of encounter, activity crowding out relationship, man-centered rather than God-centered responses, rushed "repentance" that stops short of changed lifestyles, depending on methods instead of God, and a focus on decisions rather than conversions.

2. *Don't hide God's glory.* Encourage people to testify to God's work in their lives—even when it is still in process, but especially on the victory side. Make sure people point the glory to God and not to other people, the church, a course, or a method. God may have used others, but give God the ultimate credit.

3. *Don't report it to death.* A well-known speaker and writer was said to have experienced a great move of God in his church. Some time later he was asked what had happened to the movement. His response was, "I reported it to death." Reports of God's activity often spread the flames of revival. Reporting on God's activity is important, but it has at least two dangers: (1) you may be tempted to steal God's glory and claim credit for the work, and (2) you may become so busy reporting the revival that the revival fires die out for lack of attention.

4. *Keep the home fires burning.* Don't neglect the revival fires by being gone all the time reporting on the revival fires. As the shepherd, you need to guide the process of revival and work with conserving the fruits of revival for even

deeper work or greater fruitfulness. If requests come for testimony, send the laity who have been touched by revival. They, too, can tell the stories and share their personal testimony.

5. *If you have led in a time of genuine revival, enlist a small group of spiritual advisers from your church to help you keep your local ministry in focus with outside requests.* Trust God to guide their counsel for the good of the body of Christ (the church) where God put you.

6. *Enlist prayer warriors to pray for you.* Be specific in the requests for which they pray. For instance:

♦ Pray that I will only give the glory to God and never take it to myself.
♦ Pray that I will have discernment concerning requests from outside the church or community.
♦ Pray that I will not be distracted by opposition but that I will be sensitive to God's counsel in responding to opposition.
♦ Pray for my family and the time we have together.

7. *Be cautious about media reports.* If possible, request permission to review reports before publication. Sometimes reporters may point the credit in the wrong direction or focus on methods rather than God's activity. Don't allow pride to cause you to seek out the media to tell the story. God is much more efficient in spreading the testimony of genuine revival through word of mouth. Genuine revival does not need an advertising campaign.

8. *Watch your language in every conversation concerning God's activity.* Keep your focus God-centered, not man-centered.

9. *Provide regular times for God's people to report on what God is saying and doing.*

10. *Don't stop preaching altogether.* Though some services may be devoted to testimony or confession, people need to hear the plumb line of the Scriptures. They need to know God's original intentions so they may thoroughly repent and return to God's ways and standards. Without the preaching, their repentance may be shallow and incomplete.

11. *Allow God to broaden the revival to encompass the rest of the Christian community.* Be sensitive to opportunities to share the spotlight with others or give it away. Allow others on your staff, lay people, other pastors, or other spiritual leaders to guide sessions. When space or other needs dictate, move sessions to other churches or to neutral locations. Don't try to control it.

12. *Mobilize prayer for the harvest. Pray for laborers.* Pray specifically for lost persons. Encourage groups or prayer triplets to pray for lost persons by name.

13. *Pray through John 17 for God's glory to be revealed, for unity among all believers, and for Christ to be exalted in the eyes of the world.*

14. *Be prepared to guide and call for social change after revival.* Spiritual awakening has always had a profound impact on the very basic levels of society. These changes may take place in dealing with moral, ethical, legal, or even educational issues. Be cautious, however, about getting distracted by fighting issues outside the church. God alone is Sovereign. You should march on the "gates of hell" only at the command of the Lord.

A TESTIMONY OF GOD'S GRACE: WHEATON COLLEGE REVIVAL OF '95

On Sunday night, March 19, 1995, a group of about seven hundred students gathered on the campus of Wheaton College (Wheaton, Illinois) for a World Christians Fellowship. That night two students from Howard Payne University (Brownwood, Texas) shared testimonies about the outbreak of revival on their campus the month before. The service began at 7:30 P.M. and continued to 6:00 A.M. the next morning, as student after student came to the microphone to confess sin. As students confessed sin they were immediately surrounded by fellow students who prayed with them and for them.

Recognizing that God was not through with them, an announcement was made that they would meet again that evening at 9:30 P.M.. That night black trash bags were placed along the front at the altar. Students were given the opportunity to put away things that hindered their walk with the Lord or that tempted them to sin. Five bags were filled with drugs, alcohol, pornography, secular music tapes, and even credit cards. At 2:00 A.M. God was still dealing with students. In order to give students time to rest, the meeting was concluded for the night, and another meeting was planned for Tuesday. These meetings continued for four nights as the Spirit continued to spread His work across the campus.

During the sessions before the Lord, time was given to worship and praise. Scripture reading and impromptu special music was interspersed between times of confession of sin. On Wednesday leaders recognized the need for instruction from the Scripture to keep the response on track. Three school officials spoke on dealing with temptation, sin, and discipleship for Christian growth. By the end of Wednesday's session all students who desired to confess sin publicly had done so. Students formed groups to hold each other accountable for the commitments they had made to Christ. Students who were not in a group were "adopted" by a group before they left the session.

Thursday evening's session was given to praise and thanksgiving for what God had done. Students shared testimonies of the victories they had experienced or told about what God was teaching them. At the conclusion of that session a call was issued for students to surrender their lives to full-time Christian service, and between two hundred and three hundred students responded. Testimonies from Wheaton then began to spread to other colleges, universities, seminaries, and churches. We are living in a day of God's favor when He is granting repentance to His wayward children.

SUMMARY

- ◆ You will know revival has come when God returns to His people.
- ◆ Watch out for problems that can hinder revival.
- ◆ Don't hide God's glory. Encourage people to testify to God's work in their lives.
- ◆ Don't report it to death.
- ◆ Keep the home fires burning.
- ◆ Enlist prayer warriors to pray for you.
- ◆ Be cautious about media reports.
- ◆ Don't stop preaching altogether.
- ◆ Allow God to broaden the revival to encompass the rest of the Christian community.
- ◆ Mobilize prayer for the harvest.
- ◆ Pray through John 17 for God's glory to be revealed, for unity among all believers.
- ◆ Be prepared to guide and call for social change after revival.

ENCOUNTERING GOD IN PRAYER

- ◆ Since human wisdom will fail you at such a time, ask God for wisdom from above.
- ◆ Pray for God's glory.
- ◆ Surrender yourself to be a servant for whatever God may ask.

ENCOUNTERING GOD WITH OTHERS

As you have opportunity in a small group, consider these discussion questions for chapter 18:

1. What are some of the dangers to be avoided when revival comes? How can those dangers be avoided?

2. What are some of the positive things to be done during times of revival?

3. What are some of the best ways for God to be glorified during a time of revival?

4. Of all the suggestions above, which seem to be most significant to you? Why?

CHAPTER 19

TIMES FOR CONTINUING RENEWAL

One of the reasons many churches are so far from what God intends is that we have failed to renew the love relationship with God on a regular basis. We may have made attempts at renewal or gone through the motions of revival services, but our current state indicates that we have failed somewhere along the way.

Years ago revival services lasted two or more weeks. The first week was devoted to helping God's people return to the Lord. The second week was devoted to an evangelistic thrust toward the lost. This is the same sequence we discuss in God's pattern for revival and spiritual awakening. Revival of God's people must come first. Over the years, however, we have shortened our revival services. Now many churches devote only three or four days to revivals.

Because of our commitment to reach the lost, we often have placed the primary emphasis of revival services on evangelistic messages to the lost. In doing so, we have neglected the revival and renewal of God's people.

We pray that the *Fresh Encounter* message will be a tool that God will use to bring you and your church through genuine revival. Revival, however, is going to be a recurring need for God's people. We will always be departing from God and allowing our love relationship with Him to grow cold. Begin now to plan for regular times for revival and renewal. When God brings revival, don't allow the flames to die out again. Guide God's people to return to the Lord regularly. The following ideas may give you some help in planning and conducting regular times for renewing the love relationship with God. May this revival/awakening that is coming last a generation . . . or at least until the Lord returns!

HOLY DAYS

Christian holy days (holidays) like Thanksgiving, Christmas, and Easter ought to be times of renewal. On these days and during the related seasons, place your focus on both celebration and renewal of a relationship. These are days to remember all the love God has lavished on us by sending His Son. Rather than going through time-honored traditions as mere ritual, these can be times for remembering God's love and responding to that love.

Help people come to understand what God has done that affects their lives. Help them respond to God in personal ways. The holy days may be good times to encourage the giving of special offerings for mission causes as an expression of thanksgiving and gratitude to the Lord for all He has done. They also can be times to call for repentance when people realize they have broken fellowship with God because of their sin.

PRE-COMMUNION MEETINGS

In the past century, in some other countries (and among some groups even today), pre-Communion meetings have been used as a time for repentance. On the Saturday before the Sunday observance of the Lord's Supper, an entire congregation would set aside all regular work and come together for a time of examination. The time was used for the people to confess and repent of all known sin and correct broken relationships lest they partake of the Lord's Supper in an unworthy state (1 Cor. 11:27–32). They did everything possible to have clean hands, a pure heart, and a clear conscience before God as they came to the Lord's table.

Sometimes this pre-Communion time lasted a week or two. Andrew Murray wrote a book in the nineteenth century in South Africa called *The Lord's Table*.[1] It was used as a daily study one week before the Lord's Supper to help people focus their attention on the Lord Jesus and His invitation to the table. Readers would go through a careful time of self-examination prior to the Sunday observance. The focus during the Lord's supper was on the sacrifice Christ Jesus made for us through His death on the cross. This guided people to remember the Lord's death and also anticipate His coming again. The book then provided a daily study for the coming week to reflect on the difference the Lord's provision makes in daily life related to power, sanctification, obedience, work, and fellowship with Jesus.

Restoring meaning and purpose to the observance of the Lord's Supper would help in continuing renewal. Providing time for members to examine themselves and repent of all known sin on a regular basis could be a valuable measure to keep us close to the Lord.

PENTECOST PRAYER MEETINGS

In *The Prayer Life,* Andrew Murray describes the beginning of Pentecost prayer meetings.[2] The revival of 1857–58 in America spread to South Africa by 1860. In 1861 the pastors decided to hold prayer meetings in the afternoons one week prior to Pentecost. Many hearts were warmed and deeply touched.

Since Pentecost has special significance for the coming of the Holy Spirit on the church, churches decided to spend the ten days between Ascension and Pentecost observing daily prayer like the disciples in the upper room. Over the next fifty years, the Pentecost prayer meetings were observed. Pastors circulated notes with subjects for sermons and for prayer.

According to Murray, these prayer meetings frequently were times of revival for God's people. He said they often were followed by fruitful evangelistic harvests. You might want to consider some special prayer meetings leading up to Pentecost.

PILGRIM PRAYER MEETINGS

In 1816 in Wales, William Williams was preaching about the work of the Holy Spirit. He offered this suggestion to the parish: "What if you were to consent to have Him to save the whole of this parish? 'Ah, but how can we have Him?' Well, hold prayer-meetings through the whole parish; go from house to house— every house that will open its door. Make it the burden of every prayer that God should come here to save. If God has not come by the time you have gone through the parish once, go through it again; but if you are in earnest in your prayers, you shall not go through half the parish before God has come to you."[3]

In that service was a lonely old woman with little religious background. Though very poor, she splurged and bought two wax candles to be ready for the pilgrim prayer meeting when it came to her house. Almost a year later, the discouraged woman went to the shop where she had bought the candles. She asked the owner when the prayer meeting was coming to her house. The owner felt rebuked, for none of the church members had taken the suggestion seriously. He reported the incident to the church and the pilgrim prayer meetings began. On a Sunday evening in August, 1817, the Holy Spirit came in power and swept revival through the vale.

Your church might consider having pilgrim prayer meetings, moving from house to house praying for each family of your church and community until God sends revival.

BODY LIFE MEETINGS

The church is described as the body of Christ. Every member has an important role in helping the whole body function properly. A "Body Life" meeting is a time for members of the body to care for and strengthen one another. It can be a time for testimonies, for sharing special prayer requests, for praying for each other, for rejoicing with those who rejoice, and for weeping with those who weep. It can be a time for members to share faults, weaknesses, or needs and have the rest of the body minister to the ones in need.

A Body Life meeting is a time of corporate worship and sharing that is more informal and intimate than a traditional service. Consider planning a service around the idea of Body Life. Ask members to study Romans 12 and 1 Corinthians 12, making a list of ways the members of the body of Christ relate to one another. Encourage members to share needs, request prayer, testify to God's goodness, remember God's blessings in the past, and discuss ways to help and encourage one another. Get members to think and share about how they can "spur one another on toward love and good deeds" (Heb. 10:24, NIV).

TESTIMONY MEETINGS

Using the suggestions for "Leading Times of Testimony" on page 186, provide regular times for God's people to declare His marvelous deeds among the people (see Psalm 96). God uses testimonies of His recent activity in one person's life to create a desire in another person for a similar experience of Him. As people hear of God's activity, their faith is increased to trust God for His special working in their own lives and families.

CLEANSING BY WASHING WITH THE WATER OF THE WORD

Present Scriptures related to a particular theme in a bulletin insert or in some other publication. Read the Scripture from the pulpit or guide the congregation in a responsive reading. Present a choral reading of Scriptures.

The Scriptures are not an end in themselves. They should always be pointing people to a relationship. Therefore, ask the people to reflect on those Scriptures or respond to God in some way—for instance, after the presentation of Scriptures:

♦ Suggest that people pray and ask God what He would want them to do in response to this truth. What the person thinks is not too important. What others want to tell them is not particularly important. But what God wants them to do in response to the message is very important. Point people to the Lord so that He can speak directly to His people.

♦ Ask, "Is God convicting you of any sin? Then confess it and return to Him." Notice the emphasis on what God is doing rather than what man is thinking or saying. In using questions like this you encourage people to turn to the Lord to do what He wants to do. The miracles happen when God does get their attention and lives change!

♦ Request that people get in small groups of four or five and pray sentence prayers of response to the Lord. Sometimes this is the point in a small and intimate group that a person may allow the dam of resistance to break. Then God floods in and their lives are radically changed. When this happens in a group, the others in the group encounter God, too. Testimonies from these kinds of experiences can lead to a major breakthrough in God's working among a people.

PREPARING YOUR OWN PLUMB LINE MESSAGES

Pastors and other spiritual leaders need to allow God to identify a subject that He wants to deal with in your group or congregation. Provide a listing of Scriptures with appropriate questions or activities to help people evaluate their lives against God's plumb line on the given subject. Preach or teach on the subject and then call people to respond to God and return in any area where they recognize a departure from Him. During many of the revivals in history, sermons focused on one specific sin. As the preacher dealt thoroughly with that one sin, God dealt deeply with His people. Messages might include such sins as pride, bitterness, gossip, divisiveness, greed, adultery, theft, or deceit.

CHURCH DISCIPLINE

God holds every individual accountable for his or her own sin. He expects us to respond to the conviction of the Holy Spirit in dealing with individual sin. If a Christian refuses to deal with his or her own sin, God intends for the church to deal with it. A church is made up of many members, but they are one body. If one member is living in rebellion, the whole body is accountable.

Church discipline must be undertaken in a careful, loving, and God-directed manner. When the early church disciplined wayward members, great fear came on the people, and that fear increased the level of faithfulness of all. God has commanded the church to deal with sin in the church. When we fail to take God-prescribed action, the church sins and invites God's discipline.

You probably will need to prepare your church for such a step. Because of former abuses of church discipline, we have departed from the clear commands of the Lord. Careful teaching and much prayer will be required for a church to let God guide it in this practice.

What are some of the things God says about church discipline?

Romans 14:12—So then each of us shall give account of himself to God.

1 Corinthians 12:25–26—There should be no schism in the body, but that the members should have the same care for one another. And if one member suffers, all the members suffer with it; or if one member is honored, all the members rejoice with it.

Galatians 6:1–2—Brethren, if a man is overtaken in any trespass, you who are spiritual restore such a one in a spirit of gentleness, considering yourself lest you also be tempted. Bear one another's burdens, and so fulfill the law of Christ.

James 5:19–20—Brethren, if anyone among you wanders from the truth, and someone turns him back, let him know that he who turns a sinner from the error of his way will save a soul from death and cover a multitude of sins.

1 Timothy 5:19–21—Do not receive an accusation against an elder except from two or three witnesses. Those who are sinning rebuke in the presence of all, that the rest also may fear. I charge you before God and the Lord Jesus Christ and the elect angels that you observe these things without prejudice, doing nothing with partiality.

Titus 3:10—Reject a divisive man after the first and second admonition.

2 Timothy 4:2—Preach the word! Be ready in season and out of season. Convince, rebuke, exhort, with all longsuffering and teaching.

2 Thessalonians 3:14–15—If anyone does not obey our word in this epistle, note that person and do not keep company with him, that he may be ashamed. Yet do not count him as an enemy, but admonish him as a brother.

1 Thessalonians 5:14–18—Warn those who are unruly, comfort the fainthearted, uphold the weak, be patient with all. See that no one renders

evil for evil to anyone, but always pursue what is good both for yourselves and for all. Rejoice always, pray without ceasing, in everything give thanks; for this is the will of God in Christ Jesus for you.

1 Corinthians 5:6–7, 9–13—Your glorying is not good. Do you not know that a little leaven leavens the whole lump? Therefore purge out the old leaven, that you may be a new lump, since you truly are unleavened. For indeed Christ, our Passover, was sacrificed for us. . . . I wrote to you in my epistle not to keep company with sexually immoral people. Yet I certainly did not mean with the sexually immoral people of this world, or with the covetous, or extortioners, or idolaters, since then you would need to go out of the world. But now I have written to you not to keep company with anyone named a brother, who is sexually immoral, or covetous, or an idolater, or a reviler, or a drunkard, or an extortioner—not even to eat with such a person. For what have I to do with judging those also who are outside? Do you not judge those who are inside? But those who are outside God judges. Therefore "put away from yourselves the evil person."

2 Corinthians 7:8–12—For even if I made you sorry with my letter, I do not regret it; though I did regret it. For I perceive that the same epistle made you sorry, though only for a while. Now I rejoice, not that you were made sorry, but that your sorrow led to repentance. For you were made sorry in a godly manner, that you might suffer loss from us in nothing. For godly sorrow produces repentance leading to salvation, not to be regretted; but the sorrow of the world produces death. For observe this very thing, that you sorrowed in a godly manner: What diligence it produced in you, what clearing of yourselves, what indignation, what fear, what vehement desire, what zeal, what vindication! In all things you proved yourselves to be clear in this matter. Therefore, although I wrote to you, I did not do it for the sake of him who had done the wrong, nor for the sake of him who suffered wrong, but that our care for you in the sight of God might appear to you.

2 Corinthians 13:1—"By the mouth of two or three witnesses every word shall be established."

OTHER IDEAS FOR CONTINUING RENEWAL

Some other ideas you may want to consider developing yourself include:

♦ God Watch—Encourage people to watch for God's activity around your church and community and then report to the body.

♦ Discipleship training—When a life is swept clean and not filled with a new way of living, old patterns may return (see Matt. 12:43–45). Provide training in right living to fill the void left by the cleansing of a life.

♦ House of Prayer—Make every effort to develop a praying church. Don't focus on the activity of prayer but on the relationship to the Lord of the universe.

♦ Restore meaning to worship—Many practices of worship have lost their meaning. We have a tendency to treat them as common or as mere ritual. Baptism and the Lord's Supper services ought to be significant times of worship.

A TESTIMONY OF GOD'S GRACE: PENTECOST PRAYER MEETINGS

Wellington, Texas, is a rural community with about thirty-five hundred people in the county. First Baptist Church had been through a time of renewal. The pastor, Johnny Tims, couldn't quite explain what had happened. But he said, "This church is different. We are not the same church we were three years ago. We have a spirit of unity. The people love each other. They love the Lord and are seeking to obey Him. They have a burden to pray and a burden to see the lost come to saving faith in Christ."

During 1993 and 1994, the church had not held the traditional spring and fall revival services. They had focused their attention on seeking the Lord. They had prepared to follow the Lord when He let them know what they were to do. Early in 1995, as groups and individuals were praying, they began to sense a burden to give themselves more fully to prayer. They had studied God's pattern for revival and spiritual awakening. Since they realized that somehow God had revived His people, they anticipated that they would begin to see a harvest of lost people being saved. They were burdened that they were not seeing a harvest come. As they prayed and sought the counsel of others, they sensed God leading them to a plan.

They learned from a study of the Jewish festivals that the Jews gave a family emphasis to counting up the fifty days to Pentecost. The emphasis on Pentecost is first fruits, and the early church experienced the fulfillment of the first fruits on the Day of Pentecost when three thousand were converted. They also heard about Andrew Murray's testimony regarding Pentecost Prayer Meetings the ten days between Ascension and Pentecost (p. 200). As an entire congregation they committed the spring of 1995 to an emphasis on prayer, especially prayer for a spiritual harvest.

Beginning the day after Passover, families met daily to read a portion of Scriptures and pray. The families began listing every lost person they knew personally and began praying for their salvation. This continued for the fifty days up to Pentecost.

For six weeks prior to Pentecost Sunday, the entire church went through *In God's Presence,* a study on prayer and praying together. Each Sunday every adult and youth Sunday school class spent an hour praying together and practicing what they had learned about prayer. During their worship services, volunteers spent the time in a prayer room praying for special requests submitted by members. They also began praying through a growing list of lost people in their community.

On each of the ten days prior to Pentecost, they met nightly to pray together. One night they invited all the other churches in the community to join them in prayer for their county. Some nights they divided and went to homes to pray in small groups. Some small groups went on prayer walks through town; still others went on prayer drives through the county, praying for a harvest. One night the church commissioned a team of members who were leaving on an evangelistic mission trip to Russia; together they prayed for a spiritual harvest. By the time Pentecost Sunday came, God had prepared this church as a house of prayer for the nations.

Pentecost Sunday's service became a time of testimony and sharing about what God had done in recent months. Some who had never given a public testimony told of how they came to know Christ. Four people made public commitments to the Lord that day. These were seen as first fruits in Wellington. Then the church held a dinner on the grounds to celebrate God's bounty and the provision for the physical needs of His people. One person was born again that afternoon.

During the coming months, they began to see the power of the Lord released in bringing people to Christ. Their Russian mission trip saw four hundred people come to Christ. Their church was already in a variety of prison ministries. They saw more than three hundred prisoners come to saving faith in Christ through that ministry. Members began to disciple prisoners in their faith, and they saw lives radically changed by the Lord. Even in this small community, they saw twenty-five of the people they had been praying for come to Christ. Now they continue to pray, realizing that prayer is a primary work strategy for a church and that God answers prayer.

CHAPTER 20

Praying for Revival in the Land

Our Sovereign God is the Ruler of men and nations. Throughout history He has established nations and has poured out His wrath and judgment on nations that depart from Him and live in wickedness. If our nation is to survive we must return to the Lord our God. He alone is our Hope. We must trust in Him. Read the following truths from the Psalmist and identify ways you can be praying for our nation.

> Psalm 33:10–22—The LORD brings the counsel of the nations to nothing; He makes the plans of the peoples of no effect. The counsel of the LORD stands forever, The plans of His heart to all generations. Blessed is the nation whose God is the LORD, The people He has chosen as His own inheritance. The LORD looks from heaven; He sees all the sons of men. From the place of His dwelling He looks On all the inhabitants of the earth; He fashions their hearts individually; He considers all their works. No king is saved by the multitude of an army; A mighty man is not delivered by great strength. A horse is a vain hope for safety; Neither shall it deliver any by its great strength. Behold, the eye of the LORD is on those

who fear Him, On those who hope in His mercy, To deliver their soul from death, And to keep them alive in famine. Our soul waits for the LORD; He is our help and our shield. For our heart shall rejoice in Him, Because we have trusted in His holy name. Let Your mercy, O LORD, be upon us, Just as we hope in You.

What God plans to do will take precedence over the plans of people and nations. God watches humanity and He fashions their hearts individually. If you want to begin praying for revival in the nation, start by seeking revival in your own heart and let revival begin in you.

Many people sense that many of the most desperate problems faced by our nation today are the consequences of our sin and the evidence of God's discipline and righteous judgment. God is bringing discipline on us. That has been His pattern throughout history. At times of God's judgments, no military might, technology, or human expertise will be sufficient to deliver the nation from His wrath. God has sufficient means to bring down the most powerful of nations.

Not many years ago, the world witnessed the fall of the atheistic Soviet Union. Almost overnight the walls came down so the gospel could spread throughout the nations of Europe and Asia. People are turning to Christ in unparalleled numbers. Some parts of the world are experiencing differing measures of spiritual awakening even now. Though some would debate the issue, God had a major role in the fall of Communism. His heart's desire is to see all come to repentance and a knowledge of the truth.

Today some missionaries in these areas of great harvest are praying that Western Christianity will not pollute the work God is doing. The filth, impurity, hypocrisy, lethargy, and compromise of Western churches causes God's name to be defamed in other parts of the world.

REVIVAL OUR ONLY HOPE

If God can bring down the Soviet Union to open the door for His purposes, He can do what He pleases to get the attention of any other nation that has departed from Him. Our only hope for a future in our nation is for revival to sweep our churches and spiritual awakening to touch the land. If our nation is to return to the Lord and fear Him once again, God's people must begin the repentance. Remember, the healing of our land is waiting on the repentance and revival of God's people. "If My people who are called by My name will humble themselves, and pray and seek My face, and turn from their wicked ways, then I will hear from heaven, and will forgive their sin and heal their land'" (2 Chron. 7:14).

If we are to see revival, we must meet God's requirements. We must deal ruthlessly with our stubborn pride and humble ourselves before the Lord.

Then we must pray and seek His face. Prayer is a relationship with a person. Prayer is entering into the throne room of the universe to stand before the Lord God Almighty. When God's people take prayer seriously and enter the presence of Holy God, they will recognize their sin and fall with broken and contrite hearts before His majesty.

When we come to understand the nature of our sin and when we have a broken heart about it, we will be ready to repent and return to the Lord. God stands ready to grant and enable our repentance, if we will just respond to His invitation.

Genuine and sincere praying for revival will lead us to repentance. If we are to see revival in the land, we need to begin praying and repenting at all possible levels:

+ as individuals;
+ as families;
+ as churches;
+ as businesses;
+ as communities;
+ as denominations;
+ as the larger Christian community;
+ and eventually as a nation.

PRAYING FOR REVIVAL

Are you willing to change your lifestyle significantly enough to be the kind of person in prayer that God could use to change your family, your church, your city, your denomination, and your nation? Since God's desired pattern is to begin revival through leaders, pray for the leaders:

> I exhort first of all that supplications, prayers, intercessions, and giving of thanks be made for all men, for kings and all who are in authority, that we may lead a quiet and peaceable life in all godliness and reverence. For this is good and acceptable in the sight of God our Savior, who desires all men to be saved and to come to the knowledge of the truth. . . . I desire therefore that the men pray everywhere, lifting up holy hands, without wrath and doubting. (1 Tim. 2:1–4, 8)

A TESTIMONY OF GOD'S GRACE: GOD HEALED THE UNITED STATES

The following are examples from history of one of the leaders of the United States calling his people to repent of their individual and national sins. The

Congress and the President sensed the Civil War they faced was the result of God's righteous judgment of the nation for its sins. The division of the nation was great. There was no reason why the United States could not have become two separate countries after that great war. However, the President called the nation to prayer and repentance. The war came to an end; the nation was reunited; and the land was healed. This is a testimony of how God can bring a deeply troubled nation to repentance.

During the period of the Civil War in the United States, both houses of Congress and President Abraham Lincoln sensed a desperate need for the nation to humble itself before Almighty God and confess its sins and repent before Him. The following excerpts come from proclamations issued by President Lincoln between 1861 and 1864.

Proclamation of a National Fast Day, August 12, 1861

"Whereas a joint committee of both houses of Congress has waited on the President of the United States and requested him to recommend a day of public prayer, humiliation, and fasting, to be observed by the people of the United States with religious solemnities, and the offering of fervent supplications to Almighty God. . . .

"It is fit and becoming in all people, at all times, to acknowledge and revere the supreme government of God; to bow in humble submission to his chastisements; to confess and deplore their sins and transgressions, in the full conviction that the fear of the Lord is the beginning of wisdom; and to pray with all fervency and contrition for the pardon of their past offenses. . . .

"Whereas when our own beloved country, once, by the blessing of God, united, prosperous, and happy, is now afflicted with faction and civil war, it is peculiarly fit for us to recognize the hand of God in this terrible visitation, and in sorrowful remembrance of our own faults and crimes as a nation and as individuals, to humble ourselves before him and to pray for his mercy. . . .

"Therefore, I, Abraham Lincoln, President of the United States, do appoint the last Thursday in September next as a day of humiliation, prayer, and fasting for all the people of the nation."

Proclamation of a National Fast Day, March 30, 1863

"Whereas, the Senate of the United States, devoutly recognizing the supreme authority and just government of Almighty God in all the affairs of men and of nations, has by a resolution requested the President to designate and set apart a day for national prayer and humiliation:

"And whereas, it is the duty of nations as well as of men to own their dependence upon the overruling power of God; to confess their sins and transgressions in humble sorrow, yet with assured hope that genuine repentance will lead to mercy and pardon; and to recognize the sublime truth, announced in the Holy Scriptures and proven by all history, that those nations only are blessed whose God is the Lord;

"And insomuch as we know that by his divine law nations, like individuals, are subjected to punishments and chastisements in this world, may we not justly fear that the awful calamity of civil war which now desolates the land may be but a punishment inflicted upon us for our presumptuous sins . . . We have been the recipients of the choicest bounties of Heaven. We have been preserved, these many years, in peace and prosperity. We have grown in numbers, wealth, and power as no other nation has ever grown; but we have forgotten God . . . we have vainly imagined, in the deceitfulness of our hearts, that all these blessings were produced by some superior wisdom and virtue of our own. Intoxicated with unbroken success, we have become too self-sufficient to feel the necessity of redeeming and preserving grace, too proud to pray to the God that made us.

"It behooves us, then, to humble ourselves before the offended Power, to confess our national sins, and to pray for clemency and forgiveness. . . .

"I do hereby request all people to abstain on that day from their ordinary secular pursuits, and to unite at their several places of public worship and their respective homes in keeping the day holy to the Lord. . . . All this being done in sincerity and truth, let us then rest humbly in the hope authorized by the divine teachings, that the united cry of the nation will be heard on high, and answered with blessings no less than the pardon of our national sins, and the restoration of our now divided and suffering country to its former happy condition of unity and peace."

PROCLAMATION FOR A DAY OF PRAYER, JULY 7, 1864

"Whereas the Senate and House of Representatives, at their last session, adopted a concurrent resolution, which was approved on the second day of July instant, and which was in the words following, namely:

"That the President of the United States be requested to appoint a day for humiliation and prayer by the people of the United States; that he request his constitutional advisers at the head of the executive departments to unite with him as chief magistrate of the nation, at the city of Washington, and the members of Congress, and all magistrates, all civil, military, and naval officers, all soldiers, sailors, and marines, with all loyal and law-abiding people, to convene at their usual places of worship, or wherever they may be, to confess and to repent of their manifold sins; to implore the compassion and forgiveness of the Almighty . . . to implore him, as the supreme ruler of the world, not to destroy us as a people, nor to suffer us to be destroyed by the hostility or the connivance of other nations, or by obstinate adhesion to our own counsels which may be in conflict with his eternal purposes. . . .

"Now, therefore, I, Abraham Lincoln. . . . do hereby appoint the first Thursday of August next to be observed by the people of the United States as a day of national humiliation and prayer.

"I do hereby further invite and request the heads of the executive departments of this government, together with all legislators, all judges and magistrates, and all other persons exercising authority in the land, whether civil, military, or naval, and all soldiers, seamen, and marines in the national service, and all the other loyal and law abiding people of the United States, to assemble in their preferred places of public worship on that day, and there and then to render to the Almighty and merciful Ruler of the universe such homages and such confessions, and to offer to him such supplications, as the Congress of the United States have, in their aforesaid resolution, so solemnly, so earnestly, and so reverently recommended."

May the day come in the United States and in other needy nations around the globe, that the leaders of each nation will have a holy fear of God and call the nation to prayer and repentance. "Lord, do it again!"

SUMMARY

- ♦ Our Sovereign God is the Ruler of men and nations.
- ♦ If our nation is to survive we must return to the Lord our God.
- ♦ If you want to begin praying for revival in the nation, start by seeking revival in your own heart and let revival begin in you.
- ♦ Remember, the healing of our land is waiting on the repentance and revival of God's people.
- ♦ When God's people take prayer seriously and enter the presence of Holy God, they will recognize their sin and fall with broken and contrite hearts before His majesty.
- ♦ Genuine and sincere praying for revival will lead us to repentance.
- ♦ "Lord, do it again!"
- ♦ "Restore us, O God of our salvation . . . That glory may dwell in our land" (Ps. 85:4, 9).

ENCOUNTERING GOD IN PRAYER

Are you willing to pray? If so, here are some suggestions of ways you can begin praying individually. You also may want to use these suggestions for corporate praying.

♦ Pray that God will display His holiness and bring glory to Himself in His dealings with all of us.

♦ Pray that God will do whatever is necessary to bring us and our leaders to recognize His punishments for individual and corporate sins.

♦ Pray that the leaders will humble themselves before God or be broken and brought to humility before a holy God.

♦ Pray that leaders will acknowledge that God is the Sovereign Ruler of men and nations.

♦ Pray that leaders will place their dependence on God for direction and trust Him for their help.

♦ Pray that leaders will recognize the discipline and judgments of God and call families, churches, cities, denominations, and the nation to repent and return to the Lord as their God.

♦ Pray that all the people in each grouping also will recognize the discipline and judgments of God and wholeheartedly follow the leaders back to God.

♦ Give God glory, thanksgiving, and praise when He accomplishes His purposes in your family, church, city, denomination, and your nation.

ENCOUNTERING GOD WITH OTHERS

If you really care about your nation and about your God and His righteous purposes, make a determined effort to join with other believers to pray for revival. Pray for revival to begin with you and continue to your family, church, city, denomination, and the entire nation. Rather than focusing on discussion questions, here are some suggestions to help guide your praying together.

1. Acknowledge God's presence and active participation with you in prayer.

2. Use common language rather than "churchy" words.

3. Speak for yourself using *I, me, my,* or *mine* rather than *we, us, our,* or *ours,* except when you are confessing corporate sin.

4. Save your closings (like "Amen," or "In Jesus name") until the end of the time of prayer.

5. Prepare yourselves through prayers of confession, cleansing, and reconciliation.

6. Spend time in prayers of worship, praise, and thanksgiving.

7. Spend the time in prayers of petition and intercession. Share requests as you pray rather than spending time at the beginning to list and discuss requests.

8. Pray about one subject at a time.

9. Take turns praying about that subject. Continue on that subject as long as God seems to be guiding the praying.

10. Be specific in what you are asking of God. Try to avoid vague or general requests.

11. Ask the Holy Spirit to guide your praying according to the will of God.

12. Consider God's viewpoint and give God a reason to answer.

13. Use biblical principles, patterns, and promises to guide your requests.

14. Seek Spirit-guided agreement with others in your prayers.

15. Pay attention to the directions the Holy Spirit prompts you to pray.

16. Seek to put yourself in the place of the one you are praying for so that you can "feel" what that person is feeling.

17. Listen to the prayers of others for directions or answers to your prayers.

18. Respond to the prayers of others.

19. Pray for each other.

20. When time permits, pray until God is through with you.

21. Consider writing down the subjects for which you have prayed, so you can watch with anticipation for God's answers.

22. When God answers one of your prayers, remember to thank Him and watch for opportunities to testify to His wonderful work.[1]

A PRAYER FOR REVIVAL: PSALM 85:4–9

Restore us, O God of our salvation,
And cause Your anger toward us to cease.
Will You be angry with us forever?
Will You prolong Your anger to all generations?
Will You not revive us again,
That Your people may rejoice in You?
Show us Your mercy, LORD,
And grant us Your salvation.
I will hear what God the LORD will speak,
For He will speak peace
To His people and to His saints;
But let them not turn back to folly.
Surely His salvation is near to those who fear Him,
That glory may dwell in our land.

NOTES

Chapter 1

1. Adapted from Jonathan Edwards, "Narrative of Surprising Conversions," *The Works of President Edwards* (New York: Leavitt & Allen, 1857), 231–72; and Frank Grenville Beardsley, *The History of American Revivals,* 2nd ed., rev. and enl. (New York: American Tract Society, 1912), 20–83.

Chapter 2

1. Adapted from C. L. Culpepper, *The Shantung Revival* (Atlanta: Home Mission Board, 1982); and Bertha Smith, *Go Home and Tell* (Nashville: Broadman Press, 1965).

Chapter 3

1. Adapted from Beardsley, *History of American Revivals,* 84–107; and E. A. Payne, "The Prayer Call of 1784," *Ter-Jubilee Celebrations 1942–44* (Baptist Missionary Society, 1945), 19–31.

Chapter 4

1. For further reading on the Wales Awakening, see J. Edwin Orr, *The Flaming Tongue* (Chicago: Moody Press, 1973); or Richard Owen Roberts, *Glory Filled the Land* (Wheaton, Ill.: International Awakening Press, 1989).

Chapter 5

1. "Christ-Centered Revival," *National Prayer Conference Notebook* (June 1990), 9–12.

Chapter 7

1. Beardsley, *History of American Revivals,* 216.

2. Ibid. For further reading, see J. Edwin Orr, *The Event of the Century: The 1857–1858 Awakening,* ed. Richard Owen Roberts (Wheaton, Ill.: International Awakening Press, 1989).

Chapter 8

1. Adapted from Robert E. Coleman, ed., *One Divine Moment: The Asbury Revival* (Old Tappan, N.J.: Fleming H. Revell Co., 1970). Also available is a video giving actual pictures and audio record of this revival, with interviews with those who participated—*When God Came,* Broadman & Holman. The showing of this to your family or church could be used of God to "spark revival" in our day!

Chapter 12

1. John Avant, Malcolm McDow, and Alvin Reid, eds., *Revival! Brownwood, Fort Worth, Wheaton and Beyond* (Nashville: Broadman & Holman, 1996).

Chapter 19

1. Andrew Murray, *The Lord's Table: A Help to the Right Observance of the Lord's Supper* (Fort Washington, Penn.: Christian Literature Crusade, 1985).

2. Murray, *The Prayer Life* (Springdale, Penn.: Whitaker House, 1981).

3. Lewis H. Elvet, "With Christ Among the Miners," *Glory Filled the Land,* ed. Richard Owen Roberts (Wheaton, Ill.: International Awakening Press, 1989), 20.

Chapter 20

1. Adapted from T. W. Hunt and Claude V. King, *In God's Presence* [a course on praying together effectively], (Nashville: LifeWay Press, 1995), 94.